AUTO-ETHNOGRAPHIES

AUTO-ETHNOGRAPHIES

The Anthropology of Academic Practices

edited by

Anne Meneley and Donna J. Young

broadview press

Library and Archives Canada Cataloguing in Publication

Auto-ethnographies : the anthropology of academic practices / edited by Anne Meneley and Donna J. Young.

Includes bibliographical references and index.
ISBN 1-55111-684-7

1. Ethnology—Study and teaching (Graduate) I. Meneley, Anne II. Young, Donna Jean, 1956–

GN320.A87 2005   301'.071'1   C2005-900253-0

Broadview Press Ltd. is an independent, international publishing house, incorporated in 1985. Broadview believes in shared ownership, both with its employees and with the general public; since the year 2000 Broadview shares have traded publicly on the Toronto Venture Exchange under the symbol BDP.

We welcome comments and suggestions regarding any aspect of our publications–please feel free to contact us at the addresses below or at broadview@broadviewpress.com / www.broadviewpress.com

North America
PO Box 1243, Peterborough, Ontario, Canada K9J 7H5
Tel: (705) 743-8990; Fax: (705) 743-8353
email: customerservice@broadviewpress.com
3576 California Road, Orchard Park, NY, USA 14127

UK, Ireland, and continental Europe
NBN Plymbridge
Estover Road
Plymouth PL6 7PY UK
Tel: 44 (0) 1752 202 301
Fax: 44 (0) 1752 202 331
Fax Order Line: 44 (0) 1752 202 333
Customer Service: cservs@nbnplymbridge.com
Orders: orders@nbnplymbridge.com

Australia and New Zealand
UNIREPS, University of New South Wales
Sydney, NSW, 2052
Australia
Tel: 61 2 9664 0999; Fax: 61 2 9664 5420
email: info.press@unsw.edu.au

Broadview Press Ltd. gratefully acknowledges the financial support of the Government of Canada through the Book Publishing Industry Development Program for our publishing activities.

Copy-edited by Betsy Struthers

PRINTED IN CANADA

CONTENTS

ACKNOWLEDGEMENTS

Anne would like to thank Michael Levin for laughs over cocktails over the past few years; Don Kulick, for once again being a source of editorial inspiration and hilarity; and Bruce Grant for his continual support, advice, and friendship.

Donna would like to thank Anna de Aguayo, Jennifer Lund and Alison Forrest for being stalwart friends.

We would both like to thank all of our authors who responded to our comments with grace, good humour, and intelligence. The role of editor is not always an easy one, as we've discovered. Thanks to those of you who made it a pleasant and often interesting task. Of the many friends and colleagues who have inspired and helped us (wittingly or not) a couple deserve special mention. Lindsay DuBois introduced the two of us to each other and, for many years has been a trusted friend and cherished interlocutor, one who doesn't hesitate to enlighten us when it is required. Paul Manning is a friend and colleague of a more recent vintage who has been enormously helpful in reading various drafts of our papers and the introduction to this book, in listening to us discuss our various trials and tribulations along the way, and by offering his very funny and astute commentary on the wacky world of academe. He also helped by introducing us to Bonnie Urciuoli and David Graeber. And thanks to David Graeber and Camilla Gibb, who contributed their papers at the eleventh hour with signature grace and style! Michael Lambek generously and quickly read the manuscript, fitting us into his hectic schedule. As always, he is a perceptive reader and writes with elegance.

Many, although not all, of the papers in this volume were originally presented at a symposium that we organized for the 2003 meetings of the Canadian Anthropology Society in Halifax. Thanks to the organizer of the conference, Lindsay DuBois, and the audience for their interest, questions, and comments. The original impetus for the symposium, and ultimately, this book, was Anne's research on the idea of "collaboration" in the Ford Foundation's "Crossing Borders" initiative. Thanks to the Ford Foundation for funding this research; Anne's co-researcher, Julia Harrison;

and the co-directors of the Interconnecting Diasporas project: Grant Cornwell, Eve Stoddard, Rhoda Reddock, Brinsley Samaroo, and especially Charmaine Eddy and Susan Wurtele.

It was a pleasure to work with Broadview Press. Thanks to Betsy Struthers for her excellent copyediting. We would like to thank Michael Harrison for scaring us at the beginning and Anne Brackenbury for appreciating the fruit of this fright!

Finally, we would like to thank Vaidila Banelis and Uzo Esowanne for forgiving us for our extended telephone conversation, which lasted for more than a year. Lenin, Ben, and Theo all provided welcome distraction.

INTRODUCTION: AUTO-ETHNOGRAPHIES OF ACADEMIC PRACTICES

DONNA J. YOUNG AND ANNE MENELEY

> "In short, if anthropology is not possible everywhere, it is not possible anywhere."
>
> —MARC AUGÉ

AUTO-ETHNOGRAPHIES INVITES ONE TO THINK ethnographically about the academy, so that we might consider the ways in which current intellectual practices are produced within various institutional, national, and international constellations of meaning and power. As with all social institutions, the university is subject to the tides of history, which academics, young and old, must navigate. It is not always smooth sailing. The academy is as puzzling and full of contradiction as any other field site. At times, it appears so steeped in tradition as to be both obsolete and impregnable; at other times, it seems assailable from all sides, subject to the whims of fashion. Over the past several decades, academics and politicians have frequently questioned the purpose, if not the very idea, of the liberal university. Positions on the subject swing from the conservatively nostalgic to the destructively postmodern.[1] In the first instance, the defenders worry that academic standards and the ideals of universalism and nationalism, which they believe are integral to a quality education, have steadily eroded. In the second instance, such ideals are considered the nub of the problem. We contend that neither a nostalgic longing for a university we know never really existed, nor the naive assumption that parody and disdain for one's forbears will happily destabilize an oppressive authoritarian structure, are adequate to the task of critically evaluating trends that today shape, enable, and confine academic practices.

If we are to take Edmund Leach (1984) and Sidney Mintz (1981) at their word, the ugly politics of class, racism, colonialism, and sexism ran rampant in universities of the last century. Contrary to the ideals of liberalism, many a talented scholar suffered the consequences, while others, sometimes less worthy, enjoyed prestige and power.[2] Nevertheless, Stanley Fogel's (1988: 34) claim that "(far) too little has been done to unnerve teachers and administrators of the humanities, to dismantle their taxonomies and dissipate their powers" seems, from our present vantage, petulant. Many of the essays in this collection draw attention to the trenchant internal critiques that took place in the humanities and social sciences, reshaping our practices. Fogel's contention that "(whatever) agitation has been produced has come externally from niggardly government funding agencies and the occasional truculent but impotent student" (1988: 34) seems unduly cynical. Admittedly, outside policy directives helped to reform the deplorable hiring practices of the past, and student protest helped to broaden intellectual horizons. Still, it seems utterly foolish to suggest that the influence of the professoriate is inflated at a time when the Bush administration is cavalierly threatening to slash funds to area study programs that do not fully endorse the current American agenda. Overall government cuts to universities, the tying of scarce available funds to particular policy directives, and the increasing demand to cater to students as clients, or consumers, has not been an unmitigated good. Indeed, some of these policies unthinkingly reify the logic of the late-capitalist marketplace and modes of political thinking that re-engage objectifying and utilitarian practices that scholars contributing to this volume would prefer to work against.[3]

Academics argue and debate, embrace or resist, various aspects of life and work within the academy, but they are all, to some extent, disciplined and shaped by the institution. In choosing to explore disciplinary practices within the academy ethnographically, the contributors to this volume attempt to make sense of the ways in which their own intellectual endeavours are enabled or frustrated by social-cultural and political structures both within and outside of the university. We concur with Augé, who argues that "Once anthropology, through its study of rites, takes social meaning—that is, the intellectual and institutional procedures through which human beings render their reciprocal relations thinkable and possible—as its principle object, the necessity for a generalized anthropology, one that includes the whole planet, seems obvious" (1998: xiii). An auto-ethnography of academic practices provides an excellent example of what Augé calls the anthropology of proximity. Simultaneously participants and observers, our contributors have critically examined their quotidian routines and rituals in the academy, in places where they conduct research, and in their communities.

Auto-ethnography is challenging because it requires those who are already embedded in particular cultural and social processes to subject themselves and their most intimate surroundings to the same forms of critical analysis as they would any other. As Bourdieu (1988) notes, this is a particularly difficult exercise, as one must objectify the familiar. Such reflexivity already assumes that there is no possibility of a truly uncontaminated point of view. But in highlighting one's positionalities, which may shift radically over the course of one's career, one hopes to make explicit the social and structural parameters at play.[4] It is assumed one's perspective on different experiences within the academy may shift when viewed with hindsight.

One of the strengths of this volume is that our contributors currently occupy a wide variety of positions within the academy and are at different stages in their careers: as graduate students, as part-time and non-tenure-stream faculty, untenured and tenured faculty, as editors and publishers, as administrators, and sometimes as interveners in public debates. They can be found working in a variety of international contexts. They were educated and work in both noble and commoner departments.[5] In the greater scheme of things, those working in Canadian institutions, on the periphery of empire, may even constitute a subaltern class of intellectuals.[6] While the hegemony of the American academy is palpable, as is its political power, it is not total. The essays that follow make it evident that various international networks uniting scholars who have field sites, theoretical interests, political goals, and concerns about the academy in common crosscut national academic traditions. Although not all our contributors are trained as anthropologists, all have approached the subject matter with an ethnographic sensibility, hoping to give readers a deeper knowledge of a world that many people participate in as students, but may not fully understand.

AUTO-ETHNOGRAPHY AS PRACTICE AND GENRE

Our use of the term auto-ethnography is influenced by four separate, if overlapping, genres of anthropological writing. First, there is a long and venerable history of ethnographers who have worked at home, in their own societies, producing a genre of native, or insider, anthropology. Second is a genre of autobiographical reflexivity, which came to fruition in the 1980s and 1990s in response to critiques of ethnographic objectivity. Third, there are political economies of anthropology as a profession, which explore the material and social conditions that contour academic practices. Finally, there is a genre of retrospection in which, typically, senior academics recall and critically comment on past and present trends in both the disciplines and institutions which house them. In integrating these genres, we hope to incorporate their various strengths and insights, while avoiding some of their conceits and/or excessive claims.

At Home

Although often overlooked in genealogies of anthropological thought, anthropologists and sociologists were quick to understand that the practice of participant observation could help to shed light on little understood elements of their own societies. From the very beginning, ethnographic studies were carried out at home. For instance, the sociologists Nels Anderson (1923) and Edmund William Bradwin (1928) drew on first-hand experience as hobos and labourers in the United States and Canada when completing their ethnographic studies of homeless men in the early twentieth century. Their insider status was highly valued for lending depth of understanding to their vivid accounts of transient labourers, but the transition to the academy was a difficult one for both men.

The publication of Anderson's *The Hobo* in 1923 launched a series of studies based on participant observation, which came to distinguish the Chicago school of sociology under the stewardship of Robert Park. But in moving to Chicago in the early 1920s, Anderson discovered "finding jobs was easier than adapting to an upper-level academic life" (1961: xi). He wrote:

> Still, even after the publication of *The Hobo*, when I was permitted to take the oral examination for my Master's degree, I was not able to answer most of the questions put to me. Apparently some of my answers must have amused the professors. When I was called back into the room for the verdict, Professor Albion W. Small pointed to the street, "You know the sociology out there better than we do, but you don't know it in here. We have decided to take a chance and approve you for your Master's degree." (1961: xii)

The intent of their condescension is unclear: Did Anderson show insufficient knowledge of his subject, or did he fail to understand the ways of the academy? According to Rauty (1998), Anderson could not openly acknowledge his life as a hobo until long after his thesis had been published, and universities continued to shun him until, at the age of 74, he was hired as a professor at Memorial University. [7]

The anthropologist Franz Boas encouraged the talented young writer Zora Neale Hurston[8] to return to the American south of her youth to engage in the "formalized curiosity of ethnographic research," which she described as "poking and prying with a purpose" (Hurston 1942: 174). Boas was "confident that her background and easy manner would help her to 'penetrate through that affected demeanor by which the Negro excludes the white observer effectively from participating in his true inner life'" (Boyd 2003: 143). Boas, like Park, assumed that the "native" ethnographer could gain a fuller understanding by virtue of belonging to the group under study. But Hurston soon came to understand that going home to conduct fieldwork was not the same as going home for a social visit. In *Dust Tracks on a Road* (1942) she writes:

> My first six months were disappointing. I found out later it was not because I had no talents for research, but because I did not have the right approach. The glamour of Barnard College was still upon me. I dwelt in marble homes. I knew where the material was all right. But, I went about asking, in carefully accented Barnadese, "Pardon me, but do you know any folk-tales or folk-songs?" The men and women who had whole treasuries of material just seeping through their pores looked at me and shook their heads. No, they had never heard of anything like that around there. Maybe it was over in the next county. Why didn't I go over there? I did, and got the selfsame answer. Oh, I got a few little items. But compared with what I did later, not enough to make a flea a waltzing jacket. Considering the mood of my going south, I went back to New York with my heart beneath my knees and my knees in some lonesome valley.
>
> I stood before Papa Franz and cried salty tears. (1942: 175)

With equal portions of dramatic flair and self-effacing wit, Hurston exposes the flaw in one of the central conceits of doing anthropology at home. As Marilyn Strathern notes, "What one must also know is whether or not investigator/investigated are equally at home, as it were, with the kinds of premises about social life which inform anthropological inquiry" (1987: 16). Despite Hurston's past, being educated had made her an outsider of sorts, too. As with any outsider, she had to adjust her behaviour to conform to particular social conventions and to "talk-the-talk" in ways that made sense locally. Ironically, the pressures to do so may well have been greater because of her shared history with those she wished to interview. After all, where foreigners and outsiders might be forgiven their indiscretions, putting on airs amongst your own is unpardonable.

In the end, both Anderson and Hurston were able to go home to work to the extent that they were able to relearn local idioms and engage in meaningful fieldwork. Today, they are considered pioneers in participant observation and the collection of life histories in the 1920s. Both wrote in an engaging style, and their studies are continually reprinted. To read Anderson's *The Hobo* or Hurston's *Mules and Men* is to slip into another time. Unlike many of their contemporaries, who produced sociological and anthropological monographs that now appear dull and theoretically dated, the works of Anderson and Hurston still make for compelling reading. But neither became successful academics in either sociology or anthropology, perhaps because of the style of writing each adopted. Anderson approached ethnographic writing as a form of journalism, and Hurston wrote as a storyteller and cultural translator. As Strathern notes, "Attempts to make such accounts more accessible rest either on educating the audience anthropologically, or on abandoning the traditional genre in favour of a popular one" (1987: 18). As with traditional ethnographies, such genres retained an objective stance, and the goal remained that of interpreting the life-ways of one group for another. Yet neither *The Hobo* nor *Mules and Men* engage anthropological or sociological theory in any explicit way, as would a more typical ethnographic account.[9] Nevertheless, it is unclear to us if the choice to write in these more popular forms was deliberate or indicative of a more precarious relationship to the academy.

How far could an ex-hobo or a young black woman hope to go in the American academy of the 1920s? Did Robert Park and Franz Boas regard Anderson and Hurston as potential colleagues and academics, or did they value them as those "primitive philosophers" who make ideal informants?[10] Given the extreme forms of cultural relativism that informed their understanding of "other" cultural worlds (perceived as equal, but different) is it possible Park and Boas failed to properly indoctrinate these exceptional students into the ways of the academy? And, given the times, would it have made a difference? To be frank, we don't know the answers to these questions; but they deserve attention. They are the sorts of questions an auto-ethnography of the academy should take seriously. After all, it is painfully obvious that simply doing brilliant fieldwork and finely "writing culture" did not make successful academics.[11] In the case of Anderson and Hurston, we suspect being marked as native (or woman, or Negro, or hobo) was as much a liability to career advancement in the academy as it was an advantage in fieldwork.

Reflexivity

The paradoxes and dilemmas of doing ethnographic fieldwork at home have always been there, but the theoretical implications have been rarely acknowledged. The move towards anti-colonial and feminist critiques of knowledge production from the 1960s onward drew attention to the contrived, and deeply political, borders that separated self from others and anthropologists from natives. Too often, we suspect, being labelled a native anthropologist had as much to do with racist and colonial attitudes in the academy where one studied as it did with one's unique relationship to those under study. In the post-colonial (or should we say postmodern) world, these distinctions began to dissolve and identities became unstuck, so to speak, leading some to ask, "How native is the native anthropologist?" (Narayan 1995). Whether we have come full circle, as some would argue, so that claims of nativity are now manipulated to legitimate knowledge claims and advance careers, is debatable.[12] What is certain is that the practice of doing ethnography at home invites reflexivity, as it becomes obvious that what separates us from those we study is not some essential and impermeable identity but, rather, our intellectual preoccupations.[13]

Still, a reflexivity that fails to go beyond a solipsistic dwelling on one's own experience in the field is hardly sufficient. The point is not, simply, to position oneself within the text (as sometimes happened during ethnography's "experimental moment"[14]) but to engage in a critical reflection on one's relationships with others, as circumscribed by institutional practices and by history, both within and outside of the academy. Critical detachment and the ability to think ironically are required for the forms of reflexivity we are proposing for an auto-ethnography of academic practices. As

Joan Vincent (1991: 46) notes, we need to recognize "two kinds of politics around the texts of ethnography": the politics of representation found within texts, to which *Writing Culture* (Clifford and Marcus, 1986) sensitized us, and the politics "not embedded in the texts themselves," to which Roseberry (1996) drew attention when he examined the political economy of American anthropology.

Political Economies

Roseberry (1996) detected a retrenchment of power in elite American universities during the employment crisis of the 1990s. His essay, *The Unbearable Lightness of Anthropology*, is a melancholic reflection on the seldom officially recognized class structure in American anthropological hiring, where the "stars" are in perpetual motion, lured from institution to institution by high salaries and benefits like reduced teaching loads, while adjunct professors shoulder crippling teaching burdens at minimal pay, cobbling together a marginal living through a kind of academic piece-work. In his view, this not only disadvantages students from less privileged schools in terms of their professional careers, it restricts realms of theoretical engagement and debate within the discipline. The now (sadly!) defunct magazine, *Lingua Franca: The Review of Academic Life*, published an annual list of those recently hired and tenured, showing both the university of origin and the university of hiring. The list clearly proved the overwhelming success of some elite schools in placing their graduates in jobs. The hegemony of ideologies of meritocracy (so thought-provokingly explored by de Botton in his recent book, *Status Anxiety*) is almost absolute in the academy. Consequently, those who fail in the academic job search are easily found unworthy, despite their credentials and all evidence to the contrary. Thus, the fact that there simply are not enough jobs to go around is removed from consideration. Yet anyone who has participated in a job search knows that merit is not nearly as central to determining "fit" in a department as some would have us believe (Rabinow 1991). For a discipline that prides itself on attention to inequality, we seem to tolerate a fair bit of it in our midst.

In Canada, the media routinely publishes the salaries of full professors, leaving the public with an impression of over-indulged fat cats, who appear to only work (teach) eight months of the year. Never mind that we are also paid to research and write, and that there is scarcely enough time in the precious months of summer to do either in the way that we would like to. That most faculty are not full professors, that many struggle for years to write scholarly books that bring no financial rewards and serve on boards of journals and various review committees without any remuneration, is certainly never discussed. Such exposés never include the salaries of the legions of contract teachers, who labour for a pittance, often collect no benefits, and enjoy absolutely no job security, in their calculations of university salaries. Nor do most universities include such workers in their lists of faculty. After all, they are so invisible that institutions sometimes forget to provide them with offices, secretarial services, supplies, computers, or even library cards. To an extent that would surprise many of their students, and a wider public, these people help to subsidize the universities in which they work, despite ever increasing tuition fees. Surely the time has come to ask how such exploitive relations of production, awkward alliances, competing interests, and strenuous workloads affect academic work and production more generally.[15]

For our students, the political economy of academic practices, so much a part of the quotidian reality of academics, is often opaque. While we may take pains to analyze the larger political and economic historical contexts in which anthropological theories and styles of representation develop—like colonialism, globalization, anti-colonialism, and feminism—we often fail to mention the ways in which one's theoretical approach or scholarly production might be affected by issues of class, personal networks, access to funding, conditions of hiring and where one is hired, promotion, and tenure. While studies in political economy are able to trace broad sociological and political shifts in the academy, they do not always capture the historicity of the moment or the quality of lived experience in the academy, which ethnography plumbs. An auto-ethnography of academic practices sets out to recognize the structures of political economy in the ritualized and quotidian, the deeply personal, and even the mundane experiences of working in the academy.

It is in this sense that an auto-ethnography of the academy does indeed take us home and involve us in the work and contradictions of native anthropology. Academics do, to some extent, share conceptual and institutional structures, despite variations across national and disciplinary borders. Accounting for those variations is part of the project, and it requires vigilant attention to historically specific cultural, social, political, and economic currents. For instance, De Lima (1992) contrasted Brazilian and American academies, noting that in Brazil academics achieve their fame through their ability to subtly and flamboyantly converse, while in the bookish American academy, one must publish or perish. (Although, as the novelist James Hynes (1998) acknowledges, it is entirely possible to do both. His gothic tales exploring the vanities and pretensions of academics, who in the end publish *and* perish, are enough to send chills down the spines of most academics.) Rabinow's (1991) sardonic and insightful piece on the importance of class, gossip, and flattery during an American job interview suggests points of comparison with the Brazilian academy, as does Silverman's (2002) recent reflection on the funding and subsequent impact of Wenner Gren conferences. The latter also draws attention to the fact that many academic collections have their origins in conferences, many of which are plagued by personality conflicts as well as intellectual disputes. These works draw attention to the politics, often deeply personal, that attends academic work.

Retrospection

We have found that some of the most cogent and ethnographically revealing analyses of the academy can be found in the retrospectives of senior academics, periodically published in leading journals, and in the obituaries of intellectuals written by their students and close associates. All go beyond the simple description of a scholar's career path and theoretical contributions found in most texts that introduce students to the history of a discipline to give us glimpses into their personalities and the structures of feeling prevalent at the time of their tenure in the academy. Typical of the first are Edmund Leach's "Glimpses of the Unmentionable in the History of British Social Anthropology" (1984), published in the *Annual Review of Anthropology*, and T.O. Beidelman's "Marking Time: Becoming an Anthropologist" (1998), published in *Ethnos*. Leach's revelations about the elitist, sexist, and colonial attitudes at Cambridge that diminished and stifled intellectual discourse, as well as his candid observations about his contemporaries and their turf wars, should certainly disabuse any who hold onto a nostalgic reverence for the traditional academy. Beidelman claims that being drafted into the American army to fight in Korea was a brutal experience that not only shaped his subsequent interests in psychology, history, and anthropology, it also helped to prepare him for the trials of doctoral work at Oxford. Both men take delight in scurrilous anecdotes: according to Beidelman, the eminent sociologist Talcott Parsons tried to strangle him at a cocktail party; Leach's distaste for Max Gluckman is palpable. Beyond the guilty pleasures of being privy to so much mud-slinging, these retrospective essays give us a rare insider's view of the academy on two continents at a time when anthropology was expanding as a discipline.

In this regard, Beidelman's (1974) respectful, yet surprisingly frank, obituary of Edward Evan Evans-Pritchard, Sidney Mintz's (1981) lovely reflection on his professor Ruth Benedict, and Terry Eagleton's (1988) touching tribute to Raymond Williams broaden our understanding of the vicissitudes of life within the academy throughout much of the twentieth century. Beidelman understood well that Evans-Pritchard enjoyed the privileges of an intellectual and colonial elite in an English academy obsessed by class. One of the comforts of such privilege was Evans-Pritchard's purported modesty, born of utter confidence in his intellectual worth. According to Beideleman, Evans-Pritchard's meticulous scholarship, graceful writing, enduring friendships, and abiding faith were matched only by his searing wit, disdain for intellectual pomposity, and love of ribald sociability. He was brilliant and deeply complex in very English ways. As a distinguished scholar, he was much lauded, both at Oxford, where he was made Professor of Social Anthropology, and by the state, which honoured him with knighthood. This is in stark contrast to his American contemporary, Ruth Benedict. Sidney Mintz wrote fondly of his professor's humanistic writing style, her theoretical approach to culture, and her bravery in speaking out against racism even before the civil rights movement. But he also noted how sexism affected her career and delayed her promotion to full professorship until shortly before her death. For women, the political climate at Columbia was chilly; not only did law professors refuse to attend meetings if women were present, graduate students in the department of anthropology arrogantly dismissed Benedict's work, which was considered insufficiently scientific for the times. In these ways, Mintz revealed how Benedict, as an academic, was constrained by institutional structures, political prejudice and activism, intellectual fashions, and personal inclinations.

Perhaps no essay better incorporates the various strains informing our understanding of auto-ethnography than Terry Eagleton's homage to Raymond Williams. His account of the dignity shown by Williams in the face of the blatant class prejudice he experienced at Cambridge carefully articulates a particular historical moment in the academy. Williams was one of the few scholarship students grudgingly admitted to Cambridge. According to Eagleton, the price he paid for this privilege was a sense of living on the borders: "He was always haunted by the border he had crossed from the 'knowable community' to the life of educated intelligence, and he lived in border country the whole of his life" (1988: 6). The sense of detachment engendered by this experience saturates a body of work that, in and of itself, crossed ideological and disciplinary borders and, in doing so, shattered many academic and party shibboleths. His influence, across the disciplines, was and is enormous. Eagleton writes:

> Williams had, I think, an unusually strong sense of himself as an historical figure. If he could be aware of the massive importance of his own work without the least personal vanity, it was in part because he had a curious ability to look on himself from the outside, to see his own life as in a Lukácsian sense "typical" rather than just individual. He lived everything he did from the inside, saturating his thought with personal experience; yet he also seemed able to place himself impersonally, judiciously as "an ordinary life spanning the middle years of the twentieth century" (*Modern Tragedy*). (1988: 10–11)

In this volume, we have asked contributors to adopt this spirit and to think of themselves as typical—of one's generation, institution, nation, time, and place—so as to articulate the salient features of working in the academy at the turn of the twenty-first century. In other words, we have asked academics to consider themselves as worthy subjects of ethnographic investigation and contemplation.

AT WORK IN THE ACADEMY AT THE TURN OF THE CENTURY

While several decades of thoughtful scholarship examining anthropology's historical complicity in unjust epistemological and colonial systems generated much critical reflection in the discipline of anthropology, especially as it pertains to issues of representation, our encounters with the "other," the subjects of our discourse, remain fraught with difficulty. While some might confidently declare anthropology "exotic no more"[16] (would that it were so!), those who become the subjects of our study and reflection, as often as not, remain unconvinced. As many of the essays in this volume make obvious, this disjunction between what we think we do and what others think we do contours our relationships and professional practices as teachers in the university, as fieldworkers, and as interveners in public debates. And surely this should come as no surprise to a generation of savvy intellectuals schooled to recognize the ways in which tenacious and over-determined representations confound social engagements and political practices. After all, while our anthropological ancestors helped to create some of the most enduring representations of cultural others (the Trobrianders and the Nuer come quickly to mind), they simultaneously produced images of themselves as intrepid loners and quixotic scientists. In popular imagination, the exotic primitive and the eccentric anthropologist belong together. That this was never entirely the case hardly matters to those not educated in the discipline. It is the stereotype that lives on in popular imagination and frequently bedevils our endeavours. It is both a source of amusement and angst for practitioners.

As a cultural phenomenon that seems to resonate in near and far-flung places, the salience of this caricature anthropologist for our times—supposedly post-colonial and trans-global—is intriguing. Rituals of self-cleansing and contrition are performed in anthropology classes from introductory to graduate levels, as we increasingly teach against our canonical texts.

For years, the goal of university introductory classes has been to disabuse young students of their romantic inclinations, but many hold on tenaciously to the idea of anthropology as the study of quaint customs and exotic primitives. Films such as *If Only I Were an Indian* (1994), in which the anthropologist John Paskievich travels with three Ojibwe elders to visit a band of Czechoslovakian "Indians," brilliantly turns many of these notions on their head. Still, it remains very hard going for many students. Assuredly, this has always been so, but as classes grow larger and larger in our corporate university, it can be difficult to gauge when, and if, students make the critical leaps required to proceed to a wider discussion of anthropological debates. Given the pressures to fill those introductory classes with the multitudes that ensure funding for departments, it is tempting to give the students cum clients the "National Geographic" anthropology they desire, with a view to un-teaching the serious student in upper level classes. It is, after all, easier to administer multiple-choice exams when you adopt such an approach. Anthropologists have resisted such pressures, knowing that the price paid is enormous. The reification of a racist and non-historical understanding of the world has no place in the university and certainly not in an anthropology classroom. In this regard, anthropology attempts to teach against the grain.

What we find ironic is that along with all those other "others," who have been squeezed into narrow, unhistorical, cultural categories in need of unpacking, is the anthropologist. While there may be poetic justice in finding the anthropologist ensnared in the same reductive tropics of discourse as his or her subject, the spectre of the anthropologist that confronts us in the eyes of our students and on the lips of our many interlocutors (in the classroom, on ethics review boards, in visa offices, in community cultural centers, in the places where we conduct our ethnographic studies, and in the media) can pose very real problems and dilemmas.

We do not mean to suggest that anthropologists alone bear the brunt of unfortunate stereotyping. Nor do we mean to suggest that the world outside of our academic institutions is some sort of parallel universe. Practitioners in most disciplines are typecast in myriad ways, which must surely complicate their social engagements as professionals. And our research interests and conundrums are often a direct consequence of policy initiatives imposed upon our disciplines from the outside by universities, funding agencies, and national research agendas. At least in North America, a strong current of anti-intellectualism fuels the belief that the research of most academics is not only arcane but also unworthy of public support. We are, therefore, encouraged to build bridges with a wider public and to meet a series of guidelines that sometimes seem configured to prevent us from reaching our less tangible goals.

In focussing on the particular experiences of ethnographers involved in the academy, we hope to illuminate how the academy, as an institution, is both reproduced and changed over time. As in all ethnographic accounts, the goal is to uncover the broader sweep of history and the influence of power and wider social formations in the most particular and local of settings. As such, the essays that comprise *Auto-ethnographies: The Anthropology of Academic Practices* examine disciplinary and institutional rites of passage in the modern university from the perspective of individual academics. Their deepest concerns are revealed as they explore their practices and the meanings they attach to such practices. And they do so in an engagingly lucid style; they do not hide behind a shield of arcane terminology that effectively excludes the non-specialist, nor do they confuse jargon with sophistication of thought. Their concerns are heartfelt, and they write to open up anthropological knowledge to a wider audience.

STRUCTURES OF FEELING

This volume is animated by complex structures of feeling: feelings of humility linked to an ironic awareness of our selves as social actors and feelings of quiet resolve, born of a conviction that what we have to say about the world we live in is important, even if it does not translate well in a world of sound bites and simple moral imperatives. This ironic sensibility informs all of the essays found in this collection. As such, they draw attention to the complex negotiations that attend our professional work as researchers, writers, teachers, administrators, and citizens. Two things on which all agree are that moral behaviour cannot easily be codified as ethical procedure and that the practice of participant observation, as a viable research method, needs defending.

Long gone is the sense of righteous conviction that Joan Vincent (1991) found in the political activism of 1960s anthropology, but, nevertheless, we remain politically engaged and deeply concerned about the complex and unjust world we live in. Equally gone is the chastened anthropology of the 1980s, which, caught with its hands in the colonial cookie jar, grew either defensive or obsessed with rituals of self-mortification. That period of self-critical examination affected many of our authors, who were in graduate school when *Writing Culture*, the volume that came to epitomize that time, inspired much enthusiasm and not a little controversy. While that moment profoundly shaped the research agendas of some of our authors, most discovered that choosing to do things differently, or writing differently, did little to undermine asymmetrical power structures. Further, ethical concerns do not evaporate into thin air because one is self-critical. Indeed, acting ethically requires constant vigilance, and awkward—even nasty—situations remain unavoidable. Anthropologists are not the only ones capable of succumbing to the enticements of power, and ours is, for the most part, a cautionary tale about the hubris of academics.

NOTES

1   Allan Bloom's *The Closing of the American Mind* (1987) is typical of the former; Jean François Lyotard's *The Postmodern Condition* (1987), written as a report for the government of Quebec, and Stanley Fogel's *The Postmodern University* (1988) are examples of the latter.

2   Sidney Mintz (1981) recounts how poorly Ruth Benedict was treated by her male colleagues at the University of Chicago, while Edmund Leach (1984) gives a startling account of how T.T. Barnard, a botanist who knew nothing of anthropology but was well-connected to the British elite at Cambridge, became Chair of the Anthropology Department in Cape Town, South Africa.

3   See Strathern, *Audit Cultures* (2000).

4   See, for instance, Benhabib (1992), Reed-Danahay (1997), Haraway (1991), and Okely and Callaway (1992).

5   Roseberry compares academic hierarchies to conical clan structure: "the noble line is located in elite departments, the noninheriting sons and daughters are located in colleges, sociology, and non-PhD-granting departments" (1996: 10).

6   Thomas Dunk (2002: 31) argues that Canadian anthropology was formed "by parameters of internal colonial [of first nations] and neocolonial relations [with the United States and Britain]." Dunk's critique of socio-cultural anthropology in Canada suggests that what typifies Canadian anthropology is a dependence on practitioners who were trained outside of Canada (2002: 27).

7   See Anderson, *The American Hobo: An Autobiography* (1975).

8   Zora Neale Hurston became a famous folklorist and novelist. Her novel *Their Eyes Were Watching God* (1937) is an American classic. But see also her quirky autobiography *Dust Tracks on a Road* (1942). Her correspondence with Franz Boas can be found in her published letters (Kaplan, 2002) and in the biography *Wrapped in Rainbows* (Boyd, 2003).

9   Strathern notes "This applies especially to 'ethnographies' in so far as they are perceived to be about specific peoples at specific places and times; but most books which contain ethnography comprise a mixed genre, including attempts at anthropological theory…." Strathern intends "reference to this mixed genre" when she distinguishes between ethnographic and anthropological accounts (1987: 19).

10   In *Primitive Man as Philosopher*, Paul Radin wrote that a select few within any group are "constrained by their temperaments and interests to occupy themselves with the basic problems of what we call philosophy" (1927: xxi). For a discussion of Radin's work see Darnell (2001).

11   This is, in part, the argument made in *Women Writing Culture* (Behar and Gordon, 1995). It was noted that women made peripheral to the academy had for a long time engaged in novel forms of ethnographic writing, for which they paid a heavy price. This is a fact little acknowledged in *Writing Culture* (Clifford and Marcus, 1986) that only noted textual innovations in ethnographic writing made by men.

12   For instance, Narayan (1995) questions Abu-Lughod's (1988) concept of a "halfie," noting that it always seems to be the "darker" half that grants the capacity for ethnographic insight!

13   See Strathern (1987), Okely (1996; 1992), and Todorov-Pirgova (1999).

14   See Wolf (1992).

[15] Elsewhere, Bourdieu (1994, 1988) traced the influence of class in the French academy by analyzing records of admissions and the career patterns of academics in elite and commoner institutions. Contrary to expectation, he found that many of the more innovative and influential academics of the past several decades, broadly associated with French critical theory, were housed in less prestigious schools. More recently, Strathern (2000) and Gledhill (2002) have described the particular dilemmas faced by anthropologists in England, while Dunk (2002) has appraised the discipline's present state of affairs in Anglophone Canada. All of these works make an important contribution to our knowledge of a changing academy within particular national contexts. Importantly, they demonstrate that practices of gatekeeping and the messy politics of nation, class, race, and gender not only determine the sociological profile of professional academics in particular institutions, they also influence currents of intellectual thought within disciplines.

[16] MacClancy (ed.) *Exotic No More: Anthropology on the Front Lines* (2002).

WORKS CITED

Abu-Lughod, Lila. 1988. Fieldwork of a dutiful daughter. In *Arab Women in the Field: Studying Your Own Society*. Ed. Soraya Altoki and Camilla Fawzi El-Sohl. 139–61. Syracuse, NY: Syracuse University Press.

Anderson, Nels. 1923. *The Hobo: The Sociology of the Homeless Men*. Chicago, IL: University of Chicago Press.

———.1975. *The Hobo: An Autobiography*. Leiden, NL: E.J. Brill.

———.1998. *On Hobos and Homelessness*. Intro. and ed. Raffael Rauty. Chicago, IL: University of Chicago Press.

Asad, Talal. 1973. *Anthropology and the Colonial Encounter*. London: Ithaca Press.

———.1986. The concept of cultural translation in British social anthropology. In *Writing Culture: Poetics and Politics of Ethnography*. Ed. James Clifford and George E. Marcus. 141-64. Berkeley, CA: University of California Press.

———. 2003. *Formations of the Secular*. Stanford, CA: Stanford University Press.

Augé, Marc. 1998 [1994]. *A Sense for the Other: The Timeliness and Relevance of Anthropology*. Trans. Amy Jacobs. Stanford, CA: Stanford University Press.

Basch, Linda, and Lucie Wood Saunders, Jagna Wojcicka, James Peacock (eds.). 1999. *Transforming Academia: Challenges and Opportunities for Engaged Anthropology*. Arlington, VA: American Anthropological Association.

Barthes, Roland. 1972. *Mythologies*. Trans. Jonathan Cape Ltd. Paris: Editions de Seuil.

———.1989. Research: The young. In *The Rustle of Language*. Trans. R. Howard. 69-75. Berkeley, CA: University of California Press.

Behar, Ruth, and Deborah A. Gordon, eds. 1995. *Women Writing Culture*. Berkeley, CA: University of California Press.

Beidelman, T.O. 1974. Sir Edward Evan Evans-Pritchard (1902–1973): An appreciation. *Anthropos* 69: 553–67.

———.1992. Millennium. *Cultural Anthropology* 7: 508–15.

———.1998. Marking time: Becoming an anthropologist. *Ethnos* 63(2): 273–96.

Benhabib, Seyla. 1992. *Situating the Self: Gender, Community and Postmodernism in Contemporary Ethics*. Cambridge: Polity Press.

Bérubé, Michael. 2003. Standards of reason in the classroom. *The Chronicle of Higher Education* December 5: B7–B10.

Bloom, Allan. *The Closing of the American Mind*. New York: Simon and Schuster.

Botton, Alain de. 2004. *Status Anxiety*. Toronto: Viking Canada.

Bourdieu, Pierre. 1988. *Homo Academicus*. Trans. Peter Collier. Stanford, CA: Stanford University Press.

———. 1993. *The Field of Cultural Production: Essays on Art and Literature*. Cambridge: Polity Press.

———. 1994. *Academic Discourse: Linguistic Misunderstanding and Professional Power*. Cambridge: Polity Press.

Bourdieu, Pierre, and Loïc J.D. Wacquant. 1992. *An Invitation to Reflexive Sociology*. Chicago, IL: University of Chicago Press.

Boyd, V. 2003. *Wrapped in Rainbows: The Life of Zora Neale Hurston*. New York: Scribner.

Bradwin, Edmund William. 1972 [1928]. *The Bunkhouse Man: A Study of Work and Pay in the Camps of Canada, 1903–1914*. Repr. Toronto: University of Toronto Press/Columbia: Columbia University Press.

Brenneis, Donald. 1994. Discourse and discipline at the National Research Council: A bureaucratic *bildungsroman*. *Cultural Anthropology* 9(1): 23–36.

———. 1999. New lexicon, old language: Negotiating the "global" at the National Science Foundation. In *Critical Anthropology Now: Unexpected Contexts, Shifting Constituencies, Changing Agendas*. Ed. George Marcus. 123–46. Santa Fe, NM: School of American Research Press.

Brent, David. 1999. Merchants in the temple of scholarship: American university press publishing at century's end. In *Critical Anthropology Now: Unexpected Contexts, Shifting Constituencies, Changing Agendas*. Ed. George Marcus. 361–86. Santa Fe, NM: School of American Research Press.

Clifford, James, and George E. Marcus (eds.). 1986. *Writing Culture: The Poetics and Politics of Ethnography*. Berkeley, CA: University of California Press

Darnell, Regna. 2001. *Invisible Genealogies: A History of Americanist Anthropology*. Lincoln, NB and London: University of Nebraska Press.

De Lima, Roberto Kant. 1992. The anthropology of the academy: When we are the

Indians. *Knowledge and Society: The Anthropology of Science and Technology* 9: 191–222.

Dunk, Thomas. 2002. Bicentrism, culture, and the political economy of sociocultural anthropology in Canada. In *Culture, Economy, Power: Anthropology as Critique, Anthropology as Praxis*. Ed. Winnie Lem and Belinda Leach. 19–32. Albany, NY: State University of New York Press.

Eagleton, Terry. 1988. Resources for a journey of hope: The significance of Raymond Williams. *New Left Review*, March/April: 3–11.

Fabian, Johannes. 1983. *Time and the Other: How Anthropology Makes Its Object*. New York: Columbia University Press.

———. 2001. *Anthropology with an Attitude: Critical Essays*. Stanford, CA: Stanford University Press.

Fogel, Stanley. 1988. *The Postmodern University: Essays on the Deconstruction of the University*. Toronto: ECW Press.

Garber, Marjorie. 2001. *Academic Instincts*. Princeton, N.J.: Princeton University Press.

Gledhill, John. 2002. A small discipline": The embattled place of anthropology in a massified British higher education sector. In *Culture, Economy, Power: Anthropology as Critique, Anthropology as Praxis*. Ed. Winnie Lem and Belinda Leach. 73–87. Albany, NY: State University of New York Press.

Haraway, Donna. 1991. *Simians, Cyborgs, and Women: The Reinvention of Nature*. New York: Routledge.

Hernández, Graciela. 1995. Multiple subjectivities and strategic positionality: Zora Neale Hurston's experimental ethnographies. In *Women Writing Culture*. Ed. Ruth Behar and Deborah A. Gordon. 148-65. Berkeley, CA: University of California Press.

Hurston, Zora Neale. 1978 [1937]. *Their Eyes Were Watching God*. Urbana and Chicago, IL: University of Illinois Press.

———.1984 [1942]. *Dust Tracks on the Road: An Autobiography*. Intro. and ed. Robert Hemenway. Urbana and Chicago, IL: University of Illinois Press.

———. 1990. *Tell My Horse: Voodoo and Life in Haiti and Jamaica*. New York: Perennial Library.

———. 1995. *Folklore, Memoirs and Other Writings*. New York: Library of America.

Hynes, James. 1998. *Publish and Perish: Three Tales of Tenure and Terror*. New York: Picador.

Jackson, Anthony, ed. 1987. *Anthropology at Home*. London: Tavistock Publications.

Kaplan, Carla, ed. 2002. *Zora Neale Hurston: A Life in Letters*. New York: Doubleday.

Leach, Edmund. 1984. Glimpses of the unmentionable in the history of British social anthropology. *Annual Review of Anthropology* 3: 1–23.

Lyotard, Jean François. 1987. *The Postmodern Condition. A Report on Knowledge.* Trans. Geoff Bennington and Brian Massumi. Minneapolis, MN: University of Minnesota Press.

Marcus, George. 1998. *Ethnography Through Thick and Thin.* Princeton, NJ: Princeton University Press.

———. 1999. *Critical Anthropology Now: Unexpected Contexts, Shifting Constituencies, Changing Agendas.* Santa Fe, NM: School of American Research Press.

MacClancy, Jeremy (ed.). 2002. *Exotic No More: Anthropology on the Front Lines.* Chicago, IL and London: University of Chicago Press.

Mintz, Sidney. 1981. Ruth Benedict. In *Totems and Teachers: Perspectives on the History of Anthropology.* Ed. Sydel Silverman. 140-68. New York: Columbia University Press.

———. 1998. The localization of anthropological practice: From area studies to transnationalism. *Critique of Anthropology* 18(2): 117–33.

Narayan, Kirin. 1995. Participant observation. In *Women Writing Culture.* Ed. Ruth Behar and Deborah A. Gordon. 33–48. Berkeley, CA: University of California Press.

———. 1997. How native is the native anthropologist. In *Situated Lives.* Ed. Louise Lamphere, Helena Regoné, and Patricia Zavella. 32–41. New York: Routledge.

Okely, Judith. 1996. *Own or Other Culture.* London and New York: Routledge.

Okely, Judith, and Helen Callaway, eds. 1992. *Anthropology and Autobiography.* London and New York: Routledge.

Paskievitch, John. 1994. *If Only I Were an Indian.* Ottawa, ON: Zemma Films and the National Film Board.

Pratt, Mary Louise. 1986. Fieldwork in common places. In *Writing Culture: The Poetics and Politics of Ethnography.* Ed. James Clifford and George E. Marcus. 141–64. Berkeley, CA: University of California Press.

Rabinow, Paul. 1986. Representations are social facts: Modernity and post-modernity in anthropology. In *Writing Culture: Poetics and Politics of Ethnography.* Ed. James Clifford and George E. Marcus. 234–61. Berkeley, CA: University of California Press.

———. 1991. For hire: Resolutely late modern. In *Recapturing Anthropology: Working in the Present.* Ed. Richard G. Fox. 59–71. Santa Fe, NM: School of American Research Press.

———. 1996. *Essays on the Anthropology of Reason.* Princeton, NJ: Princeton University Press.

Radin, Paul. 1927. *Primitive Man as Philosopher.* New York: Appleton and Co.

Rauty, Raffael. 1998. *Introduction to On Hobos and Homelessness*. Ed. R. Rauty. Chicago, IL: University of Chicago Press.

Reed-Danahay, Deborah (ed.). 1997. *Auto/Ethnography*. Oxford and New York: Berg.

Rorty, Richard. 1999. *Philosophy and Social Hope*. London: Penguin Books.

———. 1989. *Contingency, Irony, and Solidarity*. New York: Cambridge University Press.

Roseberry, William. 1996. The unbearable lightness of anthropology. *Radical History Review* 65: 5–25.

———. 2002. Political economy in the United States. In *Culture, Economy, Power: Anthropology as Critique, Anthropology as Praxis*. Ed. Winnie Lem and Belinda Leach. 59–72. Albany, NY: State University of New York Press.

Russo, Richard. 1997. *Straight Man: A Novel*. New York: Vintage.

Silverman, Sydel. 2002. *The Beast on the Table: Conferencing with Anthropologists*. Walnut Creek, CA: Altamira Press.

———. 2004. *Totems and Teachers: Key Figures in the History of Anthropology*. Walnut Creek, CA: Altamira Press.

Strathern, Marilyn. 1987. The limits of auto-anthropology. In *Anthropology at Home*. Ed. Anthony Jackson. 6–37. London: Tavistock Publications.

———. 2000. *Audit Cultures: Anthropological Studies in Accountability, Ethics, and the Academy*. London and New York: Routledge.

Todorov-Pirgova, Iveta. 1999. "Native" anthropologist: On the bridge or at the border. *Anthropological Journal on European Cultures* 8(2): 171–90.

Vincent, Joan. 1991. Engaging historicism. *Recapturing Anthropology: Working in the Present*. Ed. Richard G. Fox. 45–58. Santa Fe, NM: School of American Research Press.

Williams, Raymond. 1962. *Border Country*. New York: Horizon Press.

———. 1966. *Modern Tragedy*. London: Chatto and Windus.

———. 1977. *Marxism and Literature*. Oxford: Oxford University Press.

Wolf, Margery. 1992. *A Thrice Told Tale*. Stanford, CA: Stanford University Press.

PART I | INITIATIONS

W E BEGIN WITH INITIATIONS, where the focus is on fieldwork as a rite of passage for anthropologists. As neophyte anthropologists, Sylvain, Gotlib, and Cummings all entered the field well aware of the internal critiques of anthropological practice that dominated discussion within the discipline over the past several years. Although determined to be morally responsible and to do anthropology differently, they discovered that acting responsibly is not always easy or even obvious. They reflect on the ethical and moral dilemmas they must confront as they attempt, simultaneously, to adhere to new professional standards as imposed by ethics review boards and to engage in participant observation fieldwork as moral actors.

As Sylvain notes, "Filling out forms and responding to the queries of ethics committees provides opportunities to reflect on the wisdom of imposing only one ethical vocabulary, a discourse of legal persons and professional responsibility, onto what most anthropologists insist is an unstable and contradictory moral engagement." She argues that the ethnographic encounter involves "putting our own identities at risk" so that one develops new habits of perception and thus new moral habits.

Gotlib draws attention to the problematic reification of ethics review boards in the contemporary university, noting that the ethics review is as much intended to protect the university as it is to protect the subjects of research. While earlier discussions of ethical field practices tended to focus on an anthropologist's privileges with respect to her informants, power relations in the field are not always that clear cut. Gotlib found that when a discipline with less cultural capital, such as anthropology, attempts to study a discipline with greater cultural capital, such as medicine, economic clout in the form of funding may open more doors than either theoretical subtlety or ethical rigour.

Cummings is initiated into her fieldwork in Vanuatu as part of a collective research grant initiated by her doctoral supervisor. In Vanuatu, collaboration with local researchers and the production of research initiatives that benefit the people of Vanuatu are a precondition for foreign researchers. Thus, Cummings is assigned to making a video that allows young Vanuatu women to speak about current issues in their lives. Ironically, as an anthropologist,

Cummings is assumed to be interested in the domain of "kastom," which not only encompasses "traditional knowledge" but is also a domain where patriarchal relations are authorized. The young women Cummings works with are contesting patriarchal assertions that women wearing trousers are being disrespectful to the traditional domain of "kastom." They also object to the argument, made by their elders, that doing so makes them vulnerable to rape. Cummings's informants stage a sartorial revolt by wearing trousers to work; her own conformity to the dominant norms is used to chastise them. Cummings implicitly explores the ambiguities of to whom one owes loyalty as an anthropologist: to one's informants or to those who can withhold or approve further research?

These essays raise a series of questions about the implications of implementing legally binding procedures for ethical behaviour in a discipline like anthropology that engages in participant observation research in a wide variety of contexts. Together, they challenge the idea that one rule should apply equally. This is not to suggest anthropologists do not take ethics seriously. Indeed, we would wager no subject has been more hotly debated within the discipline. We are, therefore, understandably mortified when we overhear colleagues from other disciplines use the awkward phrase "to anthropologize" as a stand-in for "to objectify"!

Anthropologists increasingly ask themselves if participant observation research, the very practice that is supposed to make them anthropologists, is even possible under the new rules of governance in our universities. Yet, as Michael Lambek notes in the Afterword, the signed ethics form is simply—and unethically—a way to transfer liability to our subjects. We would add that the signature required on such forms undermines our efforts—as far as possible—to protect the identity of our informants.[1] In a place like Canada, where a university risks losing funds for faculty research grants if the procedures established by the Tri-Council Ethics Policy are not strictly followed, the university ethics committee might be inclined to protect the interests of colleagues and the university as a whole, rather than the research subjects.

NOTES

[1] Thanks to our colleague Paul Manning for conversations about the fundamental contradiction between signature and anonymity: you can have one or the other, but not both.

LOYALTY AND TREACHERY IN THE KALAHARI[1]

RENÉE SYLVAIN

> "It is not enough to be true to one's self. The self may be bad or need to be changed, or it may change unawares into something strange and new."

—LAURA BOHANNAN,
RETURN TO LAUGHTER

THE SAN (BUSHMEN) OF THE Omaheke Region in eastern Namibia are one of the most stigmatized and marginalized ethnic groups in southern Africa. Most live and work on cattle ranches owned by Afrikaner farmers, but an increasing number move between resettlement camps and the squatters' villages on the edges of urban areas, where they struggle to make ends meet by performing menial tasks for other ethnic groups and where they are the targets of racially and ethnically motivated violence. The situation of the Omaheke San is bleak, but not hopeless. They are remarkably adept at negotiating the extreme power asymmetries that structure their lives, and, even in the most marginal areas, they create and maintain a meaningful cultural life for themselves. There is love and laughter in the lives of the San, and they are determined to improve their material conditions and "go forward."

My research focussed on one group of San, the Ju/'hoansi, who live and work on white-owned farms. My commitment to research that had social and economic justice as its primary goals meant that I had to be very careful not to exacerbate the already volatile relations between the San and other ethnic groups. I also had to determine how far to participate in the lives of people who must survive through banditry. The ethical codes and research contracts currently being elaborated are too aloof to help us navigate ethical problems that arise in particular field situations, and the good professionals they help us to be are not always the same as the good persons we hope to become. For the sources of an anthropologist's moral agency, we must look at how the anthropologist is variously defined as an agent.

Specifically, we need to pay attention to the ways the anthropologist's own identity is shaped and played out in the process of conducting fieldwork.

THE IRONIC ADVOCATE

Filling out forms and responding to the queries of ethics committees provides opportunities to reflect on the wisdom of imposing only one ethical vocabulary, a discourse of legal persons and professional responsibility, onto what most anthropologists insist is an unstable and contradictory moral engagement. Our compliance with codified and contract-based ethical frameworks often implies the betrayal of a deeper commitment to other moral vocabularies. This ironic conviction was what motivated many of us to do anthropology in the first place. Richard Rorty describes an "ironist" in terms that are sure to be familiar to anthropologists:

> The ironist spends her time worrying about the possibility that she has been initiated into the wrong tribe, taught to play the wrong language game. She worries that the process of socialization which turned her into a human being by giving her a language may have given her the wrong language, and so turned her into the wrong kind of human being. (1989: 75)

It is widely recognized that fieldwork is a rite of passage: as neophyte anthropologists we go through the familiar phases of separation, liminality, and reintegration. However, in most tales from the field, this rite of passage is treated as something to be endured, survived, and surpassed in order to get down to the "real" business of gathering data and writing up one's research. "Culture shock," the dissonance that individuals often feel when first immersed in another culture, is often seen as an obstacle to knowledge, rather than an experience that can produce a more nuanced moral subjectivity. But as anthropologists who study rites of passage appreciate, these rites change the initiate's identity. The same is true for anthropologists. Our identities and our self-understanding change as we move through our initiation ritual of fieldwork.

THE HOPEFUL REFORMER

During my pre-fieldwork training in graduate school, I was duly humbled, diminished, and destabilized by the postmodern turn in anthropology. I was schooled in all the ways in which anthropology was implicated in colonial injustices, in its authoritarian predilection for silencing and then speaking for "the Other," and about how anthropology itself was suffering from an incurable identity crisis. While preparing for fieldwork among the San, I developed an appreciation for the extent to which they had been subject to racial stereotyping in the popular media and even in many early ethnographic works. So I saw myself as a reformer ready to study the intersections of gender, race, and class inequalities in a place where apartheid remained powerfully present, even after six years of independence from South African rule. My mission was to deconstruct colonial and neo-colonial stereotypes. So off I went to the Omaheke to do battle against the evils of bad discourse.

Before I could confront bad discourse, however, I had to get past the hostile Afrikaner farmers and onto their farms where the San are labourers. My anxiety only increased once I arrived in Namibia and was told by every local expert I met in the capital city that the farmers would shoot me. I decided to present myself to the farmers in very vague terms, as an "ivory-tower" ethnologist concerned primarily with a romantic prehistorical past. One of the first farmers to grant me permission to speak to his workers gave me a friendly warning: "If you interfere with my workers," he said, "I'll shoot you."

Despite the threats and the warnings, what I did not anticipate was the extent to which many farmers would enthusiastically support my research. Labour relations on the farms are based on the farmers' notions of "innate capacities" and levels of "cultural development" among different "nations." Since running a farm requires an intimate knowledge of the different "ethnic natures" of their various workers, farmers often see themselves as amateur ethnologists.

My first encounter with such a farmer taught me an important lesson about the difficulties of securing informed consent in a context marked by profound class, gender, and race inequalities. Immediately after I explained my project, the farmer turned to a Ju/'hoan woman working in his kitchen and demanded that she round up all the Ju/'hoan women on the farm and bring them to meet me at the farmhouse to answer my questions. Since the farmer insisted on observing, I had no choice but to conduct interviews with these women. I did my best to keep my questions harmless (asking if they remembered the "old time" ways), but the experience was almost as painful for me as I'm sure it was for the women.

After that encounter, I developed a coded introductory statement that my interpreter and I could present to Ju/'hoansi even if the farmer was present. In English or Afrikaans, I would explain that I was interested in learning about "old time ways." My interpreter would explain, in Ju/'hoan, that I wanted to talk to them about gender, race, and class issues. The farmer would hear the apolitical version of my project in a language he could understand, while the Ju/'hoansi heard the political version in a language he couldn't.

Upon arriving on a farm, I was usually obliged to visit with the farmer before I set off to the workers' compound. Since the Ju/'hoansi had just seen me sitting with their *baas*, drinking tea and having a nice chat, I was initially treated with distrust. I would have to earn their trust and assure them that I would not disclose the content of our conversations to their employer, who, if he learned what we had discussed, would possibly fire them or, even worse, beat them.

Farmers were not the only obstacle to getting informed consent. Before we started interviewing farm workers, my interpreter warned me that almost every farm had a *witvoet* (white-foot), "a person who walks to the farmer with the black peoples' business." So first I had to become integrated into the social life on the farms in order for the San to tell me which of the workers could not be trusted. I ended up interviewing people about innocuous matters for months before I fully disclosed the true subject of my research. The issue of trust worked both ways: I had to find out who I could trust, and I had to prove myself trustworthy. To do this, I had to redefine myself as a white woman.

NEITHER A *MIESSIS*, NOR A MISSIONARY

When I first arrived in the Omaheke, I was addressed as *miessis*, the local term for madam, reserved for use by black and Bushman servants when they are speaking to a white farmer's wife. It is usually accompanied by a subservient posture, head bowed, hat in hands. I would reply, "I'm not a madam" (*Ek is nie 'n miessis nie*). Upon hearing this, many Africans would fall back on the next likely identity for a white woman—if I was not a *miessis*, then I must be a missionary. Most abandoned this theory when they saw me smoking and heard me cursing at my truck.

The first farmer my husband and I met welcomed us warmly. He and his wife were excited to have visitors from so far away after years of isolation that came with the pariah status of their apartheid government. The farmer, a liberal thinker by local standards, explained how labour relations were shaped in the apartheid days: "When you first bring the blacks onto your farm, you take the biggest, strongest one down from the truck and beat him senseless with a *sjambok* [a leather whip]—from there you won't have any problems with the blacks on your farm." The farmer's wife asked about our experiences with the local black population. Since we were foreigners, they expected "the blacks" to get "cheeky" with us. The farmer advised us to get a deep tan (so that we would look like local whites) and to commit a few Afrikaans phrases to memory (these phrases had to be properly pronounced and preferably barked): "What do you want?" (*Wat soek julle?*) and "Are you looking for trouble?" (*Soek jy moelikheid?*). Safety, we learned, lies in being mistaken for Afrikaners, who the blacks "knew" to be capable of any form of barbarity. Initially my husband and I decided not to heed the well-intended advice, but there were episodes where we felt we had little choice.

One such occasion occurred in the squatters' village on the fringes of the black township of Epako, where many unemployed and impoverished San live. One young Ju/'hoan man, //Umte, was especially helpful as an informant, and he was one of the first San people to befriend us. One day, while my husband and I were conducting interviews and visiting //Umte's family, some young Damara men, local thugs who were constantly terrorizing and bullying the San, stole the family's donkey cart and donkeys. We heard the commotion when a group of San men set off in pursuit of the Damaras and the donkeys. The San men caught up with the Damaras, and, just as my husband and I arrived, a fight was on the verge of breaking out. The chase had taken us into an area of the township dominated by Damaras, and the San were clearly out-numbered and were about to take a beating. When the Damara men caught sight of my husband, their combative posture intensified. At that point my husband barked, "*Soek jy moelikheid?*" Every non-San person within hearing range backed off several feet. The donkey-cart was immediately returned, with profuse apologies for the "misunderstanding," and a fight was avoided. The San had a good laugh when we returned to their shacks, but my husband and I had long conversations about the ramifications of our behaviour for the San after we left.

NOW IT'S "N≠ISA"

Firewood is a chronic problem in Epako. As the squatters' village expanded over the last decade, the surrounding veld has become denuded. Now San women must travel five to ten kilometres to gather firewood. While travelling through the veld, many are beaten, robbed, and raped by young men who belong to the township gangs. They must take this risk, though, since one cannot eat without firewood to cook the staple mealie porridge.

As I got to know the San families in the squatters' village, I was eventually approached for assistance in gathering firewood. My truck would enable the San to gather a week's supply of firewood in only a few minutes if I could take them far enough from the denuded municipal lands. But gathering outside the municipal lands meant stealing from the vast farms in the surrounding area. My husband or I would drive several Ju/'hoan men 30 to 40 kilometres north of Epako. We would park the truck next to the fence-line of a farm owned by an absentee farmer, and while the Ju/'hoan men went into the bush we would deflate the truck tires. If we saw a dust cloud on the road indicating an approaching vehicle, we would give a shout to the Ju/'hoan men, who hid behind the bushes, while we pretended to pump the tires back up. We developed variations of this method to avoid suspicion—for instance, opening the hood to check the fan belt or distributor cap.

As the veld around the squatters' village denudes, the Ju/'hoansi have no choice but to venture onto the white farms to poach firewood. In response, there are increasing episodes of violence against Ju/'hoansi, including beatings and electrocution. However, if the Ju/'hoansi got caught while they were with us, the chances they would be beaten were significantly reduced. Protected by our own whiteness, we would get little more than a scolding.

Our willingness to assist in their efforts to gather firewood was one way we were able earn the trust of the Ju/'hoansi. Despite farmers' threats, we soon found ourselves "interfering" almost constantly with San farm workers. On the majority of farms we visited, we encountered very sick people, many of them children. Tuberculosis, malnutrition, and malaria were the primary ailments. The farmer was usually unwilling to drive them to town to get medical attention, or if he was willing, he would charge them more than they could afford for the petrol. Very often, we would smuggle these sick people off the farms to take them to the clinic or the hospital, and then, after they were treated, we would smuggle them back. This meant taking some risks, but, in the circumstances, it was the only way to behave morally.

Once the Ju/'hoansi had established that my husband and I could be trusted, they began to treat us differently. When I first arrived in the field, I was referred to by the Ju/'hoansi as "/tun dima" (little white woman). As I developed closer relationships with them, particularly with the family that adopted my husband and I, I was renamed "N≠isa." Many new responsibilities came with my status as fictive kin.

Once I was named, I became a relative of every woman named N≠isa and of anyone with a relative named N≠isa. In one village in the northern Omaheke, I was adopted by N!hunkxa. In accordance with Ju/'hoan practices, she would address me as "daughter," because her daughter and I shared the same name. I was expected to engage in the generalized reciprocity for which the Ju/'hoansi are famous. If I had a skirt I wasn't wearing often, I was expected to give it to my sister. An old pair of shoes I was ready to discard should be given to a relative who needed them. When I refused to provide assistance at an inappropriate time, or if I neglected to assist someone who had a legitimate claim on me, my Ju/'hoan family would chastise me by addressing me as *miessis*, implying thereby that I was behaving in an un-Ju/'hoan manner. I had to learn how to be less like a white person, whom the Ju/'hoansi characterize as "far-hearted," and more like a proper, if honorary, Ju/'hoan. I did my best to do my familial duties but, all the while, tugging at my conscience, was the knowledge that research contracts developed by the non-governmental organizations (NGOs) that work with the San contain an absolute prohibition against "hand-outs," with a special caution against gifts of clothing. Such gifts, it was believed, would instill a "dependency mentality" among the San.

WHITE BY MANY LIGHTS

As the Ju/'hoansi got to know me better, after I had transformed into what they called a "different" sort of white person, they occasionally manipulated my multidimensional whiteness. When I was on a farm, a Ju/'hoan man would approach me: "N≠isa, you must take my wife to the clinic, she is very sick. We'll hide her in the back of your truck under some blankets so the farmer won't know." On the farm, I was N≠isa, a co-conspirator, and a source of familial support and assistance. Once in town, however, I was to present myself to the clinic staff as "*die miessis*," and the Ju/'hoan patient was to be my "worker." This way we could count on the medical staff treating

Ju/'hoan patients. The same applied in any government office. If the Ju/'hoansi arrived at a ministry office on their own, they would be passed over and ignored by the civil servants at the counter. However, if I came along and insisted that my "worker" needed his or her identity documents, the forms would be provided and processed.

So I learned about power not so much because I was studying it, but because I had it. I went to the front of every queue; I was given immediate attention in any government office; I was waited on promptly in any medical clinic or restaurant. I quickly saw that this kind of power and privilege can seriously warp an individual's character. One had to be careful and very self-aware.

In the offices of NGOs I heard a rumour (only that) about a young researcher who had gone into the north to work with the Ju/'hoansi. They told me that after only a few months in the bush, he had transformed the local Ju/'hoansi into his servants, who did his cooking and laundry, kept his house clean, and waited on him. I was unable to investigate this story myself. However, the complicated and occasionally antagonistic relations between NGO workers and anthropologists led me to take it with a grain of salt. But even rumour and myth can provide moral instruction, so I saw two interpretations. The NGO workers related it as a story about the assertion of racism and white privilege, but it might also be a story about a researcher "going native" and becoming the only sort of white person the San knew how to help him be.

When I heard this rumour, I remembered the constant pressure put on me by Ju/'hoan men to hire their wives to clean and cook for me and the scandal my husband and I caused by hand-washing our own laundry—a job that whites and non-whites alike consider a job for servants. I did eventually hire a particularly desperate but proud Ju/'hoan man to wash my truck on weekends, a pointless exercise in the Kalahari, but a way of enabling him to feed his family. To not do this, I thought, would have been morally callous. But, as I later came to see, to do so was also to risk moral peril.

There were other ways in which expectations of "white" behaviour imposed themselves. One Ju/'hoan man, Debe, with whom I had become very close, was struggling with an extreme addiction to alcohol. He suffered from delirium tremens and was often on the verge of starvation and complete physical breakdown. Debe's drinking was the subject of many bitter and heated arguments between us. During one argument, he insisted that I must help him with his drinking problem, saying, "You must be like a white farmer and beat me if I drink." He accepted my vague explanations about why I couldn't administer a helpful beating, but at that moment I began to appreciate the trap that the local white people were in.

As I had more opportunities to interact with Afrikaners, I was reminded of George Orwell's essay "Shooting an Elephant," about a white police officer in colonial Lower Burma who is called upon to deal with a rogue elephant:

> I did not in the least want to shoot [the elephant] ... But at that moment I glanced around at that crowd that had followed me ... And suddenly I realized that I should have to shoot the elephant after all. The people expected it of me and I had got to do it ... And it was at this moment, as I stood there with the rifle in my hands, that I first grasped the hollowness, the futility of the white man's domination in the East ... I perceived in this moment that when the white man turns tyrant it is his own freedom that he destroys ... He wears a mask, and his face grows into it. (1984: 22)

As I watched the Afrikaners struggle with their own power and privilege, I began to recognize that they, too, were not completely free—more comfortable for sure, but not entirely free. Their moral codes had to bend to scripts of which they were not the sole authors. The director of an NGO that began working with the San in 1998 told me that the San suffered from "internalized oppression." I doubt that all the oppression from which they suffer is internal, but I want to use her phrase, turned on its head: inside even the most liberal of whites, in the political and moral environment of southern Africa, grows an internal oppressor.

Even though the whites were also in their own kind of trap, my loyalties were to the Ju/'hoansi. This usually required some form of treachery toward the farmers. I began to realize that much of my concern to demonstrate my trustworthiness to the Ju/'hoansi was not motivated by my desire to get them to open up to me so that I could gather data, but by my desire to be a different kind of white person, to distance myself from the whiteness of the Afrikaners. The abstract, disembodied expert on the construction of identity was under construction.

MY TRAITOR'S HEART

Afrikaners understood that I needed insight into the psychology of being white in southern Africa. One of the first books they suggested for my edification was Breyten Breytenbach's *The True Confessions of an Albino Terrorist* (1983), a story written by one of South Africa's most famous poets, who had spent 15 years in exile and was eventually arrested by the apartheid regime. The other was Rian Malan's *My Traitor's Heart* (1990), written by a descendant of D.F. Malan, South Africa's first nationalist prime minister and the founder of the formal system of apartheid. Were my white informants trying to tell me something? I already saw myself as an anti-racist feminist, strongly committed to class issues and social justice. But was I also a "race traitor"?

Alison Bailey defines "race traitors" as "privilege-cognizant whites who refuse to animate the scripts whites are expected to perform and who are unfaithful to worldviews whites are expected to hold" (1998: 28). On this definition, becoming a race traitor is a worthy goal. But it is clearly not as easy as this. There were many situations where animating "white privilege scripts" was the only way to behave morally toward the Ju/'hoansi. By strategically playing the role of the white *miessis*, I was perpetuating a system of racial and class subordination; at the same time, I was securing medical care for a desperately ill individual. Ethics must negotiate with power, and one dubious act may be the necessary precondition for an ethical act. However, it is from such contradictory and ambiguous situations that a moral subjectivity evolves.

By deciding not to animate white-privilege scripts (at least in most circumstances) we are compelled to seek out alternative resources for developing privilege-cognizant scripts. The attention I eventually paid to my variable whiteness was one such resource, but this involved more than just a reflexive acknowledgement of my privileged position as a white, middle-class, Western academic. The importance of this kind of reflexivity was already impressed upon me by the feminist ethnographies I had read before arriving in the field. In much reflexive feminist ethnography, the identity of the anthropologist is already given. Diane Bell states: "The issue of gender arises because we ... do fieldwork by establishing relationships, and by learning to see, think and be in another culture, and *we do this as persons of a particular age, sexual orientation ... educational background, ethnic identity and class*" (1993: 2, emphasis mine). However, none of these features of an ethnographer's identity—age, educational background, class, etc.—are fixed or static. The meaning of whiteness, for example, changes and develops more complexity as this identity is played out, manipulated, and thus redefined as we negotiate our relationships with others.

A question that has nagged much feminist ethnography is: if we accept that there is no essential category called "Women," and if we accept that women are differently situated and so have different perspectives, can a female ethnographer truly understand the experiences of the female "other"? This is an important question, but perhaps it is also useful to examine how an anthropologist comes to know what she knows about herself and others.

Since I was conducting research on Ju/'hoan domestic servants on the farms, I was especially interested in the unique kind of class and racial consciousness they developed through their relationships with their white employers. Tchi!o, my main female informant and my closest friend in the field, confided to me many times that she sees her white *miessis* as lazy, stingy, and rather helpless, yet also trapped and desperate. She also told me that she knew that her *miessis* saw her as dull-witted and incompetent. What I had in common with Ju/'hoan domestic servants was not an essential womanhood and certainly not a shared perspective on the world derived from a similar position within the socioeconomic hierarchy. But we did share similar experiences of being "outsiders-within"(see Bailey 1998: 29 and Collins 1990). Tchi!o could see, from the outside, how whites lived and how whites saw and defined her. She could see herself through the eyes of whites. I could see, from the outside, how the Ju/'hoansi lived and how they saw and defined whites. However partial and myopic the view achieved, it was through their eyes that I had begun to catch glimpses of myself.

Alison Bailey claims that "World travel must put our privileged identities at risk by travelling to worlds where we often feel ill-at-ease or off-center" (Bailey 1998: 40; see also Lugones 1987). By travelling into the world of the Ju/'hoansi, I was also travelling into the world of racial inequality of which I was a part. Of course, anthropologists are professional world travellers, but it was only by putting my *professional* identity at risk that I could better appreciate my own position in the apartheid-coloured world of the Omaheke.

CONCLUSION

Just before he describes his arrest at Jan Smuts International Airport, Breyten Breytenbach poses the following question to his imagined interrogator:

> Will it be possible one day to know where you come from, and therefore where you are, and therefore where you are heading, and therefore what you are, in which case you should be able to attach a name to it?

He answers this question for himself: "if there is one thing that has become amply clear to me over the years, it is exactly that there is no one person that can be named and in the process of naming be fixed for all eternity" (1983: 13).

I was not limited to just one name or just one identity; I had to negotiate many. But it was very important that the Ju/'hoansi give me a name, and by manipulating my fictive Ju/'hoan identity and my multidimensional white identity, they gave me an invaluable source of moral subjectivity. By the moral codes under which I signed on to do fieldwork, I became a liar and a thief. But these codes were designed to regulate the behaviour of a person with a fixed identity: a professional researcher, an expert, a disembodied observer. They were never suited to regulate relations among friends and family (even fictive kin) for someone whose identity, by the very nature of fieldwork, is challenged, put at risk, and altered.

Of course, there are those for whom the processes that destabilize the self will appear as a loss of any centre of moral gravity (see Marcus 1998, Clifford 1988, and Geertz 2000). And there are those who have raised doubts about the real depth of the doubling and decentredness that characterize anthropological fieldwork. That is, the rapport established by complicity with "natives" always has an element of insincerity and can only be sustained by ignoring the broader contexts of power that situate the ethnographer. However, that would only be so if there was a single unified self, a centre of moral agency to which the anthropologist fails to be true in the acts which express her complicity with her subjects and to which she can simply return when her ethnographic travels end. Those of us with a less abstract (and so less secure) view of the self will settle for, and even be consoled by, John Dewey's thoughts on such matters: "selfhood (except insofar as it has encased itself in a shell of routine) is in the process of making ... [and] any self is capable of including within itself a number of inconsistent selves, of unharmonized dispositions" (cited in Rorty 1999: 78). Rorty explains Dewey's pragmatist view in terms that may suit many world travellers: "Moral development in the individual, and moral progress in the human species as a whole, is a matter of remaking human selves so as to enlarge the variety of the relationships which constitute those selves" (1999: 79).

By putting our own identities at risk, by "enlarging the variety of the relationships which constitute our selves," we develop new moral habits, not just new habits of behaviour, but also new habits of perception. By trying to see ourselves through other people's eyes, we expand the community of others to whom we must justify ourselves, and so to whom we belong. Except by the standards of the previous and narrower selves we have shed along the way, this does not sound like ethical collapse or moral decay, but the very substance of moral progress.

NOTES

[1] I am thankful to the organizing committee of the 2003 Graduate Student Conference at the University of Guelph for inviting me to give the keynote talk where I first formulated the views expressed in this paper. I am indebted to Anne Meneley and Donna J. Young for all their assistance and encouragement and to Rocky Jacobsen for his thoughtful feedback. Deepest gratitude goes to the Omaheke San for sharing their knowledge and insights with me.

WORKS CITED

Bailey, Alison. 1998. Locating traitorous identities: Toward a view of privilege-cognizant white character. *Hypatia* 13(3): 27–52

Bell, Diane. 1993. Introduction 1. In *Gendered Fields: Women, Men and Ethnography*. Ed. Diane Bell, Patricia Caplan, and Wazir-Jahan Begum Karim. 1–18. London: Routledge.

Bohannan, Laura. 1964. *Return to Laughter*. New York: Natural History Library.

Breytenbach, Breyten. 1983. *The True Confessions of an Albino Terrorist*. San Diego, CA: Harcourt Brace and Company.

Clifford, James. 1988. *The Predicament of Culture: Twentieth Century Ethnography, Literature and Art*. Cambridge, MA and London: Harvard University Press.

Collins, Patricia Hill. 1990. *Black Feminist Thought: Knowledge, Consciousness and the Politics of Empowerment*. New York and London: Routledge.

Geertz, Clifford. 2000. *Available Light: Anthropological Reflections on Philosophical Topics*. Princeton, NJ and Oxford: Princeton University Press.

Lugones, Maria. 1987. Playfulness, "world"-traveling, and loving perception. *Hypatia* 2(2): 3–21.

Malan, Rian. 1990. *My Traitor's Heart: A South African Exile Returns to Face His Country, His Tribe, and His Conscience*. New York: Grove Press.

Marcus, George. 1988. *Ethnography Through Thick and Thin*. Princeton, NJ: Princeton University Press.

Orwell, George. 1984 [1940]. Shooting an elephant. In *George Orwell: Essays*. London: Penguin Books.

Rorty, Richard. 1989. *Contingency, Irony, and Solidarity*. Cambridge: Cambridge University Press.

———. 1999 [1994]. Ethics without principles. In *Philosophy and Social Hope*. Comp. Richard Rorty. London: Penguin Books

2 | DOCTORS WITH BORDERS[1]

LESLEY GOTLIB

EARLY IN MY DOCTORAL STUDIES, I attended a seminar entitled "Construction of Gender and Medical Ambiguity: Ethical Issues in Intersexuality." An articulate social worker named Tess described her involvement in the creation of a new multidisciplinary clinic. Here, children born with a range of intersex conditions were going to receive much anticipated long-term care. Intersex conditions are rare congenital disorders, which sometimes render a person's anatomical sex undifferentiated at birth (also called hermaphroditism). Medical care for these patients has been the topic of much controversy over recent years, and North American practitioners in the field have been subject to harsh criticisms (see Diamond and Sigmundson 1997, Diamond 1998, Kessler 1998). Tess and her colleagues told me their goal was to establish a clinic that would "provide an integrated sharing of clinical and social thought, evaluation and planning for parents, in a coordinated setting." The clinic was being established in an effort to respond to the protests of adult patients, as well as families of affected children, for whom biomedical interventions had been less than optimal. This was an unprecedented endeavour that would bring together urologists, gynecologists, endocrinologists, geneticists, and mental health experts, who were struggling with ideas of appropriate medical interventions. As I listened to them speak, I was impressed by their dedication and determination.

I excitedly walked away from this presentation imagining an ethnographic community of impassioned clinicians, patients, and parents, whom I would observe, interview, and casually converse with about the function and meaning of medicine in the case of sexual ambiguity. It seemed the perfect place to explore the medical management of gender non-conformity, a project that I already hoped to pursue in a local gender identity clinic. So, when I approached Tess some weeks later to inquire about the possibility of carrying out ethnographic research for my doctoral thesis, I was thrilled by her openness to the idea. She thought it was an ideal moment to conduct such a study, as the newly recruited team members were just about to see patients. Further, I learned that the director of research for the team also headed the aforementioned gender clinic. How convenient, I thought, two separate clinics with overlapping practitioner membership and a semi-shared patient population. I was convinced I had found the field sites for my ethnographic research.

Tess organized a meeting with the head psychologist, Dr. Marvin.[2] He was intrigued and readily lent his support. Dr. Marvin was used to working with students and has in the past supervised his own doctoral students. I felt that he was taking me under his wing and, given my junior status, was comfortable with this. But more importantly, I found in Dr. Marvin a person who was as intellectually curious about my anthropological interests as I was about his medical views. Our relationship was founded on a respectful and mutual inquisitiveness. It was Doctor Marvin who encouraged me to meet with the remaining clinicians at the Intersex Clinic.

The day I was to meet the other team members at the clinic, Dr. Marvin and I shared breakfast at a local hospital. He offered me some advice about how I could convincingly address the others. "These guys are the *real* doctors," he told me. "You might want to spit out your gum." In this way he flagged an important distinction between *us* and *them.* Dr. Marvin holds a PhD in child psychology, rather than a medical degree. Indeed, he was broadly read in a literature on gender and sexuality from many disciplines. He reminded me that I should address the medical doctors, nurses, and clinicians, as the experts. I entered the room tentatively and tried to find an inconspicuous seat at the back. Dr. Marvin confidently took his place at the head of the table, tapped the seat beside him, and said, "Gotlib, sit here." Slowly, the doctors, some with their own students in tow, filed in. I was at the top of the agenda. Dr. Marvin introduced me as a medical anthropologist (oddly, he never introduced me as a student) and told the others he had already agreed that I would be allowed to carry out research at his gender clinic. He explained that I hoped to expand this project to include the Intersex Clinic as well.

Even if my studies in medical anthropology had made me critically cognizant of medicine as a powerful discursive regime, I, like most North Americans, felt duly humbled by my surroundings. I had entered one of the holiest shrines of modern life. The hospital seems to combine the aspect of life most revered in the west: knowledge married to helpful utility. Doctors are powerful beings and I was proposing to study them, to "study up!" (Nader 1972). Like anthropologists elsewhere who hope to learn about powerful institutions, I approached the doctors respectfully and genuinely, as a student hoping to learn from those who hold authoritative knowledge about a subject few give much thought to. My job was to try to learn from those who are respected for their knowledge within their own profession and society.[3] From this I would be able to deduce something greater about the cultural construction of gender and its relationship to structures of power.

I was very nervous, like a fish out of water, and it was obvious. I had heard rumours that some of the doctors could be quite aggressive, and I was feeling like a child amongst the grown-ups. I tried my best to offer a clear and candid explanation of what exactly I wanted to do. I told them I was interested in learning how medicine influences peoples' ideas about gender. I explained that I would be situated mainly in Dr. Marvin's affiliated clinic, but I also wanted to include them in my research. I would like to observe them in action over a period of about a year, attend clinical meetings, and sit in on consultations with families who gave consent. I would talk to them both informally and in an interview style.

This tried and true anthropological approach worked beautifully. Following my initial presentation nearly everyone happily agreed to participate. They were very curious to know what a qualitative research project would look like. They referred to this, jokingly, as a chance to take "Anthropology 101." In return, one doctor offered to give me a real sense of the work carried on in these clinics. He said, "You can watch me in the operating room." Or, I could watch "movies" he had made, in which he claimed "to turn a penis into a non-penis." Others offered to edit some of my work.

As I was preparing to leave the room, Dr. Marvin stopped me and told me to stay for the entire meeting. I protested that I should not stay because I needed to complete the ethics review. He said, cavalierly, "Consider this your pilot research. Don't worry so much about ethics." I deferred to his judgement. The doctors proceeded to discuss the day's patient load and business. As the meeting drew to a close, a doctor arriving late stopped to say, "Welcome to the confusion; maybe you can figure it out for the rest of us." I left the meeting feeling confident and assured that obtaining ethics approval would essentially be a formality for me—all my key informants had just verbally consented. I felt I had just completed my first day in the field.

NEW PROTOCOLS

The undertaking of my fieldwork must be understood within a particular historical context. Throughout the 1990s across North America, research institutions were implementing new guidelines for ethical research with human subjects. For example, within Canada, the new policy became known as the Tri-Council Policy Statement: Ethical Conduct for Research Involving Human Subjects (1998). But similar policies were also being implemented in the United States. They were geared to making researchers in the social, natural, and biomedical sciences adhere to common modes of research governance. One of the goals was to simplify the ethics review process by harmonizing the conditions of research across the boards.

The protocol established by these new conventions proved to be particularly complex in my case, because I would have to obtain clearance from my university, *and* the hospital that housed the gender clinic, *and* the hospital that housed the Intersex Clinic. The Intersex Clinic was housed in a very prestigious hospital, and I was told that I should seek ethical clearance there first, and the other hospital would expedite their process. My university assured me they would accept the hospital's ethical review process as their own. When I met with the ethics administrator at the hospital, I was advised that I should acquire letters from the relevant doctors at the Intersex Clinic, indicating that, should I complete the ethics review successfully, they would readily sign consent forms. Clearly, the hospital was unwilling to proceed without assurance that the doctors would cooperate.

UNINTENDED CONSEQUENCES

So, I drafted a letter to my informants telling them how excited I was that they had agreed to participate in my study. I explained that *their* institution's Research Ethics Board (REB) was asking for assurance that, when I received approval, they would sign the appropriate consent forms. I delivered the letters. Days passed, then weeks. No reply. Did they forget? Had they changed their minds? I followed up with e-mails informing them that I had dropped off letters. I invited them to contact me if they had further questions regarding the study.

Dr. Marvin replied within a few hours, reaffirming his consent. Most of the others did not reply at all. Two doctors completely reneged. I was shocked that the doctor who, just a few weeks ago had invited me into his surgery, wrote that he now, "would not support such a research endeavour, as [he did] not think that it [had] a validated outcome as a research instrument." Such a statement points to a very different approach to research methods, whereby one is expected to predict the outcome. I was continually asked what my hypothesis was. I found it hard to translate my methodology into the language of the hard sciences that they employed in a way that would satisfy them. Another wrote, "Despite your statements to the contrary, I feel a third party in an observational role puts the clinic under a sort of reality television scrutiny, where we are being observed as we discover ourselves." I was confused by these replies. Clearly something had gone horribly wrong. The borders had been closed.

DO NOT PASS GO!

I could not believe this had happened. I went to the gender clinic to tell Dr. Marvin I would not be able to proceed with the study. A huge pimple on my forehead attested to the stress I was experiencing. I felt incompetent. What had I missed? Where had I gone wrong? I was prepared to accept defeat. I was, therefore, surprised when Dr. Marvin seemed to take all of this in stride. In his view, the others had simply failed to understand what I hoped to do, and it was my job to convince them my objectives were legitimate. I was advised to take a break, as all of the physicians were about to take holidays. I was told to return in the autumn and regroup. In the meantime he encouraged me to carry on with my "pilot study" in his gender clinic, while the ethics review could be sorted out.

Upon returning a month later I sought out Tess, who had always been very supportive. Tess linked me up with another researcher in the hospital who employed qualitative methods and had experience in writing research applications that made it successfully though the ethics review process. She worked with me for a period of six weeks or so, showing me how to *translate* my methodology into terms that were considered more rigorously scientific. Tess then arranged for me to give a series of more extensive presentations to groups of specialists in particular fields of medicine, even though many of them had no affiliation with the Intersex Clinic. She also advised me to provide other examples of similar research. I went to the first meeting armed with copies of Tanya Luhrmann's *Of Two Minds* (2001) and Pearl Katz's *The Scalpel's Edge* (1999). I had carefully chosen these texts, as both had been favourably reviewed in the *Journal of the American Medical Association*. I made photocopies of the reviews to hand out. In addition to this, my thesis supervisor (wisely, as it turns out) told me to disclose that I was already a recipient of substantial government and university funding. Naively, it had never occurred to me that I should reveal this information.

The night before the initial presentation, Dr. Marvin called to check up on me. He wanted to make certain I was well prepared. He asked me what I intended to wear. When I replied, "Well, my usual pants and top," he gently suggested I wear a skirt. Both Tess and Dr. Marvin attended the meeting to lend support and kindly agreed to say a few words on my behalf. The room was filled with completely unfamiliar faces and their support was greatly appreciated.

The presentation lasted about 20 minutes and went smoothly. I asked the doctors if they had any questions. I was floored when one doctor asked if this research on the cultural construction of gender couldn't be accomplished by sitting on my bedroom floor and rifling through *Cosmopolitan* magazines. I replied as diplomatically as possible, "Well yes, that would be one way to do this study, but it's not quite what I had in mind." At this point, Dr. Marvin piped up, "I don't think you are getting Lesley's point." He then turned to me and thanked me for giving an excellent presentation, thus dismissing me. While I felt I could depend on Dr. Marvin and Tess to defend my ideas, I knew I was being rescued. This left me feeling ambivalent. Later, Dr. Marvin assured me things had gone well, but I will never know what people really said.

Nevertheless, I was successful. All the relevant clinicians, aside from the "Cosmo-man," agreed to sign the consent forms. I took my dog-and-pony show on the road and over the next several weeks spoke to two other groups of specialists. Interestingly, the third group was comprised of a mix of professionals, such as sociologists and social workers, who carried out their own forms of qualitative research. Unlike the doctors I had previously spoken to, they were all women. This group told me they found my project very interesting, if irrelevant. Still, they found the idea of doing ethnographic field research in a hospital novel and were very intrigued. They cautioned me to avoid any mention of interviewing patients when I completed my ethics review application. One member of this group even agreed to complete the "scientific peer review" component of my application. In the end, each sector I had spoken to passed a resolution to endorse my efforts, and I was finally able to submit my application to the Ethics Review Board.

The actual ethics review took a number of months during which I addressed the Research Ethics Board and had a private meeting with its chair. Nine months from the day I addressed my first letters to the doctors I received permission to carry out ethnographic research. The "pilot study" came to a close.

IN THE FIELD

I am sitting at a conference table with the diagnostic team at the gender clinic. We are all listening to Nina, the intake worker. Nina is briefing the team prior to beginning an assessment for a young boy called Mark. She reads to us her notes from a telephone interview with Mark's mother. Mark is a nine-year-old boy who his mother describes as effeminate. She is worried because her family members commented that he was running like a girl. Further, Mark had confided to his mother that he would like to be a girl. The mother is feeling ambivalent because she feels she needs some guidance, but in phoning for help she also feels she has failed to accept her son for who he is.

Mark and his mother are just outside the room. I go to meet them and introduce myself as an anthropologist, explaining that I am doing a study about how the doctors talk to patients about gender. I ask her if she will agree to sign my consent form. She agrees, and the consent form is placed in Mark's file. Then two people, a doctor and his intern, lead them into a room on the other side of a one-way mirror, where they intend to conduct the assessment. It is only at this point that Mark's mother is told that we sit on the other side of the mirror, and again she is asked to give her consent. Further, she is asked if they can audiotape and film the assessment. On the spot, she agrees.

First they ask Mark's mother, "Why are you here?" She replies, "I am worried because all of Mark's friends are girls. He seems to prefer them, and the boys at school tease him and call him a *Tom-girl.*" They ask, "How long has this behaviour been going on?" She answers, "Ever since he was three or four, but lately it has been more noticeable." The questions continue in this manner. Over time they will become more invasive. For instance, they ask, "What was it like being pregnant with Mark?"

One of the interviewers turns to Mark and asks, "Mark, is there anything about being a boy that you don't like?" He responds, "Yes." They ask, "What are some of the things about being a boy you don't like?" He replies, "Well, girls get to dress-up, wear make-up, and have tea parties." They say, "Do you ever wish you were a girl?" He says, "Sometimes I do." They ask, "Do you think that boys can change into girls?" He says, "I know that I'm a boy because God made me a boy; but I still wish that I could be a girl."

Mark is sitting on the floor colouring. His back is to his mother, who speaks with some trepidation. Clearly, she is uncomfortable revealing these things about Mark as if they were a problem. She probably would have found it easier to talk about her feelings if he had not been present. But the entire philosophy of the clinic is based on openness. It is believed that the children should fully understand why their parents have brought them here. On this particular occasion I am struck by the fact that Mark resembles any nine-year-old boy. I see nothing that would indicate otherwise. But in subsequent interviews he is invited to play with a series of toys and dress-up clothing. In these sessions, during which his mother is being interviewed in another room, I note that he seems drawn to what the clinicians call "feminine play." For instance, he dresses in a blonde wig, puts on high heels, and provocatively struts about the room in a way suggesting feminine sexuality. When he realizes that he is being videotaped, he seems to play it up for the camera.

The team agrees that Mark has a gender disorder. In addition, Mark's mother drew the doctors' attention to his small penis. They wonder if this is connected to his gendered behaviour. In other words, they are not ready to rule out a biological explanation. He is referred to the Intersex Clinic for further assessment.

In a nutshell, this particular case highlights some of the assumptions at work in the gender and intersex clinics. Like other gender theorists before me, I was, and am, uncomfortable with some of these assumptions. It seemed to me that the gendered paradigm here was too limited, implying that one must be not only a boy or a girl, but also a certain kind of boy or girl. To be otherwise was to be abnormal.[4] Within the medical paradigm the team was using, males could not be "naturally" feminine. To act in such a way implied that the parents had failed to set limits on inappropriate behaviour because of their own unresolved psychological issues.

But, as it turns out, this case study is not only instructive because it highlights the questions about gender that intrigued me, it also brought to my attention some of the unspoken implications of what it means to carry out ethical research. At the time, I wasn't sure why the way in which the mother and her son were asked to give their consent made me so uncomfortable. I couldn't help but note the casual manner in which they were asked. This was in stark contrast to the ample time required to gain approval from some of the doctors whom I wished to study. Of course, I understand fully that Mark and his mother had approached the clinic for help, which changes the nature of the relationship from researcher and subject to one of doctor and patient. Still, in this case, events would unfold in a way I found deeply troubling.

Not long after this assessment took place, a journalist approached Dr. Marvin to do a feature article on the clinic. I was with Dr. Marvin when he was interviewed. The journalist posed a series of critical questions not dissimilar to ones I might ask. Indeed, had asked. I was, therefore, very surprised to find Dr. Marvin most forthcoming. In the enthusiasm of the moment, he whisked the journalist down the hall to watch the video that had been made of young Mark in women's clothing, a video even Mark's mother had not been allowed to watch. The lessons on proper ethical protocol that had been so impressed upon me during the ethical review process seemed completely lost on Dr. Marvin. His desire to promote the clinic publicly seemed to override the code of ethics by which his institution was governed. I felt the privacies of Mark and his mother had been completely violated, especially when I read the subsequent journal article, which described in detail the content of the film.

CONCLUSION

I felt very strongly that a degree of trust had been lost when I asked doctors to sign consent forms for anthropological research. The very doctors who had been willing to see me as a young student became very uncomfortable when I assumed the role and legal responsibilities of researcher, which the consent forms conferred upon me. I believe the very nature of the relationship between me as an anthropologist and those I hoped to come to know through participant observation research was altered when a legal contract was introduced. In the process, the doctors lost sight of me as a student hoping to understand how they saw the world, since, in their minds, research implied objectivity and predictability. They feared losing control over the outcome. Over time they came to understand that my results would be "subjective" at best. They contrasted this to the type of objective scientific work they were involved in. Somehow they found this distinction reassuring.

Ironically, the same routine of seeking consent did not seem as significant (for some) when they approached their patients. In the end, surely, consent forms should confer respect for the privacies and anonymity of those being studied and cared for. Certainly the doctors I studied wanted to know that they and their patients would be respected in this way. And yet, the consent forms, which contractually confer rights and responsibilities, seemed unable to address the obvious power differentials at play. The doctors themselves were granted much greater leeway in these regards. I felt some were merely paying lip service when they asked patients to sign consent forms. Further, they seemed more concerned with legal liabilities than with their patients' rights. I became convinced that it is difficult to codify moral behaviour and that an ethics review process cannot ensure that people will always act ethically. The doctors and I understand this process differently. For them ethics implies legal accountability.

I have also come to question the primary motives of ethics review boards, whether in hospitals or universities. Universities and other research institutions seem to be more concerned with issues of legal liability than they are with ethical conduct in research. Or, at any rate, once legal contracts are introduced, they appear to become one and the same. Contracts are required to guarantee continued government funding, something that may be compromised when the ethics protocol is not followed with precision. I learned this the hard way, the ethnographic way. Since I was one of the first anthropology students to go through the review, I was an ethics review "test case." I had already guaranteed my university a large amount of government and private funding when my research methods were questioned by the doctors. When I finally mentioned this to them, I became a more ethical— because well and prestigiously funded—researcher in their eyes.

I feel very ambivalent about my research experience, although, post-research, I even use the term "ambivalent" with some hesitation. In the gender clinic the parents of children considered most abnormal were labelled "ambivalent." Parental ambivalence was considered the root of the child's problem. Nevertheless, it is the way I felt. This ambivalence stems partly from my relationship with Dr. Marvin, who was an important mentor and ally in my quest to gain admission into the inner sanctum of the intersex and gender clinics. Obviously, I could not have completed this study without his active assistance and instruction. Even though I came to strongly disagree with many of the assumptions at play in his clinic, I appreciated being given the opportunity to carry out this study and then to openly disagree. This seems to me to be what honest research and cross-disciplinary dialogue should entail.

On the other hand, I could not help but note the double standards employed. I will never understand how it is that a journalist could bypass the ethics review process entirely while researchers are made to jump through a thousand hoops. Dr. Marvin's honest, if blunt, statement that it was "good for business" seems inadequate. But I will always respect Dr. Marvin's willingness to engage in an unfamiliar form of research. I know that he takes issue with my methodology and considers it insufficiently scientific. Nevertheless, he let me cross his borders.

NOTES

[1] Thanks to Anne Meneley for her suggestions on earlier drafts of this paper and Donna J. Young for her meticulous editing of the final draft. I would also like to thank Dr. Marvin and Tess for their unwavering support throughout my research.

[2] This is a pseudonym of which Dr. Marvin is aware. Further, he has read my research and now, on occasion, writes to me signing off as Dr. Marvin. Elsewhere, I have more carefully disguised the identities of the clinicians and patients of whom I write in the interest of protecting anonymity.

[3] For instance, when Tanya Luhrmann carried out her research on American psychiatry, she began as a student attending introductory classes for new psychiatrists in training (2001: 3–4).

[4] For studies that are critical of such paradigms see for example Sedgwick (1993), Kessler (1998), Dreger (1999), Rottnek (1999), and Fausto-Sterling (2000).

WORKS CITED

Diamond, Milton. 1998. Intersexuality: Recommendations for management. *Archives of Sexual Behavior* 27(6): 634–41.

Diamond, Milton, and H. Keith Sigmundson. 1997. Sex reassignment at birth: Long-term review and clinical implications. *Archives of Pediatrics and Adolescent Medicine* 151(3): 298–304.

Dreger, Alice Domurat (ed.). 1999. *Intersex in the Age of Ethics*. Hagerstown, MD: University Publishing Group.

Fausto-Sterling, Anne. 2000. *Sexing The Body: Gender Politics and the Construction of Sexuality*. New York: Basic Books.

Katz, Pearl. 1999. *The Scalpel's Edge: The Culture of Surgeons*. Boston: Allyn and Bacon.

Kessler, Suzanne J. 1998. *Lessons From the Intersexed*. New Brunswick, NJ: Rutgers University Press.

Luhrmann, T.M. 2001. *Of Two Minds: The Growing Disorder in American Psychiatry*. New York: Knopf.

Nader, Laura. 1972. Up the anthropologist: Perspectives gained from studying up. In *Reinventing Anthropology*. Ed. Dell Hymes. 284–311. New York: Pantheon Books.

Rottnek, Matthew (ed.) 1999. *Sissies and Tomboys: Gender Nonconformity and Homosexual Childhood*. New York: New York University Press.

Sedgwick, Eve Kosofsky. 1993. How to bring your kids up gay: The war on effeminate boys. In *Tendencies*. 154–64.Durham, NC: Duke University Press.

Tri Council Policy Statement Ethical Conduct for Research Involving Humans. 1998. Catalogue No.: MR21–18/1998 E. Public Works and Government Services Canada. Available online: <http://www.nserc.ca>.

3 | WHO WEARS THE TROUSERS IN VANUATU?[1]

MAGGIE CUMMINGS

WE WERE LEANING OVER THE EDGE of the pub's patio, squinting into the darkness below to see who was out and about on this hot Friday night in Port Vila, Vanuatu, when Ann-Marie turned to me, fussed with the full skirt of my hibiscus-print dress and laughed, "Nice dress, *misis*!" She found it terribly amusing that she, the *ni-Vanuatu* (indigenous) woman, was wearing jeans, a tank top, even lipstick, while I, the *misis* (white woman), wore a long, loose dress picked up for a few dollars in Vila's Chinatown.

I had come to the pub, frequented mostly by expatriates, in hopes of taking the night "off" from fieldwork. But it was a slow night, and the only person I knew was Ann-Marie. I lived near the office where she worked, and we had already had a few lunch-hour conversations about my research on the cultural politics of femininity, dress, and appearance for young women in Vanuatu. Educated overseas, single, and gainfully employed, she considers herself thoroughly modern and cosmopolitan, and that night she was dressed the part. She fascinated me because she seemed to embody one side of a contentious debate over the relationship between women's appearance and national identity in which I found myself interested (and implicated); one in which women, youth, urban life, foreign (white) influence, secularity, and modernity are disparagingly opposed and perceived as a threat to male authority, village life, indigenous ways, Christianity, and tradition. The idea that trousers are inappropriate ni-Vanuatu women's wear is part of the debate, and few of the women I knew from my collaborative research with the Vanuatu Young People's Project (VYPP) wore trousers as often, or as confidently, as Ann-Marie. Since she had brought up the topic, I decided I'd better take the opportunity to question her further.

But we had done little more than laugh about our sartorial role reversal when she cocked her head skeptically and said, "I didn't know that anthropologists could do stuff about fashion. Aren't anthropologists supposed to study kastom?" She was happy, she said, to talk to me about clothes, hair, and women's ways of "looking good," but she was doubtful about framing the discussion in terms of anthropology, kastom, or culture. The idea that she—a modern woman, after all—could tell me, an anthropologist and supposed expert, anything about kastom was absurd.

I was unfazed. At least someone was talking to me! Posed by my potential informants with equal parts authority and disbelief, "But aren't anthropologists supposed to study kastom?" was a common response when I introduced myself and my research interests. I felt pretty certain, despite skeptical suggestions to the contrary, that I was an anthropologist because, "as all graduate students in social/cultural anthropology know, it is fieldwork that makes one a 'real anthropologist'" (Gupta and Ferguson 1997: 1). *Kastom* (customary ways, tradition, and culture in Bislama, the pidgin lingua franca) is often glossed simply as "culture," and, insofar as I understand anthropology as the study of culture, my work was genuinely "anthropological," since my working definition of kastom/culture refers to "all contemporary practice, whatever its source" (Bolton 2003b: 30).

Anthropologists may be the experts on culture, but my understanding of culture was not the only one that mattered for my fieldwork. Vanuatu has been a field site for many anthropologists; ni-Vanuatu are very familiar with the discipline and its methodologies. The Vanuatu Cultural Centre (VCC) administers all cultural research, and foreign researchers must comply with the Vanuatu Cultural Research Policy in order to obtain a research permit.[2] The policy defines kastom as "traditional political, social, religious, and economic structures, and their associated practices, systems of knowledge, and material items" (Vanuatu National Research Council 1994). Of course, the term "kastom" has a complex history and many meanings (for a thorough discussion of this history, see Bolton 2003b). A third interpretation, which becomes particularly relevant when thinking about gender, is scathingly articulated by the late ni-Vanuatu poet, feminist, and politician Grace Mera Molisa, in a piece entitled "Custom":

> "Custom"
> misapplied
> bastardized
> murdered
> a frankenstein
> corpse
> conveniently
> recalled

to intimidate
women
(Molisa 1983)

These competing definitions of kastom were invoked whenever I introduced myself as an anthropologist. In this context, the scenario in which Ann-Marie, an intelligent, interesting, well-informed, well-dressed, and beautiful ni-Vanuatu woman insisted that she had nothing intelligent, interesting, or well-informed to say about the cultural politics of being a well-dressed and beautiful ni-Vanuatu woman, begins to make sense. Similarly, the way in which our clothes puzzled each other and defied our respective expectations captures the essence of the ironies and dilemmas I faced as a foreign anthropologist collaborating with local researchers to do research about women's lives. When Ann-Marie (and any number of other ni-Vanuatu) asked me, "But don't anthropologists study kastom?" it was a question about what we could expect from each other in a situation where "anthropologist," "kastom," and "native" have many, often contradictory, meanings.

Below, I discuss the ways in which these expectations came to matter in relation to what I call "the trouble with trousers"—a debate involving chiefs, young women, and the right to wear trousers. I situate the debate within its historical and ethnographic terrain, and then discuss the reactions of some of the women I knew to this debate, particularly the VYPP fieldworkers who worked on a video about the trouble with trousers. I conclude by briefly discussing the ways in which the collaborative process and the question "Aren't anthropologists supposed to study kastom?" have shed light on each other.

CHIEFS, TROUSERS, AND TROUBLE

In March 2001, five months before I arrived in Vanuatu, a group of chiefs from the island of Paama decided to ban women from wearing shorts and long trousers, claiming that they were too revealing and could *cause* men to commit rape and adultery (Cain 2001: 54). The ruling applied to Paamese women living in Port Vila as well. The ban, intermittently enforced and not necessarily very effective (see Bolton 2003a: 138 n.5), was the subject of a great amount of debate and received much local media attention. Highly contested, yet vastly influential (many other island communities followed with bans of their own), the ruling was also highly effective in explicitly and publicly linking women's bodies, dress, and behaviour to discourses of kastom, national identity, Christian authority, and modernity.

By the time I arrived, explanations for the ban were fully elaborated by a vocabulary of blame, protection, and "trouble." *Trabol* (trouble) is a catch-all term for the social problems associated with rapid urbanization and modernization in Port Vila; it is also a euphemism for sexual assault. In the dominant discourse, there is a slippage between trousers and trouble. Wearing trousers, the story goes, is a sign of the erosion of traditional ways under the influence of modern, foreign ways. Moreover, when women wear trousers, they show a lack of respect for kastom, Christian gender norms, and male authority. Women in trousers become the scapegoats for all such troubles. The blame for cultural loss is turned back on them as the threat of sexual violence, or trouble. Simply, women who wear trousers are disrespectful; disrespect incites rape. Banning trousers, therefore, is a way to protect women from themselves, while simultaneously protecting kastom and chiefly authority against modernity and cultural loss.

ABOUT VANUATU

Some background information is needed to understand why women in trousers become equated with cultural "trouble." Vanuatu is a Y-shaped archipelago of approximately 80 islands spread over 850 kilometres in the southwest Pacific. Formerly known as the New Hebrides, it was administered jointly by Britain and France from 1906 to 1980. The official languages are English, French, and Bislama; in addition, most ni-Vanuatu speak one of 113 indigenous languages. Vanuatu's population in the 1999 census was approximately 187,000. Eighty per cent of the population live in rural areas collectively referred to as "the islands"; however, population growth in the capital, Port Vila (often simply called "town"), is rapidly outstripping that of the islands. The rural-urban dichotomy is a particularly salient way in which ni-Vanuatu categorize themselves and each other. Port Vila was built as a colonial administrative centre populated by white officials and settlers. Today, the majority of its population is ni-Vanuatu (most of whom come to town for education, employment, or excitement), but town is still the symbolic centre of foreign, white, "modern" ways; indigenous ways reside in "the islands." The relationship between urban and rural is antagonistic: the exotic draw of life in town is said to be destroying kastom and indigenous ways.

KASTOM AND CHRISTIANITY

Vanuatu is a Christian nation, both officially, as suggested by the national motto, "*Long God Yumi Stanap*" (Before God We Stand), and in practice—95 per cent of the population identify as Christian. Pre-independence, under the influence of Christian missionaries, kastom was negatively juxtaposed to *skul* (Christian ways). Kastom and Christianity are no longer seen as conflicting; both are central to the nation's post-colonial national identity. Nor does kastom refer uniformly to all pre-contact cultural practices; instead, it is used to "indicate the practices and characteristics that *distinguish ni-Vanuatu from other people*" (my emphasis, Bolton 2003b: 25). Elements of kastom and Christianity have been synthesized in ways that are said to favourably distinguish Vanuatu from secular, modern nation-states. Not all elements of kastom are suited to such synthesis: "those aspects of kastom that patently conflict with Christianity—sorcery, the worship of ancestral creator beings, warfare and cannibalism are unlikely candidates for recuperation and revival" (Jolly 1994: 251). However, other aspects of kastom and Christianity mesh well, particularly for the purposes of forging a uniquely ni-Vanuatu identity, as is the case with gender, dress, and status.

GENDER, DRESS, AND STATUS

The trousers ban is sometimes miscast as "Victorian morals mistaken for kastom" (Tarere 2001). However, the relationship between gender, dress, status, and trousers exemplifies the way in which kastom and Christianity can inform and mutually enforce each other. In Vanuatu, as in the Pacific generally, "clothing was one of the most obvious markers of the changes imposed by colonialism and the mission" (Colchester 203: 1). Such changes were not imposed on a cultural blank slate. To the missionaries' eyes, scantily-clad ni-Vanuatu were simply naked savages, but indigenous styles of clothing and adornment were actually significant markers of gender and status or rank:

> If gender was indicated by a standard difference of form in dress (such as skirts versus penis wrappers [for women and men

respectively]), rank was indicated by elaboration and ornament, and depending on the context in which it was awarded, aspects of that elaboration and ornament were worn by both men and women" (Bolton 2003a: 123–24).

When Christian missionaries (especially Presbyterian missionaries) introduced European-style clothing as a way to civilize ni-Vanuatu, they were particularly interested in promoting Christian gender relations through dress. Women were encouraged to wear the "Mother Hubbard," a long, shapeless frock that resembled a nightgown. Sewing and caring for clothes (as opposed to unfeminine garden chores) became women's work, bringing women's lives in line with the missionaries' notions of proper Christian women as "docile, disciplined, and domesticated" (Douglas 2002: 2). Christian men were encouraged to wear shirts and trousers and to work outside the home. Wearing European clothing became a powerful symbol of the shift from heathen to Christian status. As well, it reconfigured gender differences as differences of *status*, in which men were linked to the (privileged) public sphere, women to the domestic sphere.

European-style dress "did not acknowledge any differences within each group based on individual status" (Bolton 2003a: 128). The status that *was* marked by the taking up of European clothes, particularly the Mother Hubbard (or "island dress," as it is known today), was collective: ironically, it was racial difference that was emphasized. For example, the Mother Hubbard, although "European in character, and ... designed to meet European notions of modesty" (Bolton 2003a: 129), was never worn by the missionary women. Clothing became a very visible marker, although on Eurocentric terms, of difference between ni-Vanuatu and Europeans, and marked gender-as-status difference as well.

It is within this context that it was possible for ni-Vanuatu (men and women alike) to tell me that *"aelan dres hemi kastom dressing blong yumi"* (island dress our kastom dress) and not contradict themselves. The island dress *does* distinguish them from other people, regardless of its missionary roots, because today it is ni-Vanuatu, not white foreigners, who uphold the properly modest and Christian gendered division of dress: women in dresses, men in trousers. Since independence, the island dress has become a powerful means of asserting national identity in black and white (and gendered) terms.

It is little wonder, then, that when chiefs banned women from wearing trousers, they made it clear that they would prefer for women not only to wear long skirts, but also to wear island dresses. In many ways, the relationship of the island dress to gender, status, kastom, and Christianity mirrors the situation of chiefs as figures of authority, for the category "chief" today is one that incorporates both indigenous roles and colonial structures (Bolton 2003a; Lindstrom 1997). Vanuatu's variety of indigenous leadership types included hereditary chiefs, big men, and "owners" of kastom knowledge; these systems were overlaid, but not necessarily replaced, by Christian leaders and indigenous colonial agents who were also bestowed the title "chief" by missionaries and the colonial government, respectively. In postcolonial Vanuatu, the Malvatumauri, the National Council of Chiefs, embodies this coming together of kastom, Christianity, and political forms of authority. This group of 22 chiefs (all men) is made up of elected representatives from around the archipelago; its mandate, embedded in Vanuatu's constitution, is to advise and consult with Parliament on kastom matters and to "protect" kastom (Jolly 1994: 254). Perhaps not surprisingly, much of the kastom policy codified by the Malvatumauri (who endorsed the trousers ban) "seems designed particularly to keep women and youth under closer control" (Lindstrom 1997: 219).

THE YOUNG WOMEN, BEAUTY, AND SELF-IMAGE PROJECT

In order to facilitate research that benefits the researcher and local counterparts equally, the Vanuatu Cultural Research Policy encourages collaboration with local researchers and requires the creation of opportunities or cultural products that benefit the local community and the nation. After reading my research proposal, Ralph Reganvanu, the director of the VCC, requested that I work with the Vanuatu Young People's Project. Established in 1997, the VYPP provides a forum for ni-Vanuatu youth to speak about their lives, particularly through research, advocacy, and video production. We designed and envisioned the video-training project, entitled "The Young Women, Beauty, and Self-Image Project," as a response to recommendations from earlier VYPP research, which suggested the need to train more young women in video production skills and to pay more attention to the gendered dimensions of issues affecting ni-Vanuatu youth, particularly girls and women (Mitchell 1998).

Emily Niras, the project coordinator, and half a dozen youth field-workers worked with me to design a questionnaire about dress, appearance, and related issues affecting young women. We invited the women we interviewed to participate in one of three video-training and discussion workshops The goal of the research and the video training was to provide opportunities in which to hear "Young Women Speak"—as we named the project report (Cummings 2002). Young women, as Ann-Marie's skepticism about her abilities as an "anthropological" informant suggest, are rarely given such opportunities. Once, before an interview, Nicky, a single woman in her early twenties born and raised in Port Vila, expressed her surprise, as so many people did, that an anthropologist would be interested in appearance, rather than kastom. I tried to explain my perspective on anthropology and its relationship to culture. She agreed to talk to me and said, "I think it's a good thing you're asking us about this topic, and asking us what women think, because most of the time we don't have a chance to tell people what we think, because nobody listens."

We designed an extensive interview questionnaire that included questions about hair, makeup, clothes, and self-esteem, but the questions about trousers elicited the most passionate, elaborate, and telling responses. When it came time to decide on a focus for the video, both the fieldworkers and the workshop participants voted overwhelmingly in favour of using the video to "talk back" to the chiefs and to their communities about the trouble with trousers. As Nicky put it, it would be a chance to tell "the girls' side of the story." The result, entitled *Wan Naes Wan* (roughly, Pretty Woman), basically takes the form of a debate in which young women and girls actually have a say. A lot of time is devoted to the question of whether or not wearing trousers "causes" rape. One chief, who appears as a spokesman for the Malvatumauri, explained that:

> There are reasons why chiefs don't like it when girls wear trousers
> or short skirts above their knees. When you dress like that, half
> your body is showing, and it attracts men. You see it happen all the
> time, that when a girl is dressed up like that, boys get turned on.
> Sure, you might argue that in some places, women still wear grass
> skirts and are nearly naked all the time, but there aren't any more
> rape cases because of it. But that's because it's kastom and it has
> meaning. But you couldn't walk around half naked in Port Vila or

Luganville, or it would cause trouble and rape. So that's why we chiefs feel strongly that young women must dress properly: because we don't want you to get into trouble or be raped. Because everyone knows that men are strong, but women aren't. When you dress like that, and show off your body, you are asking for trouble. It's better to protect yourself and your body. That's one reason the chiefs don't like to see girls wearing trousers. The second reason we don't like it is that it means that you don't have respect for chiefs or kastom (my translation, from Cummings 2002: 13).

The slippage between "trouble" as a cultural dilemma and "trouble" as sexual assault that underlies the politics of blame and protection is clear. Chiefs, designated custodians of kastom, also "protect" women and keep them out of "trouble." If women choose to cause trouble by wearing trousers, they have no one to blame but themselves—for both kinds of trouble. When women wear trousers, they stake a claim to the (male) power invested in wearing the trousers. Linking trousers to "trouble" doubly reasserts dominant relations of power, especially as they relate to kastom: chiefs (as well as elders and men in general) remain protectors of both women and kastom; women take the blame for the perceived threats to kastom and as victims of sexual assault.[3]

No woman I spoke to believed that if she wore trousers, she was "asking" to be raped:

It's not true. Say a woman is wearing trousers; she's probably just wearing them because they're comfortable and she likes them— she's not thinking it's going to attract men. If a man attacks her, it's because of he's a nasty person doing a nasty thing, not because of what she's wearing.

There are lots of cases where women are raped even though they weren't wearing trousers; they were wearing dresses or skirts. I think the chiefs just don't like to see girls in trousers, and that's why they say it.

Nor do women appreciate being made the scapegoats for the loss of kastom (or, more to the point, the shrinking reach of kastom authority).

Many women questioned the inflexible relationship between dress, respect, and kastom:

> I don't think trousers are disrespectful because they cover up my body as well as a dress does.

> Today they make trousers for men and trousers just for women. If they are women's trousers, how can they be disrespectful?

> If you're playing sports or walking around a lot, trousers cover up your legs way more than a skirt or a dress, which might blow up. Trousers are at least as modest as dresses—maybe even more.

> If people really want girls to dress kastom, they shouldn't be telling us to wear dresses, they should be telling us to wear grass skirts—and men themselves should be wearing *nambas* (penis wrappers), not trousers. If they're going to say that women who wear trousers are disrespectful, they need to be clear—disrespectful of what?

Given that a "preoccupation with rank and status is allied today with ... respect" (Bolton 2003b: 3), which in turn is allied with kastom, the answer is clear—women in trousers are less disrespectful of kastom per se than a challenge to men's authority—to the literal and figurative right to wear the trousers.

WHO WEARS THE TROUSERS?
THE IRONIES OF COLLABORATION

All of which leads me back to "Aren't anthropologists supposed to study kastom?" It is a humourous comment from natives who are both savvy about and weary of being studied by foreigners. It also implies other questions about competing definitions of anthropology and of kastom and about the relationship between them. Moreover, it draws attention to the ways in which I, as an anthropologist, as a white woman, as a feminist, and as a collaborator with local counterparts, am implicated in the research process. Whenever I introduced my research interests and myself as an anthropologist, I was asked to explain myself. I began to think that introducing myself this way, as a so-called expert on kastom, exacerbated the insecurity and ambivalence that young women feel about their relationship, through dress, to kastom. Ambivalence was built into the project itself. The project was shaped and supported by the VCC; there *is* interest in hearing "Young Women Speak," even though dominant local understandings of kastom define young, urban, trouser-wearing women as its antithesis.

I developed what I thought was a workable strategy for negotiating this ambivalence and for dealing with the question "But aren't anthropologists supposed to study kastom?" I exchanged my description of myself as "anthropologist" for "volunteer." Both categories of foreigner are familiar to ni-Vanuatu: anthropologists come to study and document kastom; volunteers come, on behalf of various development agencies, to *do* things, implement projects and provide training, to help Vanuatu to "develop" or to "modernize." The collaborative aspects of my work with the VYPP, combined with the subject matter, meant that people often suggested, "Oh, you must be a volunteer." When I said that yes, I was working as a volunteer on a research project with the VYPP, young women often seemed more comfortable and willing to talk about dress and femininity than they did talking to a cultural "expert." Embracing the "volunteer" label was a way in which to cope, as a researcher, with the ambivalence about the relationship between women, dress, and kastom. In retrospect, I fear that my adoption of the volunteer label, and the collaborative-ness of the VYPP video-training project that made it possible, actually exacerbated and upheld the politics of blame and protection that is at the heart of the debate about women's dress.

For instance, Lissant Bolton has recounted the story of the measures that were taken to protect Australian Museum staff, who were in Vanuatu cataloguing the VCC's collection of artifacts, from the customary objects' power. She states: "we were understood to be vulnerable because we were women" (Bolton 2003b: 49). I witnessed the exact opposite, in a case where the artifacts had to be protected from women. Worse still, my presence, as the knowledgeable white anthropologist, was used to strengthen the case against ni-Vanuatu women. A few of the VYPP fieldworkers decided to put into practice the challenge they posed in *Wan Naes Wan*—they began to come to the VYPP office wearing trousers, rather than skirts. Uproar ensued, if uproar is the right word for finger-pointing and angry whispers of accusation. The VYPP is housed at the Vanuatu National Museum, and my friends were reprimanded, told (though not directly, but through the office grapevine) simply that they were being dangerously disrespectful to the ancestors and to kastom by wearing trousers in such close proximity to the artifacts. If they weren't going to dress respectfully, they were told, perhaps they shouldn't come to work at all. The harshest criticism of their actions was that "Even *olgeta missus* [the handful of white women working at the National Museum, including myself] wouldn't do something as disrespectful as wearing trousers in the Museum!"

Collaborative cultural research (whether as an anthropologist or as a volunteer) with young ni-Vanuatu women, especially about dress, begs the literal and figurative question: Who wears the trousers? In this case, despite the fact that women's trousers are categorically "white" women's clothes, it was my ni-Vanuatu counterparts who were wearing the trousers (when they could get away with it); I wore skirts and dresses. I was trying to fit in, and the last thing I wanted to do was dress "like a white woman" (even if most of my ni-Vanuatu informants themselves preferred trousers). Figuratively, I was also trying not to "wear the trousers," not to over-determine the shape and outcome of the video-training and research project. One point of collaboration, I thought, is to shift the power dynamics involved in representing others by giving them a chance to represent themselves. But in the end, it didn't matter what I wore, nor whether I called myself an anthropologist or a volunteer, nor whether I was working collaboratively—my whiteness, and my apparent anthropological expertise, were invoked to the detriment of my colleagues, informants, and friends: "*Even the white woman knows better than to wear trousers in the Museum!*"

My training in anthropology taught me to think long and hard about the troublesome implications of our discipline's cultural expertise. During my fieldwork I felt enough anxiety about being an anthropologist that, rather than face further difficult inquiries about anthropology and culture, I shrugged off the label in favour of another. I felt able to call myself a volunteer, because I was working collaboratively with local counterparts. The irony is that I had not *volunteered* to collaborate but did so at the behest of the VCC in order to obtain my research permit. I loved my work with the VYPP, but my point is that collaboration was not what it seemed—and that an anthropologist by any other name is still an anthropologist. We are urged to work collaboratively with our informants as a way of making our work more relevant and more useful to local communities. Framed as a moral imperative, the "primarily redemptive" (Marcus and Fischer 1999 [1986]: xxxii) goodness of collaboration seems to emanate from an inherent capacity, regardless of the context, to negate troubling power differences by ensuring that research is relevant and useful to its subjects. I do not want to argue that collaboration is useless or irrelevant. I do want to emphasize that no matter how useful, how good, and how relevant, collaboration requires an ironic sensibility. No matter what we call ourselves, nor what others call us, if we don't own up to our authoritative voice, someone else will gladly invoke it for us.

NOTES

1   Donna J. Young and Anne Meneley invited me to participate in the 2003 CASCA session "Auto-Ethnographies of Academic Practices: Politics and Practices of Collaborative Research" and, along with Margaret Rodman, have provided much-appreciated feedback on several versions of this paper. I received funding for my 2001-02 fieldwork in Vanuatu from SSHRCC and from the York University Faculty of Graduate Studies Fieldwork Costs Fund.

2   My project was not only "collaborative" in the sense that I worked with ni-Vanuatu researchers. I was also a student collaborator on Margaret Rodman's larger, SSHRC-funded project, entitled *Gender and Race in New Hebridean Settler Space* (2000-03). My research approval was obtained in the blanket approval for this project.

3   When interviewed for *Wan Naes Wan*, neither a police spokesman nor Marilyn Tahi from the Vanuatu Women's Centre had ever heard of a rape case in which the perpetrator claimed that a woman's trousers drove him to his crime.

WORKS CITED

Bolton, Lissant. 2003a. Gender, status, and introduced clothing in Vanuatu. In *Clothing the Pacific*. Ed. C. Colchester. 119–39. Oxford: Berg.

———. 2003b.*Unfolding the Moon: Enacting Women's Kastom in Vanuatu*. Honolulu, HI: University of Hawaii Press.

Cain, Tess Newton. 2001. Convergence or clash? The recognition of customary law and practice in sentencing decisions of the courts of the Pacific island region. *Melbourne Journal of International Law* 2(3): 48–68.

Colchester, Chloe. 2003. Introduction. In *Clothing the Pacific*. Ed. C. Colchester. 1–22. Oxford: Berg.

Cummings, Maggie. 2002. *Young Women Speak: A Report on the Young Women, Beauty, and Self-Image Video Training Project*. pp. 31. Port Vila, Vanuatu: Vanuatu Cultural Centre.

Douglas, Bronwen. 2002. Christian citizens: Women and negotiations of modernity in Vanuatu. *The Contemporary Pacific* 14(1):1–38.

Gupta, Akhil, and James Ferguson. 1997. Discipline and practice: "The field" as site, method, and location in anthropology. In *Anthropological Locations: Boundaries and Grounds of a Field Science*. Ed. A. Gupta and J. Ferguson. 1–46. Berkeley, CA: University of California Press.

Jolly, Margaret. 1994. *Women of the Place: Kastom, Colonialism, and Gender in Vanuatu*. Chur, Switzerland: Harwood Academic Publishers.

Lindstrom, Lamont. 1997. Chiefs in Vanuatu today. In *Chiefs Today: Traditional Pacific Leadership and the Postcolonial State*. Ed. G. M. White and L. Lindstrom. 211-28. Stanford, CA: Stanford University Press.

Marcus, George E., and Michael M.J. Fischer. 1999 [1986]. *Anthropology as Cultural Critique: An Experimental Moment in the Human Sciences*. Chicago, IL: University of Chicago Press.

Mitchell, Jean. 1998. *Young People Speak: A Report on the Vanuatu Young People's Project*. pp. 60. Port Vila, Vanuatu: Vanuatu Cultural Centre.

Molisa, Grace Mera. 1983. *Black Stone*. Suva: Mana Publications.

Tarere, Winston. 2001. The barriers to reporting HIV/AIDS in the islands. *Port Vila Presse*, December 3.

Vanuatu National Research Council. 1994. Vanuatu cultural research policy. Electronic document, available at: <http://artalpha.anu.edu.au/web/arc/vks/contre.htm>. Accessed October 13, 1999.

PART II | COLLABORATIONS

O NE OF THE OFT-MENTIONED IRONIES of academic life is that we enter our professions attracted to the freedoms associated with the pursuit of knowledge as individuals, only to find that the bulk of our activities as academics involves collaborative effort. As the essays in this section show, our training inadequately prepares us for the rigours of teaching, mentoring, and administrating while continuing to research and write. It is not only that our training favours (indeed, encourages) critical independent thinking, our institutions continue to reward individual efforts in research and writing above all others when granting tenure and promotion.

Add to this the increasing demand from within and outside of our institutions that academics build collaborative research projects across disciplinary, institutional, and international borders, and the strain begins to show. As any academic will tell you, collaboration, while rewarding in so many aspects, does not lend itself to the speedy production of research and publication. Again, wider social transformations have powerfully influenced the work of academics and the ways in which they must position themselves to be successful. Funding initiatives set up in response to what many perceived to be a "new" era of globalization called for innovative research strategies to respond to "new" transnational fields (Brenneis 1994: 125). The results are contradictory.

As Bocking shows, even writing involves collaboration. Peer review is the main mechanism for asserting standards and quality control in the university. While some perceive this as a way of fostering careful scholarship, it can become a vehicle for the most conservative of gatekeepers to seize control. Peer-reviewed publications are key for determining the author's promotion and tenure, yet the time and the contributions of the peer reviewers are often not even acknowledged.[1] Authors make very little money (if any) from their publications, but they do get symbolic capital. Brent (1999) argues that the shift in the United States, linking book publication to promotion, has increased the importance of university presses.

Meneley and Harrison discuss the anxieties they witnessed in the Ford Foundation's "Crossing Borders" initiative, which encouraged collaborative research and teaching across three national borders in three different universities. The academics and students from the three institutions had unique styles of academic engagement, which led to countless negotiations and much fencing. As Garber (2003: 54), following Freud, notes, the "narcissism of minor differences" worked to exacerbate invidious distinctions between the disciplines rather than to create a genuine interdisciplinary space, which, as Barthes suggests, should create new objects of study that belong to no one (cited in Garber 2003: 72).

Barber highlights the uncomfortable fit between the goals of people working for development agencies and researchers, which frequently complicates such joint ventures. She notes her discomfort at development workers' tendency to distort anthropological methods by assuming that participatory methods can be "sped up" to meet a development project's much tighter schedule, missing the point of long-term participant observation, long the hallmark of anthropological methods. Barber also quizzically questions the implicit assumption in developmental discourse that promotes empowerment, but never says what purpose such empowerment should serve. Meanwhile, the neo-liberal agenda seems very well-served, indeed.

NOTES

[1]   This is in blind peer review where the referees are not known to the author. One might wonder if this is to protect the peer reviewer from the wrath of thin-skinned authors!

WORKS CITED

Brenneis, Don. 1994. Discourse and discipline at the National Research Council: A bureaucratic *Bildungsroman*. *Cultural Anthropology* 9: 23-36.

Brent, David. 1999. Merchants in the temple of scholarship: American university press publishing at century's end. *Critical Anthropology Now: Unexpected Contexts, Shifting Constituencies, Changing Agendas*. 361-86. Santa Fe, NM: School of American Research Press.

Garber, Marjorie. 2001. *Academic Instincts*. Princeton, NJ: Princeton University Press.

4 | GATEKEEPER OR HELPFUL COUNSEL?
Practices and Perceptions in Academic Peer Review

STEPHEN BOCKING

UNIVERSITY GRADUATES USUALLY LOOK back on their student days with nostalgia—memories of new friends, good times, novel experiences, a simpler life—especially when the responsibilities of work and family kick in. But one thing they rarely miss is being evaluated: the endless pursuit of the elusive "A+" essay, or the perfect test grade, a life lived according to the gospel of marks. Rarely does freedom feel so real as on that spring day when the last essay is submitted, the last exam written.

Perhaps this is why students are often surprised to learn that their professors willingly engage in careers of unceasing evaluation. Most work that professors do outside the classroom, such as writing articles in academic journals and chapters in books like this one or preparing research proposals, is eventually submitted to other academics—that is, their peers—who review its quality and presentation. They rarely enjoy this process. Indeed, like students who write papers of unappreciated genius, professors often find the evaluation of their work frustrating, even enraging. Every experienced academic can tell stories about shortsighted or arbitrary peer reviewers. Critics also condemn the tendency of peer review to reward communication to one's fellow specialists over service to the larger society, while excluding from the process all who are not "peers." In the words of one critic: "This is the paradox of journal peer review: the open sharing of knowledge through publication is preceded by secret deliberations among a few scientists acting with calculatedly restricted information, vague and unenforceable guidelines, and little accountability to authors" (Chubin and Hackett 1990: 94).

Nevertheless, academics readily submit their work to peer review and for good reason. Applicants know their hopes of landing a job in a university are slim unless they have written at least a few peer reviewed articles. The granting councils (the Natural Sciences and Engineering Research Council and the Social Sciences and Humanities Research Council are the largest sources of funding for Canadian academic research) rely on peer review in determining which proposals they will fund. Peer review, in short, is essential to academic work, serving both to certify that research is of a high standard and to direct resources towards those able to meet this standard.

But today, both the status and practice of peer review are being debated. In this chapter I provide an introduction to this debate. I will review how peer review works and why it has become so central to academic practice. I will also review critiques of peer review and explore how these critiques might be addressed. My focus will be on how peer review is used in academic journals, drawing on my own experience as a journal editor and, thus, as administrator of an extensive review process.

THE NATURE OF PEER REVIEW

The basic idea of peer review is straightforward. In the case of journals, it is the assessment of research papers submitted for publication by experts in the same field as the author(s), working at arm's length from the editor. The underlying assumption is that academics know things about the practice and products of research that non-academics (politicians, business people, or the general public) do not and that they are, therefore, the best able to evaluate its quality.

While the idea is straightforward, the process of peer review can be complex. It begins when an aspiring author submits an article to a journal. The editor forwards it to two or more readers knowledgeable about the subject, who evaluate its quality. Editors use a variety of methods to find suitable reviewers: surveying the literature to identify the authorities in the field, checking references cited in the paper itself, consulting the lists of experts provided by universities, identifying teachers of courses in the general area of the paper, and soliciting advice from colleagues or from the journal's editorial board. Some journals maintain databases of reviewers, with experts matched to topics. Authors are occasionally asked to recommend suitable readers. With the intellectual resources of universities now accessible on the Internet, the process of finding reviewers has become far easier (although it is still time-consuming). This increased accessibility has also enabled editors to draw reviewers from a larger pool of experts beyond their own personal contacts, reducing the likelihood that an "old boy's network" will monopolize assessment of papers.

Editors often provide fairly detailed guidelines to reviewers, who usually appreciate knowing exactly what kind of information the editor needs. In some cases reviewers are asked to recommend that the paper be accepted or rejected; other editors may only request that readers comment, with the understanding that it is up to the editor to decide whether the paper should be accepted. Once reviewers receive a paper, they will read it with several criteria of quality in mind: considering whether the methods are appropriate, the data are interpreted correctly, the results are presented clearly, the work of other researchers is taken into account, the conclusions are reasonable, and so on. Reviewing a paper takes perhaps four to six hours, but especially conscientious reviewers can take much longer.

Elements of the review process vary from journal to journal. For example, the process may be "double-blind," in which neither reviewers nor authors are informed of the other's identity. On the other hand, the policy of many journals is for reviewers to be given the author's name; much less often, authors are advised of the identity of their reviewers, but only if the reviewers have given permission. This question of anonymity is a matter of debate: some argue that anonymity is best, because it helps ensure a frank, honest commentary—and there is evidence, in fact, that reviewers (and editors) can be biased towards more prestigious authors and institutions, judging more rigorously unknown, but promising authors (Chubin and Hackett 1990: 104). Others, however, suggest that reviewers should be accountable for their opinions and so should sign their reviews; by this reasoning, criticisms that must be anonymous probably should not be written in the first place. Greater transparency might also be preferable to the current system, in which, particularly in smaller research communities, reviewers are often able to guess the identity of the author, particularly if he or she has a distinctive style or point of view (Chubin and Hackett 1990: 204).

Reviewers' comments may be handled by editors in a variety of ways: some give them to authors verbatim or in summary form; others provide only the recommendations or draw selectively on the reviewers' reports in making their decision to accept or reject the paper. The reviews themselves are, of course, a major factor in this decision. But they are not the only consideration: among other factors that an editor may consider are timeliness, topicality, the balance of topics within an issue of the journal, and the geographic distribution of authors. This is where the role of journal editor can often get quite ambiguous. While peer review is a key part of publication decisions, editors have a great deal of leeway in making these decisions, both in choosing reviewers and then in deciding what to do with the reviewers' advice. As a result, excellent reviews are not necessarily a guarantee that an article will be published, especially if the topic has already been exhaustively examined in the journal. (Such a decision can often be a difficult one for an author to accept.) In contrast, the author of an article that receives only modestly positive reviews may be encouraged by an editor who would like to see more discussion of that particular topic in the journal.

THE FUNCTIONS OF PEER REVIEW

These procedures are the outcome of a lengthy history. We can trace the practice of peer review back to the first formal scientific journals: the *Philosophical Transactions of the Royal Society* and the *Journale des Sçavans*, both of which first appeared in 1665. Since then, and especially since approximately 1950, peer review has become ubiquitous in academic publishing and is the chief mechanism by which academic work is certified as credible and reliable.

The emergence of peer review has paralleled the development of the concept of the academic community itself as a distinct and self-governing entity, able to set its own priorities and standards of quality. Peer review serves to demarcate this community from the rest of society, policing the boundaries between professional and amateur, because it implies that only those who do research can assess its value. It also serves, within the academic community, to define distinct specialist groups by enforcing the idea that reports of work in, say, biochemistry or literary criticism can only be evaluated by fellow biochemists or scholars of literature. It thus fulfills the disciplining function of academic disciplines, enforcing the idea that new knowledge must meet requirements regarding methods, evidence, and forms of reasoning that are particular to specific disciplines. As such, peer review exemplifies the contradictions of academic work: research and writing are solitary activities, but they are also activities conducted within particular communities. These include both the larger academic community and the communities defined by particular disciplines. Peer review has also been invoked in defense of the independence of academic research. One criticism of the increasing funding of science by private interests, particularly industry, is that it endangers the pre-eminence of peer review in assessing the quality of research or setting research priorities.

Such is the importance of peer review that, when it comes to career advancement, a single impenetrable (but peer reviewed) article in an obscure journal read by almost no-one may somehow be viewed as superior to a year of excellent teaching, dedicated service to a local non-profit organization, or industrious efforts at popular education or political advocacy. Given these functions—certifying the reliability of new knowledge while asserting that academic research should be conducted in an autonomous (albeit well-funded) community—we can understand why peer review has almost a sacred role in academia as the chief way of establishing the real value of academic work. This is also why there is often a reluctance to criticize the practice, not only because such critiques can be seen as "sour grapes" (perhaps, people whisper, critics only complain because they received lousy reviews of their own work), but because such criticisms might be seen as endangering the autonomy of the academic community.

The functions and status of peer review might also help explain why people do it. After all, since their work is usually anonymous, reviewers receive little recognition, monetary or otherwise, for their service, while the time each review takes is time that could otherwise be spent on one's own research and teaching. It is also expensive. For example, it was estimated in 1990 that just one major biomedical journal, the *New England Journal of Medicine*, had to spend about $1 million each year to conduct its peer review process, not including perhaps $1.5 to $2 million in reviewers' time (Weller 2001: 27). Administering peer review is also one of the most time-consuming parts of an editor's job. On the other hand, beyond fulfilling their duty to their research community (like jury duty, it is just something academics have to do, if the system is not to break down), reviewers may learn something new from the papers they review, getting a better sense of what work is going on before it is published. Junior scholars undoubtedly appreciate the opportunity to peer review, seeing a review request as affirmation of their expertise. Some observers suggest more sinister motives for reviewing: reviewers may want to learn what their competition is up to, or delay publication of their work, or even plagiarize it (Weller 2001: 151). Such motives, however, are likely quite rare.

THE EXPERIENCE OF EDITING

Between 2000 and 2003 I was able to observe and take part in the process of peer review as the editor of the *Journal of Canadian Studies*. During these three years, I received more than 170 papers suitable for peer review; these were reviewed by about 310 reviewers. Editing the journal was, therefore, an opportunity to learn about peer review from the inside out. Once I was appointed editor, I began noticing several things about peer reviewers. They varied widely in their ability to meet deadlines: some required more than one reminder (I would usually request a review within six weeks of receiving the paper), while others (often, I found, the most productive scholars) would return their reviews very quickly, often within two weeks of receipt. With authors anxious to learn if their paper had been accepted, the speed of reviewers was always an important consideration.

Most important, as I soon found, the reviews varied considerably in quality. Some were clearly the product of a careful reading and re-reading of the paper; a few others, in contrast, appeared to be merely sketchy notes based on a quick scan. An experienced participant in medical publishing once summarized the attributes of an excellent reviewer, and his list corresponded very well with my own experience as editor. According to this authority, the reader had to "determine their appropriateness as reviewer, maintain confidentiality, rule out bias, avoid conflict of interest, meet deadlines, cultivate open-mindedness, know the structure of scientific papers, draw upon medical acumen, employ critical appraisal skills, screen for misconduct, use tact, and eschew triviality" (quoted on Weller 2001: 161). Unfortunately, it is the rare reviewer that has all these qualities.

PEER REVIEW AS "GATEKEEPER"

As I received reviews, certain patterns began to emerge. It became evident that they could usually fit into one of two categories, which , in turn, seemed to correspond to two ways in which scholars understood the purpose of peer review and, therefore, the appropriate nature of a review. These two ways I eventually characterized as "gatekeeper" and "helpful counsel."

By "gatekeeper," I mean the view of peer review as a kind of screening device, a way of weeding out error from the academic output. By this view, reviewing is an essentially negative contribution: it means identifying mistakes in research or interpretation and ensuring that they will never appear in a published paper. This view was expressed in either of two ways. The first generated perhaps the briefest reviews of all (as little as 100 words in length), in which the reviewer simply said that yes, the methods and conclusions of the paper are sound and reasonable, so the paper can be accepted for publication. No, or very few, suggestions would be provided regarding possible improvements to the paper.

But this "gatekeeper" could also generate a very different kind of review, sharply negative, in which it is argued that the paper is entirely deficient, indeed unsalvageable, with its shortcomings described in almost forensic detail, in a harshly, even aggressively negative tone. For example, one review I received began by stating: "This essay is characterized by fuzzy thinking and sloppy writing. It would rate, at best, a 'B' if it were an undergraduate essay." Indeed, the review can be so harsh that it implies that the reviewer wishes not merely to ensure that the paper will not be published, but that the author will be discouraged from continuing in the academic profession.

Such reviews can, frankly, be briefly entertaining. But they also present a problem for the editor and a need to exercise judgement. How is one to communicate to the author that the reviews for their paper are strongly negative? This must depend not just on the paper, but also on the author. Was it written by a graduate student, who, flush with pride at receiving an "A" for the paper, assumed that it was of publishable quality? If so, it is best to provide only a selection of review comments: enough to communicate why the paper is not publishable, but without discouraging an author who is only just beginning an academic career. If, on the other hand, the paper was written by a senior academic, who might be expected to know better than to submit a less than stellar paper to a major journal, fuller communication of the reviewer's negative comments may be appropriate.

Negative reviews certainly do illustrate how the review process can serve as a screening device, in that they help to identify papers that could not be revised enough to be acceptable. This is done in several ways: by finding serious flaws in the paper itself; by exposing an author's apparent unwillingness or inability to correct the flaws; or in finding the topic too narrow or insignificant to merit publication, even if the essay itself is done competently.

Special challenges are raised by the not uncommon circumstance of contradictory reviews. Surprisingly often, one reviewer will consider a paper to be a worthwhile piece of scholarship, while another may urge its rejection. For example, a paper submitted to me by a prominent scholar elicited from one reviewer the following: "This article should be accepted for publication with minor revisions ... [It] is well-written and the argument is sound." The second reviewer, however, stated that "my concerns about this article are several, and major ... this article should be jettisoned" and went on to provide four pages of criticisms to support this view.

How can this be? How can two knowledgeable experts have such different views on what makes for a quality paper? Does it undermine the entire basis for peer review, just as a student essay with an A mark, on being resubmitted and given a C, might call into question the validity of marks?

In fact, such an outcome might be viewed as a positive thing. Editors will even often seek out the possibility of disagreement between reviewers by choosing two or three who are from different disciplines (if the paper in question is interdisciplinary) or who have different expectations. Reviewers might also assess different aspects of the article. For example, if one focusses on the research methods and the other on how effectively the results are interpreted and generalized, they will likely arrive at different recommendations if the author has conducted the study properly, but simply didn't have the imagination to do anything with the results generated. Such divergence can even be, for editors, somewhat reassuring—it indicates, at least, that a broad range of expert opinions has been drawn on in reviewing the paper (Chubin and Hackett 1990: 102).

But disagreement may also indicate that the peer review process itself is flawed—and this, certainly, is often the reaction of authors receiving a split decision. Just as students will naturally object if similar essays receive different marks from different reviewers, so do their professors. To some, it suggests the process is arbitrary: in effect, a lottery for authors. And, in fact, studies of peer review have judged it a failure as a dependable indicator of research quality: the likelihood of agreement between reviewers on the quality of an article is usually only slightly better than chance (Edwards and Schneider 2001: 230–31). In one such study, one article was resubmitted (with different names and authors' institutions, but otherwise identical) to each of 12 journals that had published it recently. Only three of the 12 were recognized as resubmissions; of the nine already published papers that were re-reviewed, only one was accepted for publication (Chubin and Hackett 1990: 103). The problem, evidently, is that while both truly stellar, and truly terrible, papers will likely be universally recognized, there are many papers in the broad middle class of quality that may well generate disagreement between reviewers.

More generally, disagreement between reviewers raises questions regarding the fundamental assumption of peer review: that there exist certain objective standards of quality that most academic peers are able to enforce. This assumption may hold when there is agreement about theories, methods, and goals, but it breaks down when there is not. When the knowledge base is contested, disciplinary divisions are deep, and there is no agreement on what questions should be asked, let alone what the right answers would look like. In short, when there is no consensus on what constitutes "good" research, deciding whether a particular piece of work is acceptable becomes a matter of negotiation. This can be especially problematic in an interdisciplinary field like Canadian Studies. Reviewers will often apply their own disciplinary standards to a paper, but if just certain ideas were drawn from that discipline to make a point that relates to some other field (for example, using a brief historical case to illustrate an argument in economics), that can leave that paper open to criticism that it did not go into sufficient depth or was not rigorous enough for specialists. And if the review process is viewed simply as a screening device—a "gatekeeper"—then the problem becomes obvious: in effect, a paper may be rejected because it does not meet certain objectives that the author was not even aiming for in the first place.

PEER REVIEW: MORE TROUBLE THAN IT'S WORTH?

The apparent arbitrariness of peer review has encouraged many critics to argue that it is not able to assure that research is of high quality. But this is not its only problem. Certainly the quality of reviews depends on the care and competence of reviewers. And just as not all academics can write or perform research effectively, neither can they all recognize good writing or research. Personal and political factors can also be important, particularly in smaller research communities. Peer reviewers may give preferential treatment to authors they know or judge their competitors more harshly. Such problems reflect a breakdown of the trust inherent in the review process: the assumption that researchers will follow a code of ethics obliging them to make a fair and conscientious effort.

Beyond the uncertain qualities of the reviewers, the peer review process exhibits more general shortcomings. It is often unable to consider fairly research of interest to non-academics. On occasion, I would receive papers at the *Journal of Canadian Studies* that, while of interest to a larger audience, failed to meet all the standards of scholarly research and so could not be published. More generally, studies that do not contribute to academic goals, but that do provide benefits to society, may fare poorly in the review process.

This is one reason why some seek alternatives to peer review. In particular, the federal granting councils are placing more emphasis on economic benefits (especially contribution to industrial innovation) when they assess research proposals.

Peer review also cannot detect misconduct reliably. Fraudulent research has taken place within institutions that live by the ethos of peer review, demonstrating that it is far from foolproof as a method for ensuring credible, honest science. Nor can peer review detect the influence of corporate or government funding. Over the last decade industry has become increasingly important in funding Canadian scientific research. This trend has generated much concern, especially because it raises doubts regarding the objectivity of science: studies paid for by industry are more likely to generate results favourable to the sponsor than are non-industry studies. This is not necessarily because such studies are of lower quality, but because it is always possible to design research questions and techniques in ways that favour the desired outcome (Bekelman *et al.* 2003). Peer review is unable to detect such subtle manipulation.

Peer review can discourage innovation. I received several papers that apply new methods or present new ways of thinking about Canada and Canadians. Such novelty, however, also makes it more likely that these papers will be criticized for employing untested methods or for failing to consider how the matters discussed relate to conventional theoretical concerns. Instead of encouraging unusual or challenging ideas, peer review can tend to favour studies that confirm existing beliefs. This, in fact, may be one of the most pervasive concerns among editors: that reviewers may resist taking a chance on strikingly new ideas that could eventually redefine a field of study, but that today go too far against the grain of convention. Stories of Nobel prize-winning research that originally failed peer review serve as cautionary tales. One should not be afraid to encourage risky ideas, while screening out the merely flaky.

For a variety of reasons, therefore, peer review can become an instrument of conventionality, discouraging innovation and risk taking. This is why papers that confirm rather than challenge existing beliefs often do better in the review process. This is also why one of the leading clichés of academic publishing is that if one wishes to design a paper to receive a positive review, one must avoid bold ideas or exploration of unknown territory. Instead, just push a short distance beyond what we know, keeping to the tried and true.

PEER REVIEW AS HELPFUL COUNSEL

Is such a bleak view of peer review necessary? In fact, it is not. The notion of peer review, as merely a screening device and an instrument designed to discourage original thought, is itself the product of an excessively narrow view of the process. But there is an alternative model of peer review, not as a "gatekeeper," but as a dialogue between reviewers and writers, a kind of conversation mediated by the editor. This model can be described as that of "helpful counsel." In it, there is, to be sure, opportunity to criticize and to discourage work that has no prospect of contributing meaningfully to knowledge. The emphasis, however, is on constructive suggestions for improvement, sometimes provided in the form of a detailed, critical discussion of up to 3000 words. The crucial innovation that permits this to occur is to view peer review as being situated at a different point in the process of creating a paper: not at the end point, but within the writing process itself, giving the author an opportunity to respond to the review comments, before a publication decision is made, and with the author's response taken into consideration in the publication decision (Chubin and Hackett 1990: 203). It is analogous to students receiving comments on essays before they are marked, rather than after.

Such an approach is more forgiving of not just the paper's imperfections, but of the shortcomings of the peer review process itself. By functioning as a dialogue, less emphasis is placed on the verdict of the reviewers (to accept or to reject), and more weight is given to their comments, which can be weighed on their own terms. There is, therefore, more opportunity to consider whether criticisms reflect, say, an overly narrow disciplinary perspective or the particular attitudes and preferences of the reviewer. And the door is also less likely to slam shut on a paper simply because it is novel or risky.

As editor of the *Journal of Canadian Studies* I tried to encourage this approach. I would rarely say simply "no" to a prospective author, unless the reviews were irremediably negative. A simple "yes" was also unusual. It is the rare paper, after all, that is ready for publication as first received (at my journal, this was probably less than 3 per cent of all papers).

Instead, my most common statement to authors was something like: "perhaps, but not yet." The reviews would constitute only the beginning of the process: authors would be invited to consider them and to re-submit a revised paper. This invitation provided the basis for working together on the paper, seeking to create the best possible article: rigorous, significant, and interesting to the journal's diverse readership.

Such a process is also closer to the original idea of peer review. One of the first motivations for peer review, centuries ago, was to maintain the practice of "witnessing," of finding a way, even after research communities had become too large to meet in one place, to at least simulate the communal experience of all members of a research community being present as experiments were being done. Witnessing was a way of certifying that an experiment had been done correctly, while at the same time building a sense of shared experience, a bond between all who had been present at the creation of new knowledge. When a reviewer provides a careful summary of the paper, indicating that the reviewer "got it," and then follows with constructive suggestions for improvement, that is closest to this model of being a "witness." This function can imply reconsidering the structure of peer review: rather than relying on individual reviewers, groups of experts with diverse skills, as independent as possible of any interests at stake, may be more likely to fulfill this witnessing function impartially (Brosnan 2000).

Peer review is fallible and does not deserve the exalted status it is sometimes accorded as the sole criterion by which the worth of an academic career is measured. It does, however, serve the essential function of creating opportunities to draw on the useful counsel usually found in both negative and positive reviews and to advise the author accordingly as to how the paper might be improved. Like the comments provided on student papers, it can enhance the accountability of academic work: improving its quality by catching errors and untested assumptions; moderating the influence of personal, social, and political factors; encouraging researchers to consider unfamiliar ideas and approaches; and building an academic community that shares certain core principles and beliefs about methods, reasoning, and the virtues of honest research.

WORKS CITED

Bekelman, Justin E., Yan Li, and Cary P. Gross. 2003. Scope and impact of financial conflicts of interest in biomedical research: A systematic review. *Journal of the American Medical Association* 289(4): 454–65.

Brosnan, Deborah M. 2000. Can peer review help resolve natural resource conflicts? *Issues in Science and Technology* 16(3): 32–36.

Chubin, Daryl, and Edward Hackett. 1990. *Peerless Science: Peer Review and U.S. Science Policy*. Albany, NY: State University of New York Press.

Edwards, Paul N., and Stephen Schneider. 2001. Self-governance and peer review in science-for-policy: The case of the IPCC Second Assessment Report. In *Changing the Atmosphere: Expert Knowledge and Environmental Governance*. Ed. Clark A. Miller and Paul N. Edwards. 219–46. Cambridge, MA: MIT Press.

Weller, Ann. 2001. *Editorial Peer Review: Its Strengths and Weaknesses*. Medford, NJ: Information Today.

5 | TEACHING AND LEARNING ACROSS BORDERS[1]

JULIA HARRISON AND ANNE MENELEY

> Two teachers in the classroom can flash ideas off one another
> in ways that are exhilarating for both of them and for their
> students. But they also need to learn each other's mental moves,
> rhetoric, and styles of thought, taking nothing for granted.
> Otherwise both they and the students will be bothered and
> bewildered rather than bewitched. Nothing works better than
> team teaching, when it works; nothing falls flatter when it fails.
>
> —MARJORIE GARBER
> ON DISCIPLINE ENVY IN *ACADEMIC INSTINCTS*

BOTHERED, BEWILDERED, OR BEWITCHED by collaborative teaching? To answer that question, we were gathered in a hotel conference room, a conference room that was, for the most part, indistinguishable from any other North American conference room: round tables with white tablecloths, notepads and pens at each place, jugs of ice water and glasses. Several speakers sat at a long table beside the podium at the front of the room. They weren't presenting papers, as one might expect, but rather offering their reflections on a series of cross-cultural, collaborative teaching seminars. Having a faculty-student postmortem of a pedagogical moment—especially one long past—is in itself unusual. But what made these seminars really unusual was that they were taught collaboratively by professors from Canada, the United States, and Trinidad, to students from the same three countries. The setting for this encounter was bland, but what people were saying, and the vehemence with which they were saying it, was far from it. The confessional mode evoked an Oprah-ish talk show more than a conventional academic discussion.

These teaching seminars were part of a Ford Foundation funding initiative entitled *Crossing Borders: Revitalizing Area Studies*. This initiative aimed to foster innovative thinking and pedagogical practices to cope with "transnational flows" of peoples, cultures, and commodities perceived to be moving with an unprecedented velocity in a globalized world. The initiative was designed to revitalize a conception of area studies that had begun to seem bounded, static, and inadequate for theorizing contemporary social life under conditions of postmodern capitalism. Partnerships between universities in different nations were to be funded; these were encouraged to be transnational partnerships in order to stimulate "border-crossings" which were themselves characteristic of contemporary times (Berresford 1999: vii). St. Lawrence University (SLU), a private liberal arts college in upstate New York, Trent University, a small Canadian university founded in the 1960s, and the University of West Indies (UWI), the national university of Trinidad and Tobago, received funding from the Ford Foundation for a proposal entitled *Interconnecting Diasporas: Globalizing Area Studies*. The goal of the project was to generate a collaborative dialogue about these various "global flows" among faculty and students from different disciplines in each of the three universities. It was after listening to the complex and often contradictory discussions surrounding the idea of "collaboration" at the 2001 faculty seminar that we decided to do an ethnographic investigation of the project as a whole, aiming to provide a kind of meta commentary on the notion of collaboration itself. As anthropologists who teach at Trent, we had varying degrees of involvement with the *Interconnecting Diasporas* project over the years. Julia Harrison attended and helped to organize aspects of the first faculty seminar at Trent in 1999; both of us participated in the second faculty seminar at SLU in 2001; and Anne Meneley taught in the second student seminar in Trinidad in June 2002. We wanted to explore how knowledge production was facilitated by collaborative processes across nation, institution, and academic discipline and inflected by the interplay of race, gender, and class, as well as the broader post-colonial political and economic shifts that affect the United States, Trinidad, and Canada differently. To this end, we conducted interviews with participants from all three institutions, including project coordinators, faculty, and students, and we conducted participant observation at some of the faculty and student seminars.

To gain insight into the globalized world, the participants were literally to "cross borders" to participate in joint faculty seminars, inter-institutional research projects, and three summer student seminars. It is this latter aspect of the project that we discuss here. When we gathered for the final meeting of the *Interconnecting Diasporas* project in 2003, it was, in part, to facilitate student and faculty reflections on the teaching seminars via roundtable discussions. Two of these teaching seminars had taken place a year earlier, the other, three years earlier. However, it was clear that the emotion generated by this collaborative experience still lingered or, in some cases, rankled. For instance, consider the following responses from the collaborative teaching staff of one seminar: one professor theatrically exclaimed that it had been the worst teaching experience of her life; her co-teacher said that it had been wonderful, belying his palpable discontent at the time; and a third announced, somewhat belatedly, that he had thought the whole notion of collaborative teaching was nonsense from the beginning.

The Rashomonic-like qualities of the narratives we heard are striking. Although it is not news to contemporary anthropologists (or Kurosawa, for that matter) that there is no objective truth or unified account out there for us to capture in this context or any other, our informants' accounts of their experiences often diverged so sharply that we wondered if everyone could be talking about the same event.

These self-reflective roundtables on teaching and learning were only part of the final faculty seminar. Participants also took stock of the "outcomes" of the project, to consider to what use the Ford Foundation funds had been put. The issue of "outcomes" was to prove central. In our interviews we heard considerable anxious talk about the relative paucity of material evidence of scholarly productivity resulting from the grant. As contemporary academics are all too aware, the material outcome of knowledge production in the form of scholarly publications has increasingly—for better or worse—become the signs of our scholarly worth. We are reminded of Weber's memorable argument about the Calvinists, where material signs came to be taken as signs of salvation or damnation.

Those we interviewed often mentioned the student seminars as tangible signs of "real outcomes": courses co-taught by professors from each of the three universities to students from all three institutions. At the very least, one might suspect, the syllabus would be co-produced, there would be shared teaching and discussion responsibilities, and there would be consensually assigned grades for the students. All of this would embody, it was said, concrete evidence of collaborative learning. The central themes of the project as a whole were to be the specific subject matter of the student seminars: transnationalism, globalization, diasporas, and social justice. The premise of the seminars was that a transnational set of professors and students, juxtaposed in a classroom, would in and of itself generate insight into a globalized world.

THE STUDENT SEMINARS

Each student seminar included a range of lectures, class discussions, workshops, and field trips. The first seminar, held for three weeks in June 2000 at SLU, was titled *Globalization and Diaspora: Changing Relationships to the Land*; eight students from each institution participated. The syllabus for this seminar (known as the environment seminar) stated that the goals were to "explore the ways in which globalization and the diasporic movements of people have impacted and continue to impact the environment and people's changing relationships to the places and spaces they currently inhabit." These themes were addressed in class and explored via field trips in the area surrounding the SLU campus in upstate New York.

The second seminar, entitled *Globalization* and *Diaspora: Social Justice and Comparative Multiculturalism*, was held at UWI in 2002; again, students and faculty were recruited from all three campuses.[2] This seminar (nicknamed the social justice seminar) aimed to address how "hyper-fast forms of globalization" affecting "capital, communications, labour, consumption, and cultural forms requires new methods of inquiry and new hybrid disciplines, especially in area studies," with particular reference to issues of social justice in the multicultural contexts of Canada, Trinidad/Tobago, and the United States. Discussions, readings, and lectures focussed on transnational or comparative issues, but the field trips to Trinidadian events and landmarks, and many local political issues, infused much of the classroom experience.

A key element of the final conference involved the participation of a selection of students from all of the seminars in a roundtable called "Learning Across Borders" on the second day of the conference. Faculty from the social justice and environment seminars were part of a parallel roundtable on the third day, called "Teaching Across Borders." The students and the faculty in the "Learning" and "Teaching" roundtables were boldly candid in their commentaries about their experiences, so much so that some suggested that as painful as they were, these discussions were one of the most beneficial elements of the entire project. Participants unabashedly laid out the issues and complexities of "border crossings" nationally, institutionally, and often personally.

CO-TEACHING

The seminars were taught by one, or in some cases two, professors from each institution. Professors from a range of disciplinary backgrounds were brought together.[3] For example, in the environment seminar, the faculty included an associate professor, a physical geographer at SLU; a social policy analyst, who was a sessional instructor in Trent's Women's Studies program; and a full professor of botany at UWI. Everyone agreed that teaching in the seminars was emotionally charged, but what varied was *which* emotions were remembered and articulated. The professor from SLU claimed to have had a "great time." The UWI professor, who clearly recognized that things had not gone as smoothly as they might have, acknowledged that "You must pull the good out of it ... but the experience was very traumatic at the time." The Trent professor said, "It really was an incredibly angst-filled experience, as much as it was a wonderful experience." Discipline, institution, culture, gender, generation, rank, and personality differences were all explanations that these professors gave us when contemplating the considerable tensions between them, tensions that very much coloured the experience for faculty and students alike.

What was not shared was a concept of what "teaching collaboratively" entailed. Tellingly, instructors tended to use "I" as opposed to "we" when they reflected on their experiences of collaborative teaching. For instance, one faculty member said, "*I* enjoyed it because *I* was able to teach [what *I* wanted] ... *I* was quite satisfied with what *I* did ... *I* don't think my two colleagues got the same level of satisfaction." Or as another said, "*I* wanted to teach what *I* was comfortable with, what *I* had been teaching in my classes" (emphasis added). In the environment seminar, the host faculty member presented a completed syllabus to her co-teachers, without consulting them about the content. According to one informant, this act immediately established a hierarchy, with an aggressive edge, between supposedly equal colleagues. Many students noticed the tensions between their professors, but most were uncertain of their causes. Counter-intuitively, perhaps, some students felt that aspects of these differences actually enhanced their learning, as it exposed them to alternate ways of thinking in academic cultures of which they had been previously unaware. What students found more troubling and detrimental to their experience were those tensions that they could clearly attribute to what they labelled "personalities." Some of the Trinidadians assumed that the Canadians and Americans, as neighbours and fellow members of First World countries, would be in alliance, but in fact the tensions were often at their most profound between the American and Canadian faculty, positioning, in more than one instance, the UWI instructor as an important mediator between the two.

The coordinators of the project—two professors from each university— had decided that part of the problem in the first summer seminar had been a result of lack of collaboration among the faculty prior to the seminar's inception. In order to facilitate more cooperation from the beginning, the Canadian and American professors of the social justice seminar made a short trip to Trinidad a few months before the start of the summer seminar. After a brief discussion over drinks one balmy Friday evening in Port of Spain, a syllabus was speedily assembled without any discord, but also without consideration of the other dimensions of teaching. For instance, there was no discussion about how the class itself was to be conducted, an omission that was to have many repercussions, none of them positive. In this seminar, as in the first, the professors did not establish beforehand some agreed-upon ground rules for interaction in the class between professors, between professors and students, and between the students. As a consequence, the classroom interactions were often chaotic.

Most of us know how to establish codes of classroom comportment with our own students; after the first year or two, we learn our institutional cultures and can predict the nature of our students. We can't "read" the students of other institutions—or their standards of comportment—nearly so easily. Nor, when co-teaching across institutional and national boundaries, is it clear which teaching conventions should dominate. Our pedagogical practices and implicit ethos about effective teaching and learning are thrown into sharp relief when contested by others. At the "teaching across borders" roundtable, one Trinidadian professor humourously remarked that when he first walked into the classroom, he was shocked to find the chairs arranged in a circle and the professors addressing students by their first names and vice versa. The Trent professor who had set the first name basis protocol and arranged the desks in this fashion had not given it one conscious thought, and likely wouldn't have, had her colleague not pointed it out.[4]

Institutional differences were clearly evident in student behaviours as well. The Trent students noted that it was their inclination—what they see as both their right and obligation—to engage in dialogue with their professors and to reflect critically on what they've learned. This set them apart from the SLU students who, as one Trent student noted, were "led along more in their education." It was not by chance that the most serious critiques of the seminar came from Trent students. Some UWI students, in the social justice seminar in particular, were somewhat ambivalent about the expectation that they should unquestionably show up for every session and field trip, especially since they weren't receiving credit.[5]

What proved particularly troublesome in the social justice seminar was the verbal interaction in class between students. One student, trained in consensus-based participatory action networks of the sort Graeber (this volume) discusses, was profoundly disturbed by what she understood as inegalitarian speaking patterns within the classroom. Questions posed by the professors, she said, were answered by the most aggressive or confident students. The UWI students were particularly prone to interrupting each other and the other students, which was perplexing for the Canadian and American professors, since they were not familiar with accepted verbal modes of interaction in Trinidadian classes and could not turn to their Trinidadian co-teachers for advice, as they were not present in the class for the first half of the seminar.[6] Uncertain of the politics of imposing North American standards of classroom interaction, both the Canadian and the American professor did not establish clear rules at the beginning, as they would have done at home. The Trent students, however, were so disturbed that they approached professors outside of class to voice their concerns. They suggested that, instead of having a question posed where anyone who wanted could answer it, that we have go-arounds, giving everyone a turn to voice an opinion. Space was made the following day to put forward the suggestion to the class. The American students, until this point virtually silent in class, were quite vociferous in their opposition to this proposal, saying that they would speak when they wanted to. (One of the American professors joked that the "radical egalitarianism" of the Canadians had seemed rather oppressive to some, whatever its noble intents.)

INTELLECTUAL BORDERS

The disciplinary and intellectual differences between the professors were not probed in any meaningful manner prior to the seminars. When one professor rhetorically asserted, "I am a Marxist," the others were most unusually caught without comment, although one quietly quipped, "Well, aren't we all?" Myriad academic disciplines claim Marx as an ancestor, and as there is seldom agreement between scholars who consider themselves Marxists, this assertion was hardly informative enough to ameliorate the real differences in academic perspective and resulting tensions among faculty in the social justice seminar.

One student astutely identified the larger problem underlying the personality conflicts between the professors in the environment seminar as an epistemological one, another one of the dangerous borders that this project was attempting to bridge:

> For [one professor] the study of human culture was a branch of the natural sciences and demanded some sort of scientific method.... But [another] professor ... came from a feminist women's studies background of some sort, but she at least was more open to the sort of inquiry that I wanted to do. ...you don't presume that culture is something concrete somewhere that can be studied like geologists study rock formations. The tension was a personal conflict ... the people didn't like each other, but it also manifested itself ... in terms of their scholarly background and their scholarly dispositions.

Another student wrote in his journal, kept during the seminar, that he had the "feeling like [he] was trapped in a bad marriage always dreaming of escape." His evocation of a "bad marriage" metaphor expressed a sense that the project—like marriage—was designed to create a common bond, a union, and common goals. As in a bad marriage, our informant suggested, more time was spent on miscommunication and at cross-purposes. The analogy was wryly recognizable to the professors!

The stories we heard about both of these seminars suggested that it was far from a generative communitas of collective learning. Several students expressed frustration at the failure to achieve what they saw as the larger goal of the project, crossing borders—national, disciplinary, cultural, hegemonic—in order to create a shared intellectual space wherein debate and exchange could take place. Indeed, as one student said, "there were [as many] borders erected as borders crossed." The tenacity of these "borders" and the complexities of their crossing—the latter a reality to which the original grant proposal seemed naïvely blind (at least from an anthropological perspective)—stifled what some students (and some faculty) felt was the essential need to reflect critically on the concepts being used. No one stopped to consider what key terms like "globalization," for instance, might mean from different disciplinary or national perspectives. As one student said:

> The great fear at the time was globalization as a homogenizing force, and the cure-all was some sort of heterogeneity, preserving particularity, and so forth. How does one do that without just descending into some sort of relativism. [Assuming that] there's something inherently good in particularity and specificity of the local and so forth.

The participants' perspectives on "globalization" ranged from the neoliberal to the radical. While some had been arrested in anti-globalization demonstrations, others produced dewy-eyed reflections on globalization's production of creative and unusual juxtapositions of people, commodities, music, art, and ideas. A few participants managed even to see the project as "global voices" assembled to talk. In short, it was like a reverse Tower of Babel: everyone was speaking the same language, but what they meant by the concepts "globalization," "diaspora," or "social justice" differed markedly.

"Multiculturalism" was another deeply problematic term. It has very distinct lineages in the United States, Canada, and Trinidad. The only thing that is really held in common is that the term is highly ideological in each national context. Yet, even this fact was not properly addressed, and, indeed, in the class discussion in the social justice seminar, American students implied that "multiculturalism" was a benign, or almost progressive move, while several Canadian students critiqued their country's multicultural policies as a screen behind which prejudice and disadvantage was hidden. Some of the Trinidadian students produced comments that North Americans would consider veering on racist, although they acknowledged that at least race was kept in the forefront of discussions in Trinidad and not buried beneath polite pieties. Clearly, the work that needed to be done to get beyond merely commenting on the existence of concepts such as globalization, diasporas, race, history, and multiculturalism as forms of border crossings in more than a banal sense was not being done.

To the outrage of most of the students, one professor suggested on the first day that issues of gender and language would not be central to the discussions. Such dismissal was unconscionable to many in the classroom, including his stunned co-professor.[7] Language issues, in fact, inadvertently showed themselves to be the most publicly controversial concern of the entire seminar. While everyone was gathered together, one student issued a sharp criticism of the program, what she thought was the heavily mediated engagement with ordinary Trinidadians. For instance, she asked why, instead of having a professor lecture about Trinidadian sugar cane production and its transnational circulation, was a sugar cane worker not brought into the classroom to speak to the students? Instead of gently reminding the student that hauling a labourer into a classroom to be questioned by privileged university students might produce a deeply uncomfortable—not to mention ethically questionable—experience for him, the senior faculty member moderating the discussion said that that it would have been impossible to do this as the dialects of these rural people were so strong as to be unintelligible to the North American students. When this comment caused a minor uproar, the moderator then made matters far worse by implying that the Trinidadian students in the seminar, students at his university, couldn't speak English properly either. By the time this troubled discussion, rife with misunderstanding, ended, the uproar was major: everyone in the room was shocked, some were livid, and a few students were even in tears. It was a rare moment of complete unity amongst members of all three universities, generated by what was either interpreted as, at best, a clumsy handling of an awkward situation or a deliberate attempt to demean students in front of foreign colleagues. As one student said,

> We were made to feel as Trinidadian students less. We were all feeling equal, we all being equal. When we're sitting and talking, when we were in classes, we were allowed to speak when we wanted. We understood that everybody came from different backgrounds and cultures and experiences, and it was beautiful. And then somebody says to us, "Oh no, go back to your place. This is where you belong because you're "third world"…

The North American student had inadvertently hit a very sensitive nerve, a generational one, whereby the professor was associated with an older mode of identifying with the colonial ideas about superiority and the younger generation with a new mode of national pride. The problems encountered in the project were not all transnational ones; sometimes tensions within each country and institution fed into the larger dynamics in often unpredictable ways.

EXPERIENTIAL VERSUS CLASSROOM LEARNING

One of the most frustrating aspects of both seminars for the students was simply exhaustion. As well as a heavy reading load, the students were taken on many field trips that were in themselves learning experiences. However, what they learned there was not integrated into the classroom discussion. This was a source of deep frustration for faculty members as well. As one of them said, "I don't have a problem with field trips, but the problem was there was no critical understanding as to what we were hearing." Some of the field trips did provide rich material that was potentially relevant to the course objectives, but not all of which was embodied in the journey's final destination. One student in the first seminar noted that they had occasion to cross the actual Canadian-American border several times during the various field tips in the course of visiting a dam and the Akwesasane reserve, both of which span the national borders. In the process, the political economy of passports was clearly evident. The Trinidadians, the Kenyan student from St. Lawrence, and the Thai and Mexican student from Trent were scrutinized much more thoroughly before being allowed across the border, while the Americans and Canadians had no problems whatsoever. As this astute student pointed out, this was a moment when it became abundantly clear that some borders were more difficult for some to cross—and there are clear reasons of prejudice and of unequal national power that have a long history. Yet this tangible enactment of the politics of border crossings was not brought back to the classroom for reflection or analysis.

CONCLUSION

One of the idealistic goals of the summer seminars was to allow the students a chance to examine the intellectual issues surrounding globalization and culture in an intimate, intense setting. While students had many complaints about how the professors handled these issues in the classroom, a couple of incidents made some wonder how committed they themselves were to "crossing borders." On one field trip to an Indo-Trinidadian religious festival known as "Pooja 2002," the students were given money to buy food from the myriad stalls. Yet, on the way home several students, who had eschewed the opportunity to cross a "cuisine border," asked the bus driver to stop so that they could buy lunch from a Kentucky Fried Chicken franchise. This incident provides food for thought about the ironies of an exercise intended to generate a critical perspective on globalization by "crossing borders"; sometimes "home" seems more appealing.

As anthropologists investigating funding initiatives like *Crossing Borders*, and the pedagogical practices associated with them, we have different interests than the project coordinators, who were obliged to account for the success or failure of the project in terms of material outcomes. Our concern with success or failure is only with respect to the concerns that the participants voiced about it. The student seminars were supposed to provide evidence of tangible results that had been generated from the *Crossing Borders* project, some kind of literal embodiment in the students of the worth of the project as a whole. Ironically, most students insisted that they had learned precious little in class, but that the learning that did happen took place outside, with their peers, and in their "consumption" of a foreign environment. Yet, their final projects indicated otherwise. When given an assignment that moved away from the abstract concepts toward an actual empirical case, they rose to the challenge in very insightful, often moving, and sometimes even humourous ways. For instance, in the social justice seminar, the final assignment was to take the theoretical material presented in class and exchange life histories with each other, highlighting how their lives had been caught up in global processes. An American student related the life history of a Trinidadian woman who had grown up in one of the last subsistence farming communities in Tobago; one reflected on how unequal media flows resulted in a Trinidadian woman naming her child after a character in The Love Boat; another related how a Chilean student at Trent felt Canadian for the first time in Trinidad; an American student of Dominican origin at SLU reflected on how people wouldn't let him be an American without a hyphen indexing his "other" origin; and a Canadian woman used a Trinidadian woman's experience of racial prejudice in Quebec to reflect on the hypocrisy of Canadian multicultural policies, which serve to shield poverty and racism from public view by celebrating a harmonious tolerance of difference that a "cultural mosaic" supposedly entails.

One thing that was abundantly clear was that, in the project as a whole, the commitment to literally "crossing borders" was taken very seriously. Perhaps too seriously. The differing selection criteria of the students, the fact that they were at different levels, and the fact that one-third of the students did not stand to benefit in the same way as the others did, made the classes much more difficult to teach. The disciplinary differences the lack of agreement on the analytical terms—made for a discussion that was often confused and confusing. Many felt that, to go beyond a kind of banal sense of learning (the idea that if you gather together "global voices," you're bound to learn something about "globalization"), you needed to have some common ground at the centre.

The *Interconnecting Diasporas* student seminars were inspired by noble goals. Reflecting on pedagogies to achieve better teaching and learning across borders is hardly a project that can be faulted. The summer student seminars of the *Interconnecting Diasporas* project, as in the larger *Crossing Borders* project, and anthropological theorizing of the 1990s, revealed some of the naïve assumptions and admirable, if idealized, optimism about the ability to re-imagine pedagogies across borders through structured engagement in collaborative teaching. What took many by surprise was the location of unexpected borders that had to be crossed: many found them buried in the implicitness of what is considered "normal" behaviour, what anthropologists call "practical consciousness." As one participant said at the final conference, no matter how desirous some involved in the project were of moving beyond their own hegemonic positions, what the entire undertaking did was to reinforce these. Yet ultimately, what may have made the endeavour seem unsatisfactory to many participants is the pervasive "audit culture" in which it is embedded. Such an unforgettable experience may well bear fruit in years to come in ways that are yet intangible and hence uncountable. Time will tell.

NOTES

[1]   This ethnographic project was itself one of the research programs funded by the *Interconnecting Diasporas* project under the auspices of the Ford Foundation's *Crossing Borders* initiative. Thanks to the students and professors in the *Interconnecting Diasporas* project; one could not ask for more articulate and critically aware "natives"! Donna J. Young and Paul Manning read this paper and offered their usual witty and insightful comments.

[2]   Running currently in Trinidad was an arts seminar, entitled *Globalization and Diaspora: Cultural Performance, the Arts, and Identity*. However, given the considerably different experiences of collaboration in an arts environment, we've chosen not to discuss this seminar here. See Meneley and Harrison for more details on this seminar.

3   Who ended up teaching seemed to be driven by motives ranging from a passionate interest in the idea of, or previous experience in, collaborative teaching; a sense of obligation to one's colleagues who were managing the larger Ford project at each institution; a genuine interest in the subject under study; or even, in one case, the modest financial remuneration offered.

4   Trent professors with small classes often specifically request a classroom with moveable chairs for just this reason. At both SLU and Trent, it is common for students to call professors by their first names and virtually unheard-of for professors to address students by "Mr. So and So." In this respect, as in others, UWI was a much more formal and hierarchical institution than either Trent or SLU.

5   Before the seminars even began there had been a lapse of collaboration as different selection criteria were used at each institution. Trent sent the students who were deemed to have the most to offer and who had high academic standing, SLU invited the students who they thought would benefit the most, while the UWI students were told that it would be useful for them to attend. The students were also at different stages in their academic careers. Most UWI students were graduate students; SLU students were second-year undergraduate; and Trent sent upper-year undergraduates. To further complicate the classroom dynamics, the SLU and Trent students received graded academic credit for their work in the seminar. The most contentious issue was the fact that the UWI students did not get any credit for the courses. The UWI grading system at the undergraduate and graduate level, like its British model, is based respectively on final examinations or one's thesis. There is no space in this system for credit to be given for an *ad hoc*, one-of-a-kind, extracurricular course, no matter how substantive its content and structure. This imbalance emphasized the fractured nature of the initiative in the minds of many of the students and also made it very difficult to teach the seminars, as several of the instructors commented.

6   The Trinidadian professors did not feel that having all professors in the classroom at once was a productive use of anyone's time and energies; they showed up only when required to lecture. This absence caused considerable tension in itself, but was particularly crucial for classroom interactions.

7   Although after the final roundtable, he claimed that he actually had not said what everyone thought he had said, he noted that the misinterpretation had had as consequential an effect as an accurate one.

WORKS CITED

Berresford, Susan V. 1999. Preface. *Crossing Borders: Revitalizing Area Studies*. New York: Ford Foundation.

Garber, Marjorie. 2001. *Academic Instincts*. Princeton, N.J.: Princeton University Press.

Meneley, Anne, and Julia Harrison. The Politics and Practices of "Collaboration" in the Crossing Borders Project: Three Solitudes or Transnational Communitas? (manuscript under revision).

6 | ETHNOGRAPHY'S EDGE IN DEVELOPMENT

PAULINE GARDINER BARBER

ANTHROPOLOGISTS ENTERING "THE FIELD" are often perceived in disconcerting ways. In countries that receive aid, they may encounter development projects funded by foreign governments, Canada included. While working in their field sites, anthropologists can be mistaken for development workers whose presence may signal potential material benefits for strategically located individuals and groups. As a consequence, anthropologists may receive unwelcome attention, although they are unable to offer material aid. And when anthropologists are actually attached to development initiatives, they may feel uneasy because people they meet in the field do not always understand the reasons for their involvement. For example, some anthropologists become involved in development projects to secure funding for fieldwork and to enable collaboration with researchers from host countries. Such collaboration might even be construed as a form of praxis, because the opportunity to work with international colleagues presents an opportunity to give something back by contributing resources, learning more deeply, and sharing friendship. Is this as straightforward as it might seem? This chapter considers the relationship between anthropology and development and how the forms of intervention differ and converge, usually uncomfortably.

ENCOUNTERS

My first encounter with how development entices, entraps, distracts, facilitates, and sometimes negates anthropological endeavours occurred shortly after my first tenure-track appointment at a Canadian university.[1] The coordinator of a large project, a partnership between environmental sciences institutes at my university and a university in the Philippines, approached to ask me to volunteer to represent the university at a forthcoming workshop in the Philippines on "rapid (participatory) appraisal methodologies" for coastal communities. She hoped to persuade me to attend. Several things about this request struck me as peculiar, even though I admired her good judgement in selecting an anthropologist for her mission. My suitability, it seemed, hinged on the stereotypical notion that anthropologists are experts in negotiating non-Western culture. Since participatory appraisal methodologies borrow heavily from anthropology, she argued, I had much to contribute.

It seemed to me that there was a questionable assumption lurking behind this idea, namely, that anthropological methods are generic, ripe for dislodgement from their proper dialogue with relevant theories and regional histories, and, therefore, translatable across different contexts. Such ideas have been popularized by development gurus like Robert Chambers (1983) and often criticized by anthropologists who encounter development in their field sites. Indeed, the development industry—and it is an industry—has encouraged the proliferation of resource materials for training various development practitioners to "perform" participatory appraisals in remarkable haste. To be fair to Chambers, the promotion of these methods was to help development workers gain more knowledge about the communities they visit. Chambers's audience is comprised of those experts (not exclusively foreigners) who arrive in unfamiliar contexts to deliver or administer aid with little inkling of their cultural surroundings nor the means to analyze complex issues of power and inequality in field sites. A further market for the methodologies is the burgeoning global traffic of non-governmental organizations (NGOs), with their paid workers and volunteers from all walks of life, educational levels, and political persuasions who participate in development at "the grassroots level." The incredible popularity of "participation" discourse is also linked to its promise to include development's beneficiaries. Widespread enchantment with "participation" discourse led Cooke and Kothari (2001) to propose, provocatively, that participation has become a new "tyranny."

As many anthropologists, myself included, recognize, so-called participatory methods offer, at best, a superficial reading of selective aspects of daily life. For most anthropologists, the methods are useful for commencing the research process or for supplementing other sources of ethnographic knowledge. However, others who use the participatory tool kits do so to "empower communities"; thus, the methods become the *end in itself*, not a tool to further understanding of social complexities. Indeed, shortly after I travelled to my first Philippine workshop, I attended a workshop in Canada for NGOs run by Robert Chambers. When I asked about the purpose of empowering communities, he appeared angry and did not reply. I found this mystifying. Why empower the poor? Apparently to be empowered! Anthropologists have become highly critical about empowerment discourse and its misguided logic, namely, the assumption that if people understand more about local circumstances they may be empowered/inspired to introduce changes (Cooke and Kothari 2002; Parpart, Rai, and Staudt 2002; Peters 2000). But, anthropologists argue, without significant shifts in the distribution of resources in local communities, the avenues for change remain extremely limited.

Perhaps the most peculiar aspect of my colleague's invitation to join the research team was her indifference to my limited knowledge of the Philippines. Again, it was as if our methods automatically made us experts on *all cultural others*. I considered myself qualified to discuss issues relevant to gender and unionized Western workers, not poor rural Filipinos who were likely unemployed and certainly not unionized. If any foray outside of Canada were to tempt me then, I reported, it was to Mexico, since Canada's involvement with North American free trade agreements exposed all manner of injustices in Mexican factories that begged for critical ethnographic enquiry.

Again, I acknowledge the coordinator's excellent judgement since some of the globalization issues that drew me towards ethnographic work in Mexico were as germane to the Philippines. Located in Southeast Asia, the Philippines was also colonized by Spain for several hundred years, leaving Roman Catholicism as the dominant religion. In the twentieth century (until nominal independence in 1946), the United States was the colonial power, adding another layer of cultural complexity. While Filipinos negotiated, contested, and often resisted colonial domination, never completely replicating colonial institutions (Hedman and Sidel 2000), some tracings from both colonial periods are apparent in their daily life. For example, to work in the Philippines is to encounter some familiar aspects of American popular culture selectively translated with a Filipino twist. Spanish idioms and practices also linger. Most obviously, I recognized historical labour arrangements in sugar haciendas as reminiscent of situations described in Latin American ethnography. Both Mexico and the Philippines have chosen similar (and troubling) paths toward economic development. In both countries you can find export processing zones where low-waged workers, predominantly women, assemble electronics and sew clothing for Western markets. They work under conditions that would be forbidden by law in factories located in Western countries. So my colleague's argument was certainly correct, as there was much common ground to be explored.

But my invitation was not founded on my expertise in gender and work issues. Moreover, like Donna J. Young in this volume, I had deliberately forged my ethnographic interests in a personal history and political geography that situated my research within my own culture. I had no desire to constitute an ethnographic "other" in a non-Western field site. My doctoral and postdoctoral field research was located in Canada, in industrial Cape Breton, where I studied the effects of history, class, and culture in the resistance politics of fish plant workers. While it is true that the workers I studied lived proximate to the ocean and worked in a fishing-related industry, I never described their communities, or their lives, as "coastal." Indeed, I write critically about ideological tropes like "community" and "coastal." Such constructs, I argue, assume too much about livelihoods and social relations. They homogenize differences amongst people and conflate places with local occupations and identity. Rather, my interest lies with the dynamics of global capitalism and economic restructuring: how the legacy of the development of capital in the coal mining industry casts a shadow over class, culture, and community identities in Cape Breton's old coal towns long after the industry's demise.

In short, I had good reasons to question the logic of the invitation to participate in this project in the Phillipines, to be reluctant about entering into an encounter with development, and to brood about the relevance of my prior experience. However, I set my concerns aside. I travelled to the workshop and, in the process of learning about Philippine livelihoods and political economy, became fascinated with ethnographic puzzles concerning the same globalization scenarios I had studied in Cape Breton. And thus began a longer term study of Philippine development, migration, and identities. I now turn to how this interest was shaped, in effect, against the predetermined logic of the development project I found myself entering.

THE WORKSHOP

It was early in the 1990s that despite my reservations, I travelled to the Philippines. The workshop included a trial application of some participatory methodologies in several "coastal" sites in Bais Bay, located some 60 kilometres outside of Dumaguete, in Negros Oriental. Community meetings focussed upon fishers' routines and needs. Locals at the meeting knew what we were there to discuss, so they concentrated upon fishing issues, plus other predictable difficulties of daily life stemming from their low incomes and lack of services. Since most of the visitors were trained in marine science and environmental analysis, they explored issues in the physical environment. My mind wandered, distracted by the novel surroundings and incredible heat, as plans were drawn to produce inventories of fish stocks and sea grasses. Because of my interest in livelihood complexities, I became curious about some modest, yet observable, differences in household wealth as I strolled the periphery of the open-sided building in which our meeting was held. I had an excellent view of the daily activities underway all around us.

I was such an incongruous figure in that time and place, a tall woman with pale skin flushed from the intense heat, that Daisy spotted me immediately through her window. She quickly emerged, her curiosity getting the better of her morning's planned trip to the market. She responded to my questions about local livelihoods, how people sustain themselves and make a living in the absence of reliable employment, with her own complicated story of sequential migration experiences. She had recently returned from her third overseas labour contract in Hong Kong and was now brooding as she waited for the next contract to arrive in the mail. Her house, made of visibly aged native wood with thatched roofing, seemed modest, even by local standards. It did not fit the pattern I later learned to read of housing upgrades as symbolic evidence of migration "success." She told me she lived with her son, then a young college graduate. He would soon embark on his own journey seeking work as the only work available locally was for unskilled labour and that was scarce. There was occasional day labour on small sugar haciendas or on municipal work crews, and sometimes men could find work on modest fishing crews using handheld nets. All such employment was sporadic, and opportunities were distributed through complex social arrangements. The presence of sequential international aid projects also provided periodic employment for guards, drivers, and technicians, but such prospects were unlikely for commerce graduates such as Daisy's son or for people like herself, who apparently lacked local patronage networks.

While Daisy was scornful about the prospects for community economic development— she had observed the comings and goings of development workers for over 10 years—she was less cynical about her own future. Despite her modest dwelling, she described herself as relatively well-off. Her wealth was in livestock—cows and pigs farmed through contractual arrangements with neighbours. I was curious about the discrepancy between Daisy's seemingly modest living circumstances and the more cosmopolitan flair she brought to our conversation. A subsequent conversation with Daisy's neighbour (one of the few women invited to the development meeting) provided further clues when she spoke of her poor neighbour whose husband had a drinking problem. The neighbour was Daisy, the husband a drain on her resources and perhaps the reason for her cynicism.

This encounter with Daisy piqued my interest, and in time I would investigate those women who come from "fishing households" in the poorest coastal *barangays*[2] in Bais, but who routinely migrate to work so that they can send remittances home. Over several trips to Bais in the intervening years, I noticed Daisy's house was increasingly dwarfed by improvements her neighbours made to their homes, but I never saw her again. Daisy had returned to Hong Kong, her invisible presence maintained through her modest farming enterprise and ongoing claims to property. Likely she maintains savings in Hong Kong for her own future, perhaps free from the claims of those who failed to respect her efforts and contributions.

In my mind, this initial encounter with Daisy came to represent my discomfort with development priorities. My colleagues were so preoccupied with what were obviously pressing environmental issues, they overlooked the significance of extra-local contributions to regional livelihoods, such as migration. Back at the university, analysis of the "workshop field data" all too smoothly linked poverty to environmental degradation and livelihood security to environmental sustainability.[3] Consequently, their approach to pragmatic livelihood solutions was reductive, narrowed into a singular focus on fishing. The influence of the wider political economy seemed irrelevant to the task at hand. The conversation never touched upon the reasons why the Philippines is deeply indebted to the World Bank and the International Monetary Fund, nor on the acute disparities in economic wealth found in many Philippine communities. Every Filipino I have ever met recognizes the severity of national indebtedness and unusually high national poverty rates. Filipino academics were no exception, and they taught me a lot about such topics in our casual conversations outside of workshop time. However, eco-centrism prevailed inside workshop activities.

As I reflect again on the workshop, it seems hardly surprising that discussion of livelihoods missed the significance of new gender patterns of labour migration, flowing across the country, the region, and increasingly, the world, to become the bedrock of the Filipino economy. Because the primary economic actors in coastal areas were presumed to be men, women's livelihood activities were treated as less significant in their own right. So the question of women's labour migration did not even arise in our livelihood assessments. But, as my subsequent research on gendered livelihoods in Bais clarified (Barber 1995), women's labour is more varied than men's, and women often contribute the greater share of a household's income in this, and apparently many other, Philippine communities (Illo and Polo 1990; Tacoli 1995).

FURTHER WORKSHOPS

When my involvement with this development workshop was over, I sought additional opportunities to return to the Philippines, which came through research fellowships and additional university partnerships funded by the Canadian International Development Agency (CIDA), plus independent scholarly research grants. I went on to explore gendered livelihood practices in several Bais *barangays* and elsewhere in the Philippines, following up on my hunch about the significance of migrants' remittances. Still, I continued to work in areas that were the recipient of development aid and attention, and my unease about such projects remained.

The environmental concerns identified at the workshop were subsequently translated into a series of linked "community-based resource management" activities.[4] Several modest initiatives targeted "livelihood diversification" and were premised on the logic that this might ease pressure on environmental resources. But because an eco-system approach was used, an environmental logic prevailed over socio-political understandings and dictated procedures for the whole project. The political geography of the bay included three different municipalities, each with a different history and a cast of political actors with their own interests and dispositions towards environment and development. Inevitably, competition between groups in the different jurisdictions erupted into conflict over resources. Such political realities made the idea of an eco-system and community-based approach to environmental management unworkable at the time. It was born of an imported idealism far removed from the vagaries of a history that had left over half of the population of Bais, totalling some 66,000 people, extremely poor and technically landless. Eventually, the primary action area was narrowed to the Bais municipality and its 35 quite diverse *barangays* located along the coast and extending into the uplands.

During this time, I was always identified as a "visiting researcher," not as a member of the project staff, nor as a development worker. While in Bais I found temporary accommodation in a government training centre in the poorest *barangay*, on a small island joined by a causeway to the city. Most of my fieldwork was confined to those coastal areas where livelihood issues were sufficient to retain my interest. As a result of my affiliation with the development project, I obtained ready access to municipal officials and community leaders and to the knowledge of local researchers and development staff. The situation was, in many ways, ideal. But I often felt compelled to disassociate myself from the agenda set by the wider project. Still, it is difficult to convince others you are there as an independent researcher when you seem, so obviously, to be participating.

The project in Bais was embedded in a more ambitious project, which sought to bring together the expertise of environmental and social scientists in three different Philippine environments: urban, upland, and coastal. Bais, the third site to be included, commenced at the mid-point of CIDA's funding. As with the other sites, an elaborate planning forum, called in Bais an "agro-eco-system" workshop, was organized. Here, the project was introduced to invited local community officials and strategically selected interested parties. I was not present for this, but project documents confirm what the title for the workshop suggests. The environment, its degradation and potential restoration, dictated the agenda. Six program goals were established:

1. To empower the people;
2. To have coordination in the conduct of development projects;
3. To improve the watershed;
4. To attend to other environmental concerns;
5. To establish an information system;
6. To improve household income. (Abregana 1994)

Item six translates as encouraging "people to engage in appropriate livelihood activities" and describes most social contact initiated through project activities. In what can only be described as a "victim-blaming logic," project meetings linked destructive uses of the environment to local poverty. It was reasoned that if alternative and more sustainable income generation projects could be identified, pressure would be removed from over-taxed natural resources. The first item, empowerment, reflected how significant this idea has become in post-Chambers development discourse. In this instance, as always, empowerment was ideologically charged with moral suasion; people's use of the environment (not social inequality), by default, becomes the problem. The environment seems more amenable to change. And so there commenced a concerted effort to remedy seemingly fixable scars in the environment, for example, by encouraging people to plant and tend tree seedlings along upland river courses where severe erosion contributes to flooding, thus causing siltation in the Bay. Siltation destroys fish breeding habitats; hence, the logic of the eco-system approach. Meanwhile, the two sugar refineries illegally discharging processing wastes into the bay seemed beyond official reproach and were not represented in various participatory dialogues!

Action teams set about working with "the people" in various locations; each team was led by local academics with different disciplinary backgrounds and ideas about how to enlist local community actors in the project's mission of more sustainable environmental interactions. The teams met with different responses in each community they entered. Ultimately, there was little in the way of immediate tangible results in either the environmental or social aspects of the agenda. At the end of the initial two years of funding, trees had been planted and various inventories made of marine species. The funding was terminated at this point, and the remainder of CIDA's development effort turned to the other two projects, which were of longer duration and, therefore, more amenable to results-based management.[5]

In my view, the Bais project was prematurely terminated. Continuing to "observe" from my outsider/insider vantage point, I visited the area on subsequent trips to the Philippines. One of the most striking unrecorded consequences of the Canadian project was the mayor's conversion to environmentalism, influenced by extensive conversations with Canadian project staff and local environmental scientists, who took every opportunity to promote the various concepts and technologies they felt might repair the Bay's eco-system. He proudly described his environmental initiatives to me in a chance encounter after the project's termination. Most impressive was the promotion of the city as an eco-tourism site. Local attractions included a dolphin-watching boat tour and a mangrove forest reserve, home to rare species of wildlife. Members of city staff were also experimentally growing high value crops (orchids and mushrooms) for promotion in livelihood scenarios. And an effort was launched to convince fishermen to honour a no-fishing zone, a modest marine sanctuary that might relieve pressure on breeding stock. These accomplishments matched aspirations voiced by the initiators of the CIDA project, so the work continued well beyond its life. Interestingly, city officials took on the role of the outsiders who had instigated development, namely, those Canadian academics working on CIDA goals, partnered with Philippine academics. Given these apparently positive efforts at reversing environmental degradation in Bais, you might wonder about my critical tone. Despite the rhetoric of partnership and participation, I argue that the imperatives and momentum for the project continued outside of the reach of the majority of local people.

THE POLITICS OF NEO-LIBERALISM

One of the most confounding aspects of the neo-liberal policies and practices that now dominate global development agendas is that, at first glance, they appear sensible and to fit with a commonsense understanding of the world, at least for those people living in capitalist economies. Neo-liberal discourses encourage people to be independent, self-reliant, and, most particularly, to take economic responsibility for themselves. This in part explains the seduction of "empowerment," which nests comfortably within neo-liberal ideologies. Investment and individual financial risk-taking are also promoted. Policies encourage entrepreneurial activities and discourage reliance on government assistance of any kind. Market competitiveness supposedly fuels economic growth and new opportunities. Individual rather than collective goals are encouraged. In many poor regions of the world, in the absence of other economic possibilities, tourism is seen as a development opportunity that has the potential, proponents argue, to be sustainable if an appropriate market niche is cultivated. But neo-liberalism remains unconcerned about the social distribution of development's rewards.

I confess I find the idea of eco—or any other—tourism in Bais challenging, not the least because of wealth disparities and the absence of basic services (water, sewage treatment, garbage collection) for the majority of households hugging the shoreline. For tourism, perhaps the most significant of these deficits is an acute water shortage. Project efforts to remedy this floundered. Water pipes were constructed with CIDA's support, but many households did not receive the water. Enterprising individuals took advantage of the new supply by bottling water for sale to customers further down the supply line. Sugar haciendas took advantage of it for irrigation purposes. It was a classic development *faux pas*; the introduction of a new, valuable resource emphasized pre-existing social class differences, providing an advantage to some who, while still relatively poor, were already better off than their neighbours. In keeping with national policy priorities, an attempt was made to establish a community water board, one that was gender balanced since local academics recognized that women's daily routines were most compromised by water scarcity. Women cared deeply about water. This too floundered in part because of testy politics and the multiple claims on women's precious time. So, to my anthropologist's eye, pressing issues of power, social class, and gender proved intractable during and after the life of the project. This is why anthropologists insist that development must take account of social relations and engage with questions of social inequality and wealth distribution. It also explains the vigorous debates over the purpose of development; perhaps it is not really intended to redistribute wealth. Rather, as critics of neo-liberal ideologies suggest (Hulme and Edwards 1997; Schild 2000), through development interventions, people are drawn into the market as entrepreneurs, even if in small-scale businesses and even if this occurs at the expense of others who may be further disadvantaged by the making of necessities like water, into commodities, for instance.[6]

Ironically, in the Bais eco-tourism endeavour, we see the greatest measurable success from the project unrecorded by CIDA. True to his promise, the mayor arranged for a tourist hotel to be built at the summit of a hill overlooking the bay and mangrove reserve. In translation the hotel is called "The View from the Hill," *Bahia de Bais*. Here we see the greatest potential for economic development to occur, but only for rich investors. Development "success" here is combined with the exacerbation of social disparities and injustices. The hotel represents the managed environment (recall the project was about environmental management), a site of consumption for those privileged enough to afford to stay there. Glaringly, the hotel is well beyond the economic horizons of the fishers and farmers along the shoreline who are most in need of access to environmentally sustainable, equitable material and social resources. In 1997, I spotted a national newspaper column (*Philippine Daily Enquirer*, 20 May 1997) promoting the hotel as place for elegant dining and good food. But, as the journalist noted, the hotel is "a far cry from life down at the foot of the hill"! Notable also is the fact that the hotel was built without a prior environmental impact assessment, even though this is legally required. An expansion was projected, but I have yet to follow up on this.

In thinking about the hotel and the wealth disparity it symbolizes, I am reminded of the parallels with other aspects of Philippine development where employment prospects are limited by the cheapening of labour through national indebtedness. Hence, Bais women, who work long hours every day raising livestock, selling fish in the market, and doing whatever they can to raise cash for school and medical supplies, as well as the food staple, rice, are like the factory workers who make our clothes and Filipina (like Daisy) who work as housekeepers and nannies all over the world. They are situated in difficult political and economic circumstances which they address using all the resources at their disposal. In this effort they are empowered as economic actors yet dis-empowered by economic inequalities (Barber 2002). Ethnography's edge in this example enables us to see the connections, to consider the bigger picture that the environmental angle of the intervention, what I have called here eco-centrism, obscures.

And yet, for some residents at least, in the Philippine communities described here, development continues to represent potentially positive change. This is less true for those at the bottom of the hill, but even there some households continue their experiment with the marine sanctuary and report a slight improvement in their catch. Mainly, the social status quo holds steady. Subsequent international agencies have arrived, each with a differing set of priorities in accord with global development themes. But little has changed for the majority of residents unless they are recipients of remittances from migrant relatives overseas. Enterprising locals who already hold a modicum of power carry over some small initiatives from aid project to aid project, again mainly through the creative manipulation of resources. So the anthropologist observes while development exits!

COMPLICITIES AND CONCEITS

This chapter examines the paradoxes of practicing anthropology in neo-liberal times. It questions the uneasy relationship between development and anthropology, showing how the differing agendas of action versus research produce tensions. The imposition of development in local communities, even when the rhetoric of partnership[7] and participation is present, feeds into pre-existing inequalities and power relationships that exist on many levels: between nations, between the collaborating partners, between the development experts (foreign and local) and the communities they work in, and between the actual recipients of development assistance.

I became convinced that anthropologists may indeed have a political edge over some other researchers they meet in the field, and this is due to our critical theoretical traditions and training in ethnographic methods. We begin with broader critical questions and allow more time in the field to explore possible, even unanticipated, realities. But those of us who work with development workers, or receive funding from development agencies, risk losing this edge.

I have additional concerns, which are related to the ways I first arrived inside a development project, with which I began this chapter. What happens to the time of anthropologists who get enticed into the development enterprise through invitations such as mine? Basically, their energies and focus become mobilized, sometimes voluntarily as in my case, sometimes more coercively relative to career aspirations, the needs of colleagues, and university departments. Often development collaborations include the promise of funding and affiliations with overseas institutions and colleagues, which are enticing and hard to refuse. Moreover, funding agencies now require the incorporation of the social sciences, ethnography, gender expertise, etc., in these development projects. So we travel: for institutional, personal, and collegial reasons. As we travel our research attention becomes fragmented, our time appropriated along with our labour. This means the focus of our research is redirected and pre-designated. Are we co-opted? Maybe. Certainly I am suggesting frameworks, agendas, and priorities are pre-established. Ultimately, this raises political questions, as well as epistemological and methodological concerns.

My discussion about an ambivalent relationship has then an ambivalent ending. Yes, I have been able to fashion a research focus out of my appropriated labour conditions. This is arguably positive—I think. I find myself unable to refuse any conversation about Philippine development. I take any and all opportunities to travel to the Philippines even when I know university partnerships are time-consuming and offer little or no time for actual research. This is particularly frustrating because much project activity begs for more scholarly ethnographic analysis, which does not get done because projects cannot afford the research time ethnography demands. Moreover, increasingly, interdisciplinarity is valued. Interdisciplinarity suggests that while anthropologists are appreciated for their specialized knowledge and research methodologies because it contributes to the work of others, the actual respect accorded their work is diminished. Sometimes anthropological knowledge is trivialized. Impatiently, our expertise and critiques are brushed aside by the argument that social analysis can be done by any researcher, regardless of discipline.

And still I continue my dance alongside development. My personal (professional) gains lie with my research agenda set in the nooks and crannies of partnerships. Also valued are scholarly collaborations and friendships, nurtured through a national effort that requires most Philippine academics to engage with development. They have less choice about this than we do, but their motivations and rewards are also different! The costs for outsiders like myself are enormous in terms of time and effort. There are also constraints in available writing time because of travel. To write requires that we dedicate ourselves to immobility even when development beckons. In closing, I quote anthropologist James Ferguson, an astute observer of the development machinery. He acknowledges the deep entanglement between anthropology and development, conjoined as evil twins:

> Like an unwanted ghost, or an uninvited relative, development thus continues to haunt the house of anthropology. Fundamentally disliked by a discipline that at heart loves all those things that development intends to destroy, anthropology's evil twin remains too close a relative to be simply kicked out; "after all," anthropology says to itself, "these issues, even if theoretically suspect, are of great practical importance." (Ferguson 1997: 170).

NOTES

[1] The idea of development is contested (Crush 1995). Some argue development furthers bureaucratic goals that at best have a neutral effect, but that often worsen conditions for supposed beneficiaries (Ferguson 1990). Others debate the origins of development in relation to American foreign policy goals (Escobar 1995; Cowan and Shenton 1995).

[2] A *barangay* is the smallest political unit in the Philippines. The three coastal *barangays*, in which I worked, contained approximately 1,600 households in 1990.

3   The 1980s and 1990s saw increased attention to environmental concerns. In the Philippines, the environment was recognized as having a direct relationship to human rights in the new constitution of 1987. Following the political uprisings that ousted corrupt President Marcos from power, the Philippine's fourth constitution was put in place to frame Philippine public policy. On the global stage, the Rio Convention on Sustainable Development (1992) espoused principles for the environmental responsibilities of nations.

4   Again, the global and local policy logic for the CIDA project makes sense. The Philippine Constitution provides the mandate for the concern to have communities participate in environmental management. The preferential rights of small-scale fishers are protected, as 15 kilometres of municipal shores and many components of coastal management lie with local governments, in contrast to the situation in Canada. Interestingly, both ecology and social justice are featured prominently in the Constitution.

5   Because of audit culture (Strathern 2000) in development, even university partnerships are tied to indicators of success and "results-based management." Despite difficulties involved in understanding social relationships and the cultural subtleties of micro-power flows, attempts are made to "measure" success. Ironically, this increases the potential of skewed development efforts and the likelihood that development will not benefit those who need it most.

6   Ironically, the neo-liberal slant in development can also facilitate greater scrutiny and control (both international and national) over people's lives even when it professes, paternalistically, to encourage individual, or local autonomy and independence. We see this in the Philippines with the introduction of new regulations, taxes, etc., being implemented in local communities where previously social understandings prevailed. Foucault's theories of regulation and discipline help explain this (see Ferguson 1990).

7   See Jenson and Philipps (1996) for an interesting critique of the pervasive rhetoric of partnership discourse in neo-liberal political and economic agendas.

WORKS CITED

Abregana, Betty. 1994. Attempts at community-based resource management: The development action project in the Bais Bay Basin (August 1991-December 1993). *Silliman Journal* 37: 9–26.

Barber, Pauline Gardiner. 1995. Invisible labour, transnational lives: Gendered work and new social fields in coastal Philippines." *Culture* 15(2): 5–26.

———. 2002. Envisaging power in Philippine migration: The Janus effect. *Rethinking Empowerment: Gender and Development in a Global/Local World*. Ed. Jane Parpart, Shirin Rai, and Kathleen Staudt. London: Routledge.

Chambers, Robert. 1983. *Rural Development: Putting the Last First*. New York, NY: John Wiley and Sons.

Cooke, Bill, and Uma Kothari. 2001. *Participation: The New Tyranny?* London: Zed Books.

Cowen M., and R. Shenton. 1995. The invention of development. *Power of Development*. Ed. J. Crush. 27-43. London: Routledge.

Crush, Jonathan (ed.). 1995. *Power of Development*. London: Routledge.

Escobar, Arturo. 1988. Power and visibility: Development and the invention and management of the Third World." *Cultural Anthropology* 3(4): 428–43

———. 1995. *Encountering Development: The Making and Unmaking of the Third World*. Princeton, NJ: Princeton University Press.

Ferguson, James. 1990. *The Anti-Politics Machine: "Development," Depoliticization and Bureaucratic Power in Lesotho*. Cambridge: Cambridge University Press.

1997. Anthropology and its evil twin: "Development" in the constitution of a discipline." In *International Development and the Social Sciences: Essays on the History and Politics of Knowledge*. Ed. Frederick Cooper and Randall Packard. 150–75. Berkeley, CA: University of California Press.

Hedman, Eva-Lotta, and John T. Sidel. 2000. *Philippine Politics and Society in the Twentieth Century: Colonial Legacies, Post-colonial Trajectories*. London: Routledge.

Hulme, David, and M. Edwards. 1997. NGOs, states and donors: An overview. In *NGOs, States and Donors: Too Close for Comfort?* Ed. D. Hulme and M. Edwards. 3–22. New York, NY: St. Martin's Press/Save the Children.

Illo, Jeanne, and Jaime Polo. 1990. *Fishers, Traders, Farmers, Wives: The Life Stories of Ten Women in a Fishing Village*. Manila: Institute of Philippine Culture, Ateneo de Manila University.

Jenson, Jane, and Susan Philipps. 1996. Regime shift: New citizenship practices in Canada. *International Journal of Canadian Studies* 14(Fall): 111–35.

Parpart, Jane, Shirin Rai, and Kathleen Staudt (eds). 2002. *Rethinking Empowerment: Gender and Development in a Global/Local World*. London: Routledge.

Peters, Pauline. 2000. *Development Encounters: Sites of Participation and Knowledge*. Cambridge MA: Harvard University Press.

Schild, Veronica. 2000. Neoliberalisms' new gendered market citizens: The "civilizing dimension" of social programs in Chile. *Citizenship Studies* 4: 275–305.

Strathern, Marilyn (ed.). 2000. *Audit Cultures: Anthropological Studies in Accountability, Ethics, and the Academy*. London: Routledge.

Tacoli, Cecilia. 1995. Gender and international survival strategies: A research agenda with reference to Filipina labour migrants in Italy." *Third World Planning Review* 17(2): 199–212.

———. 1998. My paradigm or yours? Alternative development, post-development, reflexive development. *Development and Change* 29: 343–73.

PART III | INTERVENTIONS

THIS SECTION EXAMINES SOME OF THE IRONIES that attend our attempts to meaningfully share our knowledge with a broader public. For all that universities are increasingly asked to become more relevant and to accommodate society's many needs, an academic's intervention in public debates is not always welcomed. While students, funding agencies, and politicians have no compunction when it comes to meddling in the practices of the academy (after all, they remind us, we pay your salaries), our knowledge born of research is often belittled and dismissed. We are told that we live in an ivory tower and that our abstract theories are irrelevant, or worse. So it is very heartening when our knowledge, occasionally, serves the needs of others, although this might happen in the most unexpected of fashions.

Solway notes the transformation of her research in Botswana over the last 30 years, from youthful and confident expert to collaborator with indigenous Batswana politicians working to claim minority rights in the new state. It is with pleasure that she finds that the meticulously detailed work of Schapera, an anthropologist who worked in southern Africa in the colonial period, is newly resurrected to become instrumental in this struggle.

Unfortunately, our expertise or scholarly reflections and understanding are not always appreciated. Sanders' attempts to intervene in the case of the "Thames Torso," by questioning the Metropolitan Police and Scotland Yard's quick assumption that the mutilated body parts found in the river represented a form of "African witchcraft," are rebuffed. As Sanders points out, cultural anthropology appears very much a weak language in the face of the forensic knowledge and the investigative theories of the police. While forensic anthropology popularized in TV crime shows and detective novels describing dead and decaying corpses captures the public imagination, the detailed cultural anthropological knowledge of living beings is marginalized and de-legitimized. Even the police seem to sideline anthropological knowledge in favour of more sensationalist (and racist) accounts.

When Swedenburg was called as an expert witness on behalf of a criminal's right to practice his religion (Nation of Gods and Earths) in an American prison, the prosecution asked, "But have you done fieldwork with them?" The prosecution's attempted strategy for dismissing Swedenburg's authority as an expert was encapsulated in that simple question, which reduced the breadth of anthropological knowledge to the domain of "been there, saw that." Thankfully, his well-rehearsed expert witness testimony prevailed. Ironically, it was most persuasive for him to employ an outmoded definition of religion, dependant on the idea that the possession of religious ideas is universal, as are human rights. Although this line of reasoning has been critiqued in the discipline, a functionalist approach with claims to scientific and factual truth resonates much better in a justice system predicated on such ideals.[1] Thus, he was able to convince the judge that this religion deserved the same respect as any other.

Our interventions are often ignored, or over-scripted, by those who invite them. For all the work anthropologists do in cultural translation, it is not easy to meaningfully translate our own ideas. In decidedly anti-intellectual times, academics, or at least anthropologists, appear to have very little real power. (For those who doubt this definition of our times as anti-intellectual, we wish to remind you that George W. Bush is the most powerful man alive). We are told we live in ivory towers, and our abstract theories, little understood, are denounced as irrelevant.

NOTES

[1] See Crapanzano (2000) for a compelling examination of literalism as an American belief system that influences their legal system.

WORKS CITED

Crapanzano, Vincent. 2000. *Serving the Word: Literalism in America from the Pulpit to the Bench*. New York: The New Press

7 | ANTHROPOLOGIST AND ACCOMPLICE IN BOTSWANA[1]

Jacqueline Solway

I have been working as an anthropologist in Botswana for over 25 years. A *consequence* of long-term fieldwork is recognition of how *inconsequential* one is. One of the most powerful lessons I have learned is modesty about my own role and about the power of my own predictions. I have learned to be cautious about adopting the present as a point of departure from which to judge the significance of our anthropological past. A perspective smugly rooted in the present can distort the work of the past by dismissing it or, worse, by judging it in terms of present standards. Anthropological theory has developed through the critique of our ancestors, but there are pitfalls to generational complacency. We must guard against positioning ourselves as more knowledgeable than past generations and characterizing our struggles as more righteous than theirs. This is not only because we too will be subjected to critique by the next generation.

I describe here the metamorphosis of my own fieldwork over the last quarter century. Then, to borrow and twist Geertz's (1984) clever term "anti anti-relativism," I offer a few anti anti-morality tales. This is not to suggest that I am against morality, or that I endorse immorality, but rather that I am critical of the myopic moralizing in which anthropologists, including my younger self, too often engage.

YOUTHFUL HUBRIS

My fieldwork experience likely resembles that of many scholars who worked in Africa during the last quarter century. My work in the 1970s seemed, at the time, to have enormous political urgency: Botswana was a newly independent country in the throes of what appeared to be a major transformation of rural political economy that would impact upon the livelihoods of most of the population. There were plans for land reform, and researchers like me were invited by the government to participate in the process. There were so many of us, researchers from a number of disciplinary backgrounds and countries, as well as expatriate volunteers and civil servants. We were young and enthusiastic. We fed off each other, eager to contribute our expertise in a meaningful way, confident that we could make a difference. There were very few young educated Batswana[2] at the time, a situation that, fortunately, has entirely changed now. But then we had no local peer group to foil or interfere with our own sense of self-importance. Our local counterparts were older civil servants, most of whom had minimal education by current standards. We saw them, in large measure, as representatives of the old school: conservative, unimaginative, and reluctant to rock the boat. We believed that we could play a role in policy, influencing the general direction of the country. Suffused with youthful hubris, we believed that our advice—despite our short acquaintance with the country—was correct and should be taken seriously. We were enchanted with our own sense of instrumentality.

I cringe now at our naiveté and our arrogance. And recognize, ironically, that one might interpret us as carrying on a sort of colonial practice, despite our self-avowed political distancing from the colonial project and our condemnation of it.

SHIFTING SANDS

The majority of us were studying rural political economy. Little did we know how rapidly, literally and figuratively, the sands beneath our feet would shift. The social and economic system I so painstakingly and lovingly documented and analyzed in the late 1970s transformed dramatically. When I returned to the field after an absence of only six years, I asked my informants if they still carried out certain practices previously vital to the local economy. Some responded, "Oh, we did that long, long ago (*bogologolo thata*)!"

Fundamental to this quick transformation was the virtual elimination of employment opportunities in South Africa by 1980; the agro-pastoral system practiced by most rural Batswana existed only in conjunction with oscillating wage labour migration, primarily to the South African gold and diamond mines. More significant were the vast diamond deposits that lay beneath the Kalahari sands. Botswana's first diamond mine, Orapa, opened in 1976, and the second, more valuable mine, Jwaneng, opened in 1982. Botswana is now the world's largest producer of high quality diamonds (Taylor and Mokhawa 2003: 262). The incredible infusion of mineral wealth transformed the country's social and economic landscape as well as its topographical one. By African standards, Botswana has been fortunate. It moved from abject poverty at independence in 1966 to relative prosperity at present. A thriving middle class has emerged. The mineral wealth has been used to create an ever-expanding social safety net that has mitigated the harshest poverty and prevented famine during severe droughts. However, Botswana has not entirely eradicated poverty. In fact, prosperity has rendered poverty more painful to endure as the sense of relative deprivation has become more pronounced.

Education expanded with the mineral boom. By the 1980s, the role of foreign researchers in policy circles seemed suddenly eclipsed by an increasingly sophisticated generation of educated Batswana who began to fill civil service positions. Another effect of local wealth that sidelined expatriates and deflated their egos was the diminished importance of foreign aid. During the devastating drought of the 1980s, Botswana, like other countries of the region, received considerable external aid, but because of its domestic resources, it was able to implement its own drought relief in the form of subsidies and schemes that differed from the sort international agencies would have instituted (Solway 1994b).

While my own interest in rural political economy has not waned, I have found my more recent research agenda set by my desire to understand what seems to be of greatest local concern now. To my great surprise, the remote Kalahari area where I worked became a hotbed of political opposition by the 1990s. Among the most compelling reason for this politicization was the attempt on the part of the Bakgalagadi residents of the region to valorize their previously disparaged identity. They are contesting their former subjugation to the dominant Tswana people by attempting to gain national institutional recognition and inclusion.[3]

I could not have predicted this transformation from my early fieldwork. Yet the movement has been so profound, and has animated so much of local life, that I found myself compelled to understand it. In the process, the topic led me from the margins, both geographically and politically, to the centre, as I discovered that what I observed in the Kalahari was becoming a national phenomenon. Increasingly, marginalized groups (minorities which, in Botswana, refer not to relative numbers but to any group that is not one of the eight Setswana-speaking "tribes" listed in the Constitution, who enjoy permanent representation in the House of Chiefs, the upper house of Parliament) were asserting their identities, claiming rights, and seeking greater inclusion in the state's institutions. As individual members of minority groups became part of Botswana's urban middle class, they retained very strong links to the rural areas. The technocratic know-how of these urban-based professionals and their connections to national power, in tandem with an increasingly politicized rural populace, were both key to the vibrancy and impact of these movements (see Werbner and Gaitskell 2002; Mazonde 2002).

As I followed the activities of the Bakgalagadi political movement, I met its leaders and eventually some of the leaders of equivalent organizations. Many of these people have become my subjects, my peers, my friends, and my collaborators. Indeed, I am in the process of co-authoring a paper with the leader of the Coalition of Minorities in Botswana. One of our themes is that the Coalition's challenge to the state to amend the Constitution is necessary for democracy to truly develop and flourish. My colleague employs a classic local metaphor to characterize democracy: it is like a snake, slippery and sly, never to be left unchecked. And like a snake, democracy must shed its skin periodically and be renewed.

My research, now largely urban-based, is conducted in conjunction with local scholars and activists who help set my agenda. The key articles that I found while sifting through archived newspapers, the key quotes that I unearthed after weeks of pouring through government documents, especially parliamentary records, are used repeatedly in the Coalition's reports and papers. But Coalition members have also provided me with invaluable resources for my individual work.

I could not have done this work 20 years ago; the people I am working with would not have accepted me as a peer, nor would they have trusted me. Maybe some still do not. But the extent to which I am trusted is contingent upon having known some of these people, or their colleagues and friends, for decades. Conversely, I could not do the kind of fieldwork I did 25 years ago now. Family and teaching responsibilities would not permit such an extended stay. And, as each year advances, my ability to endure the hardships of bush life diminishes.

Immediately upon arriving in Botswana in 2002, I met with the newly formed Coalition of Minorities. I participated in writing a report to the United Nations (UN) Committee on the Elimination of All Forms of Racial Discrimination.[4] Botswana, like many countries, had failed to submit annual reports. In March 2000, one of the minority organizations wrote to

Kofi Annan, the UN Secretary General, complaining that Botswana had not complied with all aspects of the CERD convention. Botswana was compelled to respond with a report; the Coalition of Minorities prepared a report responding to that of the government. We worked on the report virtually the entire time I was there. It was sent to the UN in early August 2002, and later that month Coalition members attended a meeting in Geneva on the Convention. The Botswana government was subsequently exhorted to adopt recommendations regarding minority rights.

RECLAIMING COLONIAL ANTHROPOLOGY: ISAAC SCHAPERA, FROM CULTURAL PARIAH TO CULTURE HERO

It was in working on this report that a moment of particular and ironic poignancy occurred. The Botswana government had always justified its policy of granting institutional recognition only to the Tswana on the basis of two premises: (1) that the Tswana constitute the numeric majority in the country; and (2) that it would be impossible to recognize all languages and ethnic groups, especially through representation in the House of Chiefs, because at least 97 exist. Recognizing all of them, it was argued, would make the House too unwieldy. These two purported facts had become part of the state's hegemonic self-portrayal that justified the status quo and showed the futility of any attempt to change it. Non-Tswana no longer blandly accepted these principles as truth. However, the data to prove or disprove what the state hoped would be taken for granted were not readily available. The last census to ask about "ethnic identity" was in 1946. However, it had been summarized and analyzed by the anthropologist Isaac Schapera in his 1952 book, *The Ethnic Composition of Tswana Tribes*.

The Ethnic Composition of Tswana Tribes is one of Schapera's more obscure publications; copies of this book are not easy to locate, but I knew there was a photocopy in the University of Botswana library in the special non-circulating "Botswana Collection." After some effort, I persuaded the very busy head of the Coalition of Minorities to come to the library and examine the book. When it was brought from the stacks, she looked at it with amazement. Her jaw dropped open, and she said, "This is it, this is where they are getting everything." It was an epiphany. But, as she soon pointed out, the state and its supporters interpreted Schapera's work rather expediently to bolster their own position. Schapera, she noted, actually said something quite different. He did not state that there were 97 ethnic groups or tribes in the country, as members of the government cited repeatedly, but noted that in the census over 97 "stocks," in his words, were self-identified. In Botswana, as elsewhere, people maintain multiple identities, and they are often multilingual. The identification of ancestry is not contingent upon current active membership in a local collectivity. The 1946 census data also revealed that the minorities, taken together, might well constitute a numeric majority in the country. In certain important districts, Batswana are clearly the numeric minority. The Coalition of Minorities already knew this and operated under that assumption. Schapera's book added proof, but it was the recognition of what was meant by "97 stocks," i.e., that these were not necessarily extant ethnic groups but self-identified ancestral associations, that was so significant for the Coalition in arguing their case.

We then "stole" the book, took it back to the head's office, and photocopied it. I later returned it to the library. The Coalition's UN report, mentioned above, made extensive use of Schapera's work. It was invaluable both to counter the government's conservative stance and to suggest a reasonable alternative whereby a manageable and representative number of groups could be proposed for House of Chiefs membership. There is no small irony in this. He was a colonial anthropologist par excellence; he carried out much of his research in conjunction with the colonial administration and some of it at its request. At first scorned by many in the newly independent country of Botswana as a colonial crony, Schapera's reputation has altered over time.

Colonial anthropology has been examined in the discipline itself. In the 1960s and 1970s, especially with the work of Gough (1968) and the edited volume of Asad (1973), the discipline underwent an important phase of auto-critique. The anthropology of Anglophone Africa, in particular, has been subjected to critical scrutiny that has revealed a complicated relationship between the anthropological enterprise and colonial authorities. Britain's policy of indirect rule depended upon rule through African leaders and institutions; there is no doubt that anthropologists' accounts were useful in delineating these. In addition, the dominant theoretical paradigm of the period, structural functionalism, contributed to a perception of Africa as composed of self-contained, self-regulating, and self-perpetuating societies that were outside the forces of history. Such atomized units were not only seen to be amenable to colonial rule but, in many instances, to benefit from the changes European stewardship via colonialism could deliver to otherwise "self-contained" and static societies. However, upon closer examination, the role of anthropology in the colonial endeavour seems far less certain. In fact, the colonial administration made use of far fewer professional anthropologists than is often assumed to be the case. Anthropologists collected what the colonial authorities perceived to be an excess of useless data, for example, on rituals and the like. They could even be an embarrassment; they often flouted colonial hierarchies by socializing with Africans and/or advocating on their behalf (James 1973; Moore 1994).

Nonetheless, even in the absence of direct collaboration, "anthropological knowledge" played an important role in colonial rule; "the official view was that it was usually easier and more efficient to teach anthropology to a British political officer than it was to put up with the peculiar ways of anthropologists whose interests were not always congruent with those of the administration" (Moore 1994: 19). In addition, while it is clear that the anthropologist "cannot be seen unambiguously as a willing agent of colonialism" (James 1973: 42) she/he remained dependent upon the colonial authority's permission and, quite often, on its material support. Despite the political inclinations of the individual anthropologist, which ranged from complicity to rebelliousness, "appearances of co-operation had to be kept up" (James 1973: 42) if they chose to continue their work. Identifying and interrogating the connections between anthropology and the colonial project were necessary and healthy. It continues to be important to bring into relief the multiple forms and relationships of power that impact upon how we conduct our research, analyze our data, and write our texts. But sometimes the hand wringing can be a little too intense. Some of us were, perhaps, a bit over zealous in our dismissal of colonially "tainted" works.[5]

Schapera and his work were inextricably linked to the colonial regime; he was well aware of this and engaged in public debate on the proper relationship between anthropology and administration (James 1973: 68). But now both the contemporary state and its citizens revere his encyclopedic documentation of Tswana society. This has not always been the case. When I first went to Botswana in the late 1970s, Schapera was a non-person. Students graduated in the social sciences from the University of Botswana without having heard of him. Perhaps excising him from local consciousness was a necessary post-colonial stance to take in the early years of independence, but since the mid-1980s there has been a significant revival of his work and legacy. A street in the capital is called Schapera Close; a scholarship has been established in his name at the University; several local publications have been dedicated to him; people turn to his work for ritual templates when customs such as initiations are reintroduced; and a wonderful museum, featuring many of the photographs and artifacts that he contributed, was established in the village where he conducted most of his fieldwork. His texts are now required reading in numerous disciplines. In a powerful move to fully reclaim his corpus, the University of Botswana established a research program in his name, the "Recovering the Legacy of Isaac Schapera Project," which held its first conference in 2000. Students and researchers in multiple fields are pursuing work that in myriad ways builds upon the substantial legacy of theories, resources, and ideas that he left behind. In addition to his prolific published writings, photographs, and artifacts, there are seven kilograms of fieldnotes, mostly genealogies written on thin airmail paper, which he donated to the project (Heald 2003).

Schapera's voluminous works are the sources through which much current jurisprudence and legal practice, ritual, and historical background is understood. His work on customary law not only forms a significant part of contemporary legal training in Botswana, it has also been used to very good effect in some controversial cases. Law, for Schapera, was always situated in a set of social, material, and historic circumstances, and, of course, many of these have changed since the 1930s. Because he so carefully contextualized law, progressive chiefs, lawyers, and judges have been able to utilize his work to illustrate circumstances in which customary law, as it operated in the 1930s, may be inappropriate in today's social context. Moreover, these legal experts have been able to use his careful documentation to suggest ways in which customary law may be reinterpreted or reformulated to conform to contemporary circumstances. His work, for instance, has been used to advocate on behalf of women exercising property rights that would have been denied to them by more conservative voices evoking a timeless notion of customary law.

Some of the legal cases utilizing Schapera's work have been high profile and precedent-setting. In 2000, a case captivated public attention: a lower court had granted compensation to an aggrieved wife in an adultery case. Citing Schapera's *A Handbook of Tswana Law,* the chief of the superior court overturned the decision, arguing that society recognizes that "a man like a bull cannot be confined in a kraal" (*monna poo ga agelwe lesaka*) and therefore tolerates male adultery, but not female. Schapera's *Handbook* (1938) was subjected to the court of public opinion as much as the legal judgements in question. Numerous newspaper articles argued against the second ruling; some called for a rejection of Schapera's *Handbook* as a colonially tainted and outdated work, but others called for a more measured reading of the book. To quote one, "The Handbook ... was written as a living document that would change as the culture ... changed." The article argues that the lower court ruling would have been "in line with the many times that Schapera mentioned modifications in traditions" (*Botswana Gazette* 12 April 2000). Several commentators were quick to point out that apart from any other changes in Botswana society, the current HIV/AIDS pandemic afflicting the country was sufficient in itself to sway social opinion against any tolerance of adultery. Although this case clearly demonstrates that there is no unified agreement as to how his texts are to be interpreted or drawn upon, the central role of his meticulously documented texts for legal deliberations within Botswana is evident.

I could give countless examples to illustrate the transformation of Isaac Schapera from colonial pariah to culture hero. As already noted, especially compelling for me was the extraordinary significance of his text for the Coalition of Minorities in constructing their challenge to entrenched powers. Ironically, these are powers that Schapera may well have contributed to entrenching, but his thorough texts enable alternate interpretations. This transformation is one example of an anti anti-morality tale (or, perhaps equally appropriate, anti anti-critique) and of the dangers of generational complacency.

In closing, I return to my own fieldwork: I particularly enjoy the collaborative nature of my current research. While I would be neither so morally superior nor naïve as to claim that I have abrogated my authorship, I recognize that authorship is shared. In addition, I have become an accomplice as well as an anthropologist, roles that are increasingly blurred. I am sure my narrative will sound familiar to anyone working with Aboriginal peoples in North America, but it is a newer role in Africa where power relations have tended more often to relegate Africans to the role of research subjects. Even in the joint research projects that have become the norm for certain large funding agencies, African scholars have complained loudly that they tend to get cast as data collectors, despite their official designations as "co-investigators," while the data is then whisked back to the north where it is analyzed and put into final written form (Mkandawire 1997). The analogy to global economic power relations in which raw materials extracted from Africa are processed and acquire added value in the West is all too obvious and all too poignant.

"REAL POWER" AND "FAUX ANTHROPOLOGISTS"

One final irony that flows nicely with my theme of deflating my own self-importance concerns the politics of research permits in edgy research. One is rarely more self-important than when one perceives oneself as potentially subversive enough to be seen as a threat to a government. Was I going to be able to obtain a research permit for my "hot" and politically sensitive topic? Botswana has maintained a very open research environment, and I have had several research permits in the past. On short exploratory visits I have entered on a tourist visa, gone to the Office of the President, which is responsible for research permits, explained my situation, and have always received a letter indicating that I am a researcher in good standing (whose thesis and publications are in the archives and libraries for anyone to see) and that I am in the process of applying for a permit. In 2000, I applied for a formal research permit. While in Botswana for a conference, I delivered the multiple copies of the application in person to the Office of the President. I knew that the topic of my research—the politics of inclusion and exclusion—was very controversial and the source of some political contestation at the time, so I was not surprised when I received a letter acknowledging receipt of my application without the usual green light to proceed.

When I returned in 2002, still without a research permit, I revisited the research office and encountered the same woman I had met two years prior. She was a bit cagey regarding the status of my application, so I resubmitted. I went back to her office on a few occasions. After she felt a bit more comfortable with me, she explained that the government was cutting back on research permits. People were coming into the country claiming to be anthropologists and then filming Bushmen in the Kalahari in order to expose their plight and Botswana's supposedly inhumane treatment of them. The main offenders are a British based NGO, Survival International.[6] They have launched an aggressive international campaign to embarrass the Botswana government publicly over its Bushmen policy, especially its controversial move to eliminate the provision of services to people, most of whom are Bushmen, living in the Central Kalahari Game Reserve. Water, medical, and educational services have been provided for them in settlements only outside the game reserve. Many within the country are critical of the government's policy, but few have any time for Survival. The heavily funded, very public attempts to spoil Botswana's reputation and to have its diamonds boycotted as conflict diamonds or "diamonds of despair"[7] have done more to damage Bushmen relations with other citizens than anything in post-independence history. In addition, Survival does the Bushmen no favour by perpetuating an image of them as ossified Stone Age relics. More pernicious is the way in which local human rights organizations working with Bushmen and the government to find creative alternatives to the existing problems have been sidelined as a result of Survival activities. The head of the local human rights organization, *Ditshwanelo*, which has done very important work on behalf of Bushmen, especially in cases of prisoners' rights, states that the situation with Survival is just another example of North/South power relations.[8] It is like a new form of colonialism.

The last time I left the office that grants research permits in August 2002, the woman in charge turned to me and said, "You're not going to go film the Bushmen are you?" I smiled and assured her that I did not own a movie camera. She smiled back at me, and a few months later a research permit arrived. The irony here is that it was not my edgy or politically sensitive research that interfered with my gaining official permission. Rather, external agents posing as anthropologists were damaging anthropology's reputation and undermining the legitimate research efforts of real anthropologists. I do not wish to imply that I believe my work is politically irrelevant. Certainly my collaborators in Botswana are keen for my input and participation, and I derive a good deal of satisfaction in working with local activists who are struggling for rights and recognition that have been denied them in the past. But I suppose what I have learned, as part of an anti anti-morality tale, is not to take myself, or the moment, too seriously.

NOTES

[1]   I thank Anne Meneley and Donna J. Young for organizing the panel at which this paper was first delivered. Derek Hall made useful suggestions during discussions of this paper and Michael Lambek, as always, has been a source of ideas, reality checks, and comfort during my travails.

2   Tswana is the noun root; its form changes with prefixes. Bo refers to land, Ba to people, and Se to language and culture. The country's name reflects relations that existed between powerful Tswana chiefs and early British imperialists. There are numerous other ethnic groups and languages; their erasure from the public sphere mirrors their political marginality.

3   This transition is captured in the title of a paper I wrote: "From Shame to Pride: Politicized Ethnicity in the Kalahari, Botswana" (Solway 1994a; see also Solway 2002).

4   This derives from the 1969 UN Convention to End all Forms of Racial Discrimination (CERD) to which Botswana was a signatory.

5   My appreciation of the richness and scholarly integrity of Schapera's work grows ever stronger. While some may criticize the seemingly antiquated theoretical approach that informed his work, no one could accuse him of ignoring history or of presenting peoples as isolated entities. Books such as *Migrant Labour and Tribal Life* portray people in the full throes of numerous historical and political processes. This proves that pat critiques of structural functionalism often do not do justice to the subtlety of the work of colonial anthropologists.

6   Survival selected the Bushmen of Botswana as their high profile case for the past several years. They have been extremely effective in fundraising and in gaining publicity. A website, <http://www.survival-international.org/bushman.htm> is devoted entirely to this cause. In response to Survival's aggressive campaign the government of Botswana has added a link to their own website <http://www.gov.bw/basarwa/index.html>. This link is the most obvious on the government's website and is the only one that flashes in different colors.

7   Survival has received extensive coverage on the BBC and obtained spots on other prominent media sources. They have organized demonstrations and picketing of Botswana's overseas embassies and at jewelry outlets selling Botswana diamonds.

8   Alice Mogwe, personal communication, 2 August 2002.

WORKS CITED

Asad, T. (ed.). 1973. *Anthropology and the Colonial Encounter*. Atlantic Highlands, N.J.: Humanities Press.

Geertz, C. 1984. Distinguished Lecture: Anti anti-relativism. *American Anthropologist* 86(2): 263-78.

Gough, K. 1968. Anthropology: Child of imperialism. *Monthly Review* 19(1): 12–27.

Heald, S. 2003. The legacy of Isaac Schapera (1905-2003) (obituary). *Anthropology Today* 19(6) 18-19.

James, W. 1973. The anthropologist as reluctant imperialist. In *Anthropology and the Colonial Encounter*. Ed T. Asad. 41-69. Atlantic Highlands, N.J.: Humanities Press.

Mazonde, I. (ed.). 2002. *Minorities in the Millennium*. Gaborone: Lenstwe La Lesedi.

Mkandawire, T. 1997. The social sciences in Africa: Breaking local barriers and negotiating international presence. Bashorun M.K.O. Abiola Distinguished

Lecture presented to the 1996 African Studies Association Annual Meeting. *African Studies Review* 40(2): 15–36.

Moore, S.F. 1994. *Anthropology and Africa*. Charlottesville, VI: University of Virginia Press.

Schapera, I. 1938. *A Handbook of Tswana Law and Custom*. London: Frank Cass and Company.

———. 1947. *Migrant Labour and Tribal Life*. London: Oxford University Press.

———. 1952. *The Ethnic Composition of Tswana Tribes*. Monographs in Social Anthropology No. 11. London: London School of Economics.

Solway, J. 1994a. From shame to pride: Politicized ethnicity in the Kalahari, Botswana. *Canadian Journal of African Studies* 28(2): 254–74.

———. 1994b Drought as a revelatory crisis: An exploration of shifting entitlements and hierarchies in the Kalahari, Botswana. *Development and Change* 25(3): 471–95.

———. 2002. Navigating the "neutral" state: "Minority" rights in Botswana. *Journal of Southern African Studies* 28 (4): 711–29.

Taylor, I., and G. Mokhawa. 2003. Not forever: Botswana, conflict diamonds and the Bushmen. *African Affairs* 102: 261–83.

Werbner, R., and D. Gaitskell. 2002. Special issue: Minorities and citizenship in Botswana. *Journal of Southern African Studies* 28.

Newspapers

Mmegi Monitor, 14–20 March 2000.

Botswana Gazette, 5 April 2000, 12 April 2000

8 | THE TORSO IN THE THAMES: IMAGINING DARKEST AFRICA IN THE UNITED KINGDOM

Todd Sanders

In London, England, on 21 September 2001, the torso of a young black boy was found floating in the River Thames. Within a month the London Metropolitan Police reported that it may have been the result of an African ritual murder. This theory, in varied forms, has underpinned media reporting on the Thames torso case to date.

Throughout the Thames torso investigation, the London Metropolitan Police—known as "The Met"—have worked very closely with the media. They have issued numerous press releases, held television and radio press conferences, and collaborated with Channel Four on a documentary, which follows inspectors on their investigation across South and West Africa and London. The Met have also maintained a public website and featured the case on BBC *Crimewatch*. This chapter considers how the police-media engagement surrounding the Thames torso investigation has led to the production and reproduction of particular images about Africa and Africans. These include the idea that Africa and Africans can be meaningfully discussed in the singular; that the things they do are morally perverse; and that these alleged perversities are, with globalization, increasingly unravelling the moral fabric of British society. The fact that the Thames torso investigation has underscored rather than undermined a series of images of African Otherness has grave implications for how the police and media manage and communicate information to the general public. What is more, it raises serious concerns about the role anthropologists play in the broader public sphere: about how we understand and represent our ethnographic subjects and our ability—or, in this case, inability—to get our views heard.

THE TORSO IN THE THAMES: A BRIEF CHRONOLOGY

The discovery of a boy's torso, clothed in orange shorts, in the River Thames was first reported in late September 2001. Speaking at a press conference at Catford Hill police station, Detective Superintendent Adrian

Maybanks said a sharp-bladed instrument had been used to cut up the boy, whom he described as black Afro-Caribbean, around five years old. The shorts on the torso had washing instructions in German (BBC 2001a). A few months later the Met would give the boy a name: Adam.

Within days, news reports began to appear suggesting a possible link between the Thames torso and a murder the previous month in Holland, where a white girl's dismembered body was found in a lake (BBC 2001c). The Thames torso case, with its possible connections to the Dutch case, was aired on BBC One's *Crimewatch*. In spite of numerous calls from the public, no new leads were found (BBC 2001b).

By mid-October, the media were reporting a new—albeit tentative— theory: that these two cases *were* possibly linked and, furthermore, that both were the result of "ritual murder" by "African witchdoctors." Newspapers used a South African term, *sangoma*, to describe these "witch-doctors" who, they claimed, use "body parts in their ointments and potions" for witchcraft (BBC 2001d). Detective Inspector Will O'Reilly of the Met's Serious Crime Group, the man heading the Thames torso investigation, explained that this theory was "flagged up to us by the pathologist who said that it may be a ritualistic killing" (Bennetto 2001; ThisisLondon 2001). O'Reilly also told the press, "It's one of many lines of inquiry we are look-ing at; we are not ruling anything out" (BBC 2001d).

In late January 2002 the police held a press conference. They made public, first, that a South African pathologist specializing in African *muti* killing was being flown to London to carry out a second post mortem on the torso, and, second, that detectives had discovered seven half-burnt candles wrapped in a white sheet in the Thames (BBC 2002f; Vasagar 2002). The name Adekoye Jo Fola Adeoye was written on the candles and sheet, noted detectives, as they displayed the sheet for the press and world to see. O'Reilly said that, "The circumstances of this murder are unique. If the murder is ritualistic, we believe it is the first in this country. We know with some certainty that the candles and the sheet form part of a ritualis-tic ceremony. We can't say if they are connected [with the torso], but at the moment we are linking them" (Vasagar 2002). Media reports suggest the police had linked the name on the sheet to West Africa in general and the Yoruba in particular (Walsh 2002). They also suggest that detectives had abandoned the idea of a link between the Thames torso and the dismem-bered Dutch girl,[1] though the Met and Scotland Yard were now liaising with detectives in Germany and Belgium where three other "similar" cases had been reported (Vasagar 2002).

A few days later, police held a conference at the National Police Training College in Bramshill, Hampshire, where detectives from across the United Kingdom—and an eager press—listened to the South African pathologist's findings: "It is my opinion that the nature of the discovery of the body, features of the external examination including the nature of the wounds, clothing, and mechanism of death are consistent with those of a ritual homicide as practised in Africa" (BBC 2002j; Guardian 2002; Peachey 2002).

By February, the Met had ruled out the sheet and candles as evidence in their investigation. Working with officers from the New York Police Department, they had located and interviewed Adekoye Jo Fola Adoye in New York. His parents, who live in London, had apparently performed a ceremony with the items in question to celebrate the fact that he had survived the September 11 attack on the World Trade Center (BBC 2002a; Flanagan 2002).

In March 2002 the police began publicizing the fact that they were conducting forensic tests on the torso. These included DNA, "bone mapping," and other high-tech tests that aimed to determine the victim's ancestry, place of origin, and residence (BBC 2002b; BBC 2002i; Flanagan 2002).

In April 2002, O'Reilly and Scotland Yard's Commander Andy Baker travelled to South Africa to ask Nelson Mandela to appeal for help to identify the boy's murderer. Mandela agreed and made a "world-wide appeal" at a press conference in Johannesburg (BBC 2002c). While in South Africa, detectives consulted with the South African police Occult Crimes Unit. Together with reporters, a television crew, and local police, they visited a market where traditional medicines and animal parts were sold. A "traditional healer" named Credo Mutwa detailed for detectives and media how the Thames torso's missing limbs were possibly used for magical ends and provided gruesome details of ritual killings. Mutwa also suggested that the killers would have been closely related to the victim and that they were followers of *obeh*, which he claimed was a West African form of witchcraft. The healer told detectives they should "look in West Africa, from Nigeria onwards for where these people are from" (Flanagan 2002).

In May, in the UK, detectives began searching for a man suspected of murder 34 years ago. In 1969 the headless torso of a baby black girl was found hidden in the bushes in Epping Forest, Essex. However the main suspect—her father—fled the country before he was apprehended (BBC 2002k). O'Reilly told the press: "We are looking at the 1969 case because of the ritualistic overtones. The father was down on his luck and apparently carried out the killing to change that" (Bennetto 2002; Sawyer 2002). Also in May, police from across Europe met at The Hague for a one-day conference. Commander Andy Baker reportedly said: "We knew about a couple [ritual murders] already, it's pushing double figures across Europe now" (Allen 2002; BBC 2002g).

In June police and newspapers reported that the genetic tests on Adam pointed to a West African origin. Additionally, analysis of stomach contents and bone chemistry suggested that the boy could not have been raised in London. A story in *The Observer* suggested that the police had modified their previous theory, claiming that they now believed "Adam was bought as a child slave in West Africa and smuggled to Britain solely to be killed" (Bright and Harris 2002).

The following month a Nigerian asylum-seeker was arrested in Glasgow and flown to London for questioning. This reportedly followed a routine visit by social workers, who reported seeing "strange voodoo-like items" in her home. A more thorough search of her flat revealed "several objects associated with curses, including whisky jars containing chicken feathers" (Thompson 2002). DNA tests on the woman, however, confirmed she was unrelated to the torso. She was released on bail and soon thereafter deported to Nigeria after a failed asylum application (Allen 2003; ThisisLondon 2002b).

In September, police pathologists identified a "concoction" of minerals and other matter in the boy's lower intestine, which, according to the media, "police believe was fed to him as part of a ritual killing" (BBC 2002d; Davenport 2002). And, in October, Scotland Yard sent a delegation to West Africa "to collect samples and carry out research" (ThisisLondon 2002a). According to *The Independent*, a team from Scotland Yard travelled to Nigeria and took samples from soil, rocks, and meat in a 10,000 square kilometre area (Allen 2003). A television crew also accompanied the police on at least part of the journey.

In November 2002, a sensationalistic story on the Thames torso hit the headlines: "Human flesh on sale in London" (Barnett, Harris, and Thompson 2002; BBC 2002e). The story appeared with two photos, side-by-side: one of a bare-chested boy from Benin, ceremonially sacrificing a goat; the other of a desiccated crocodile head seized by police in London. The story told how Thames torso detectives, together with environmental health officers, had raided a north London shop in search of illegal African bush meat—and possibly human flesh. The idea was that Adam was trafficked from West Africa to the UK for the sole purpose of ritual murder and that his body parts were sold alongside bush meat for occult purposes. A police spokesman told the press: "There is an ongoing search for Adam's head and limbs, and there is evidence to suggest a link between those who are involved and the trade in illegal animal parts and meat products" (Barnett, Harris, and Thompson 2002; BBC 2002e). One story reported the Heathrow airport's meat transport director, who took part in the raid, as saying: "The intelligence we are receiving suggests human flesh is coming into this country" (Barnett, Harris, and Thompson 2002).

In late January 2003, *Torso in the Thames: Adam's Story* aired on Channel Four. This hour-long documentary, the product of many months' media-police collaboration, chronicles the case as just described. It takes viewers from the Thames where the torso was found to various press conferences in the UK; to Mandela's public appeal in Johannesburg; with British and local police to the South African "traditional healer's" home and to an open-air market; to West Africa where a British detective is shown asking an African elder if there are any children missing from his village; and back to London, where the case continues. The documentary neatly encapsulates the broader message now being conveyed to the general public: the Thames torso is the tip of a massive and malevolent iceberg, pointing to a thriving underground transnational trade in African children and body parts for occult purposes.

DISCUSSION

The time, energy, and resources the Met and Scotland Yard have devoted to this case, the public statements they have made, and their repeated, expressed anxieties over the case suggest that they are committed to solving this crime. Yet en route, and contrary to their stated aims and objectives, the police and media have reproduced a much older and more unsettling story about Africans and African Otherness. We can usefully discuss such matters under the headings of homogenization, identity, and globalization.

Homogenization

One recurrent feature in the imagery surrounding the Thames torso investigation has been the reduction of difference to uniformity. Media imagery has consistently cast Africa, geographically speaking, as an undifferentiated entity. Black bodies come from black Africa, which is why "African ritual murder" and "African witchcraft" are purportedly meaningful categories in the first place. This is also why a black body can be linked to West Africa because of a sheet and candles and simultaneously to South Africa and South African *muti* killings by a pathologist's report. Clearly, though, West Africa is not in South Africa. Nor is it nearby.

Such homogenizing assumptions similarly underpin the idea that Nelson Mandela is or can be Africa's spokesman. When in Johannesburg, for example, O'Reilly told the press: "Mr. Mandela is one of the most influential men in Africa, and we hope people will listen to his appeal. It could well be that the boy's parents do not know he is dead because news from Britain is unlikely to have reached them. Hopefully this will help" (Nettleton 2002). While Mandela is an influential figure in Africa and elsewhere, the assumption that Africans will pay special attention to him because of this is questionable. Nor is it clear how, if Africans cannot receive news from abroad, they will see a televised broadcast of Nelson Mandela from Johannesburg. Furthermore, the suggestion that Africans do not, or are unlikely to, receive news from outside Africa is simply untrue.

The images produced of "Africans and their culture" have also been homogenous. Take the following comments—illustrative of many others—made by O'Reilly when in Johannesburg: "We have come here not because we think Adam came from South Africa, but because this is where the experts are who can help us understand this culture and belief system" (quoted in Flanagan 2002). Speaking of an African "culture" and "belief system" in the singular is more than mere semantics and highlights a tendency that pervades media reports on this case. Such implied homogeneity suggests that all Africans share a single culture, and it thus matters little where, exactly, one gains an understanding of it: in South Africa, West Africa, or elsewhere. The same can be said for monolithic media phrases like "African ritual murder," "African voodoo," or "African witchcraft."

In short, the imagery produced in the Thames torso case has continually reduced multiples to singulars, treating vast geographic, cultural, and social differences as though they simply do not matter. Similar reductive tendencies become evident when we consider the images surrounding identity.

Identity

The Thames torso case raises several issues surrounding identity. Most apparent is the guiding trope—*us* versus *them*—that underpins the images produced. In different contexts, the "us" shifts between "the Met," "British," "European," and "white," while the "them" shifts between "African," "black," or "Other." In this imagery, the two halves of this opposition are not cast as equals. Africans and the things they do are routinely glossed as inferior. The things Europeans or British do, in contrast, are glossed as superior. One of the most obvious ways such asymmetries manifest themselves is in the dogged dichotomy between reason and unreason as articulated through the lens of "science" and "superstition."

Throughout the investigation, Africans and African diaspora in the UK have been presented as people who hold weird, inexplicable, and morally bankrupt beliefs. They are said to carry out and believe in Voodoo, witchcraft, ritual murder, human sacrifice, selling human body parts, etc. Such matters are sometimes reported to the accompaniment of a flurry of adjectives and adverbs, all of them derogatory: *primitive, gruesome, horrific, barbaric, sinister*, etc. (ABC 2002; Bright and Harris 2002; Oliver 2002). Such reporting conjures and reinscribes "Darkest Africa" imagery, immortalized by Joseph Conrad's 1902 novel, *Heart of Darkness*. In Chinua Achebe's words: "Heart of Darkness projects the image of Africa as 'the other world,' the antithesis of Europe and therefore of civilization, a place where man's vaunted intelligence and refinement are finally mocked by triumphant bestiality..." (Achebe 1988: 252).

Equally common in this case are news reports that coldly and uncritically note such "African oddities"—like the sale of human body parts—as if they were widespread and commonplace practices in Africa (BBC 2002h; Davenport 2002). Other reports, following an identical logic, detail in shopping-list fashion the supposed market value of human body parts (Independent 2002; ThisisLondon 2001). Still others provide radically decontextualized statements that, while ostensibly meant to inform, serve solely to make Africans and their purported beliefs and practices look foolish. Consider the following iconic statement: "Police suspect the killers may have been practising a rare variant of the 'muti' ritual. Muti killers tend to remove the genitals, breasts and extremities of their victims, as their screams release the 'magic' of the internal organs for the potions, but do not dismember their victims" (Walsh 2002).

Such imagery of Savage and Superstitious Africans has continually been juxtaposed with its imaginary opposite, the Civilized, Rational, Science-minded Europeans. This is how one journalist established this opposition:

> A tour of a *muti* medicine market in downtown Johannesburg provided the officers with an idea of the significance of traditional medicine and witchcraft in sub-Saharan African life.
>
> Tables spilled over with decaying animal parts and jars of congealing fat. The men from the Met mingled with the regular *muti* customers. Stall holders appeared evasive about the medicinal properties of their wares, insisting only that it was "powerful" stuff, guaranteed to cure all ills.
>
> The traders were clearly uneasy to see South African officers attached to the occult unit, who had accompanied their London colleagues, scrutinising the malodorous piles.
>
> "You could probably get human body parts down here if you know what to ask for and how to ask for it," said Captain Lynne Evans from the Pretoria-based unit.
>
> Meanwhile, scientists in the UK are using several ground-breaking techniques to pinpoint Adam's home country. They believe he comes from West Africa, possibly Nigeria, Ghana or the Ivory Coast.
>
> By analysing elements found in the body's bone structure— nitrogen, oxygen, sulphur content, for example—and pollen and parasite samples extracted from the gut, experts are confident of being able to identify the boy's home to within the nearest mile (Flanagan 2002).

While Africa and Africans are variously tarred as irrational, superstitious, and morally corrupt, the Met has consistently portrayed itself and is portrayed in the media as methodical, rational investigators seeking to uncover the Truth through the application of science and technology. We might call this the Crime Scene Investigation or CSI mentality, after the

TV show—the mistaken view that the world can be reduced to "just the facts" which speak plainly and unequivocally for themselves. Here, too, adjectives and adverbs reign supreme, though this time in a markedly different tenor: Met detectives are routinely said to be using "groundbreaking" and "extraordinary" forensic tests (BBC 2002i; Davenport 2002; Flanagan 2002; Nettleton 2002).

Thus, the media imagery surrounding the Thames torso case relies on a fundamental dichotomy between "us and them," and the two sides of this dichotomy stand in an asymmetrical and inverse relationship. While *we* represent the pedestrian, rational, scientific, and morally righteous, *they* represent the exotic, irrational, superstitious, and morally indefensible. This particular imagining of self and other raises an inescapable corollary that comes with globalization.

Globalization

If one buys these images about self and other, "us" and "them," then globalization poses particular conceptual and practical problems. Key among them is that globalization logically implies a meeting of worlds, which in this case implies that a corrupt and morally bankrupt "them" threatens a sensible and moral "us." A savage and superstitious Africa threatens to undo the moral fibre of a righteous Europe through globalization.

Countless news reports and police statements surrounding the case allude to this imagined quandary. Take one example, reported on BBC News, which posited a link between the murdered Dutch girl and Adam. "The way in which both bodies were cut up has raised the fear that a form of black magic performed in South Africa could have come to Europe" (BBC 2001d). Such imagery has not, of course, been single-handedly invented by the media, but has been co-produced in dialogue with Thames torso detectives.

In January 2002, Scotland Yard's Serious Crime Group Commander, Andy Baker, made the following comments to *The Scotsman*:

> Our fear is it is the first of many. The rumours are it is opening up. I don't want to raise the fear factor but if it is a ritualistic *Muti* murder others will follow, according to South African authorities. With the movement of people around the world and the spread of this culture it is bound to come here because we have a high

African population. If the murder was ritualistic we believe this is the first in this country. Our inquiries abroad suggest there are many of these types of murders across the world (McDougall 2002).

O'Reilly has expressed similar sentiments to the press: "The ritual killing of children is an absolute reality. We do not want this to gain a foothold in this country" (Thompson 2002). The vice-chairman of the Metropolitan Police Independent Advisory Group similarly noted: "We are talking about either witchcraft, ju-ju or voodoo…. In promoting cultural diversity we import the good and the bad. If this is a ritual killing then unfortunately— as bad as it may sound—we have imported those aspects of culture into mainland Britain" (BBC 2002l).

Recent anthropologists have had much to say about how people in different parts of Africa deploy idioms of witchcraft to discuss locally specific anxieties about modernity, creeping commodification, and globalization (Moore and Sanders 2001). It is thus not uncommon to find Tanzanians deliberating over structural adjustment policies in a language of trafficking in human skins for occult purposes (Sanders 2001); Nigerians who discuss economic changes in idioms of selling human body parts (Bastian 2003); and South Africans who, in attending to rumours about migrating zombie labour forces, critique a rapidly changing post-Apartheid political economy (Comaroff and Comaroff 2000). It is interesting that in the Thames torso case we find not Africans but the British police and media using "African witchcraft" and "African ritual murder" in similar ways: to express concerns about our rapidly changing world and their place in it. The imagery surrounding the Thames torso case plainly voices popular British anxieties about otherness, globalization, immigration, and multiculturalism, and raises the grave possibility of having "our" life-world unravelled by "their" cultural practices.

CONCLUSION

While some socio-cultural anthropologists might raise objections to the foregoing analysis, they would, I believe, be in the minority. Some non-anthropologists will take exception on the grounds that there *have* been documented cases of what appears to be ritual killing in different parts of Africa. If this is true, so the reasoning goes, then the police may be onto something. And consequently this chapter is a pointless, if not counterproductive, exercise in semantics and deconstruction.

The point worth emphasizing however is that such practices in Africa are—like Satanic child abuse killings in the UK and North America—extremely rare, even if the popular imagination in both places suggests otherwise. In all such cases, the savage imagery and moral panic far outstrip the number of actual killings, which are either negligible or absent (Gulbrandsen 2002; La Fontaine 1998; Sanders 2001). Anthropologists have long known this. The Thames torso detectives know it too. O'Reilly even noted that, in 2000, only three such cases were reported across the whole of Africa (Guardian 2002). Yet the imagery produced through police-media engagements suggests something altogether more sinister: that ritual murder or human sacrifice is, in one journalist's words, "a crime common in sub-Saharan Africa" (Davenport 2002). And, moreover, that such practices are so excessive that they are now spilling over from a morally corrupt Africa onto the innocent shores of the UK. Thus, even if this case *does* turn out to be ritual killing—even if an African witchdoctor waltzes into Scotland Yard tomorrow and says "I did it!"—it matters little. The damage has already been done with the derogatory imagery generated, where old stories are refracted through new lenses, and where Savage Africans and Civilized Europeans are locked into life-or-death struggles over science and superstition, good and evil, morality and immorality, us and them. Lest there be any doubt about how the general public reads such troublesome imagery, one need only consult Channel Four's web discussion on their Thames torso documentary. In the telling words of one viewer: "Thank goodness such evil atrocities as this have been brought to our attention. Investigation in our civilized society here may well help stamp out such barbarism elsewhere."[2]

Such images, though novel in their specifics, hardly spring from thin air. They draw on a lengthy Western history of demonizing Others and are refracted through specific contemporary constellations of power, namely, the police and media. This, in turn, raises other issues. Can the police and media, singly or together, be held accountable for the negative outcome of their actions, however unintended? Should they be?

Since I have no privileged knowledge of the Met's or media's aims in this case, imputing motive can only be guesswork. For the Met, at least two possibilities present themselves. On the one hand, if their aim is to undermine in the popular imagination derogatory images of Africans, then plainly their communication strategy has failed. If, on the other hand, their aim is to convey an image of concerned and hardworking Met detectives, following any lead, however trivial, to bring the killer of a young black boy to justice, then their communication strategy has proved a resounding success, at least for some. One viewer's web comments on *Torso in the Thames: Adam's Story* speak volumes here: "an inspiring account of dogged police work and forensic science ... a damning indictment of the frequency of such crimes in African countries to make such efforts by our own police worthy of note."[3] The problem however is that whatever the case—whether the Met has not managed, mismanaged, or over-managed the information released from their investigation—the outcome has been the reproduction of derogatory images of Africa and Africans. This point is one they might ponder very seriously.

Nor is the media entirely innocent. Here, too, it is impossible to know whether the production of Dark Continent imagery has been witting— aiming perhaps to sell newspapers with sensationalist headlines (see Works Cited)—or unwitting, in which case journalists, the BBC, and others appear simply to believe the derogatory supposed "facts" they have been reporting about Africans. On 31 January 2003, for example, BBC Radio Four aired a piece on the Thames torso. The reporter noted that police believe the boy was "kidnapped or given up by parents who saw it as an honour to have their child killed in ritual sacrifice known as *muti*." An honour to have one's child killed? It should worry the BBC and others that such wild, inflammatory and racist conjecture can today pass itself off as responsible journalism.

No doubt the Met and media, if pressed, would blame each other for the negative images produced. Both, I suspect, would claim they are only reporting the facts. But neither can legitimately luxuriate in a radical postmodern position claiming the complete detachment of author from text. Both must consider their complicity in the production of such harmful images. They must also develop future communication strategies that undermine rather than underscore the very ideas of Otherness all involved ostensibly seek to eliminate.

And what of anthropologists? Have we, too, been complicit in the (re)production of such derogatory images? Where are the public anthropological voices attempting to nuance complex African life-worlds and to disrupt and undermine such patent Othering discourses? What role should we—or can we—play in these debates?

Given the nature of this case, the police have consulted many anthropologists and Africanists. A number continue to advise them today. For the record, I rang the Met in 2001 to see what assistance I might offer as an Africanist anthropologist who writes on witchcraft and to express concerns over how the case was being pursued and represented to the public. We had, I believe, three conversations in all. The evidence they then offered that the Thames torso was African ritual murder, all of which has since been made public, I found utterly unconvincing, and I politely told them so. They did not ring again. On discussing the case at the American Anthropological Association meeting in November 2002, I was surprised to discover that three of my Africanist colleagues—one from Europe, one from the United States, and one from South Africa—had also been contacted by Scotland Yard. They, too, spun a line similar to mine. They, too, were not consulted further. It is difficult to know where in the equation alternative voices might reasonably be inserted, or how they might be heard.

The media have been no more receptive to anthropological disruptions. In early 2002, I sent brief commentaries on the Thames torso to London-based newspapers, *The Times*, *The Guardian*, and *The Independent*. Not one was published. Perhaps they were poorly written. Perhaps other stories were more pressing. The broader point, though, is that while we should question the role anthropologists play in the public arena, and our own possible complicity in the production of Othering images, the very real issue remains of how we navigate these broader power structures in order to communicate our anthropological commonplaces. If Asad (1986) is right to suggest that the languages of Third World societies are "weaker" in relation to Western languages, then we might equally say that anthropology is a weaker language in relation to alternative Western idioms like those spoken by the media, police, and general public. In this context, anthropology's authoritative voice—a topic much debated and critiqued since the 1980s—is not as authoritative as some commentators would have us believe. The distressing and depressing *Heart of Darkness* imagery surrounding the Thames torso case stands, I believe, as testimony to this truth and to the seriousness of the task before us.

NOTES

[1]   Dutch police discovered that the girl was killed by her parents.

[2]   <http://www.channel4.com/culture/microsites/T/thinktv/comments/jan03_torso_comments.html>. Accessed 20 February 2004.

3   <http://www.channel4.com/culture/microsites/T/thinktv/comments/
jano3_torso_comments.html>. Accessed 20 February 2004.

WORKS CITED

ABC. 2002. Police lay wreath for Thames torso victim. *ABC Newsonline*, 22
    September. <http://www.abc.net.au/news/newsitems/200209/s682467.htm>
    Accessed 25 September 2004.

Achebe, Chinua. 1988. An image of Africa: Racism in Conrad's *Heart of Darkness*.
    In *Heart of Darkness: An Authoritative Text, Backgrounds and Sources, Criticism*.
    Ed. Robert Kimbrough. New York, NY: Norton and Co.

Allen, Nick. 2002. Police to investigate string of "ritual killings." *The Independent*,
    28 May. <http://news.independent.co.uk/uk/crime/story.jsp?story=299698>
    Accessed 25 September 2004.

———. 2003. New clue for police in torso murder hunt. *Independent*, 1 February.
    <http://news.independent.co.uk/uk/crime/story.jsp?story=374510> Accessed
    25 September 2004.

Asad, Talal. 1986. The concept of cultural translation in British social anthropol-
    ogy. *Writing Culture: The Poetics and Politics of Ethnography*. Ed. J. Clifford and
    G. E. Marcus. 141–64. Berkeley, CA: University of California Press.

Barnett, Antony, Paul Harris, and Tony Thompson. 2002. Human flesh "on sale
    in London." *The Observer*, 3 November. <http://observer.guardian.co.uk/
    uk_news/story/0,6903,824972,00.html> Accessed 25 September 2004.

Bastian, Misty L. 2003. "Diabolic realities": narratives of conspiracy, transparency
    and "ritual murder" in the Nigerian popular print and electronic media. In
    Transparency and Conspiracy. Ed. H.G. West and T. Sanders. Durham, NC:
    Duke University Press.

BBC [British Broadcasting Corporation]. 2001a. Murder hunt as child's torso
    found. *BBC News*, 23 September. <http://news.bbc.co.uk/1/hi/uk/1558833.stm>
    Accessed 25 September 2004.

———. 2001b. "No new leads" in torso case. *BBC News*, 28 September. <http://news.
    bbc.co.uk/1/hi/england/1567828.stm> Accessed 25 September 2004.

———. 2001c. Police focus on Dutch torso "link." *BBC News*, 24 September.
    <http://www.news.bbc.co.uk/hi/english/uk/england/newsid_1558000/
    1558833.stm> Accessed 30 January 2002.

———. 2001d. Witchdoctor investigation in torso case. *BBC News*, 16 October.
    <http://news.bbc.co.uk/1/hi/england/1602477.stm> Accessed 25 September 2004.

———. 2002a. Candle clues ruled out in "muti" killing. *BBC News*, 14 February.
    <http://news.bbc.co.uk/1/hi/england/1821411.stm> Accessed 25 September 2004.

———. 2002b. Dredging up Africa's dark side. *BBC News*, 19 April. <http://news.
    bbc.co.uk/1/hi/england/1938923.stm> Accessed 25 September 2004.

———. 2002c. Mandela makes Thames torso appeal. *BBC News*, 19 April. <http://news.bbc.co.uk/1/hi/england/1938580.stm> Accessed 25 September 2004.

———. 2002d. New lead in torso murder inquiry. *BBC News*, 20 September. <http://news.bbc.co.uk/1/hi/england/2270679.stm> Accessed 25 September 2004.

———. 2002e. Police examine "flesh for sale" claims. *BBC News,* 4 November. <http://news.bbc.co.uk/1/hi/england/2396697.stm> Accessed 25 September 2004.

———. 2002f. Ritual killing link to dead boy. *BBC News*, 25 January. <http://news.bbc.co.uk/1/hi/england/1780990.stm> Accessed 25 September 2004.

———. 2002g. Ritual killings "pushing double figures." *BBC News*, 27 May. <http://news.bbc.co.uk/1/hi/england/2009876.stm> Accessed 25 September 2004.

———. 2002h. SA police nab "head" man. *BBC News*, 16 May. <http://news.bbc.co.uk/1/hi/world/africa/1991406.stm> Accessed 25 September 2004.

———. 2002i. Tests to identify Thames torso. *BBC News*, 8 March. <http://news.bbc.co.uk/1/hi/england/1861192.stm> Accessed 25 September 2004.

———. 2002j. Thames torso "was human sacrifice." *BBC News*, 29 January. <http://news.bbc.co.uk/1/hi/england/1788452.stm> Accessed 25 September 2004.

———. 2002k. Torso police reopen old case. *BBC News*, 24 May. <http://news.bbc.co.uk/1/hi/england/2007198.stm> Accessed 25 September 2004.

———. 2002l. Voodoo "practised in UK." *BBC News*, 8 March. <http://news.bbc.co.uk/1/hi/uk/1861393.stm> Accessed 25 September 2004.

Bennetto, Jason. 2001. "Witch doctors" may have mutilated boy. *The Independent*, 17 October. <http://www.independent.co.uk/story.jsp?story=99865> Accessed 30 January 2002.

———. 2002. Chief suspect from 1969 ritual killing linked to torso in Thames inquiry. *The Independent*, 3 December. <http://news.independent.co.uk/uk/crime/story.jsp?story=298288> Accessed 25 September 2004.

Bright, Martin, and Paul Harris. 2002. Thames torso boy was sacrificed. *The Observer*, 2 June. <http://observer.guardian.co.uk/uk_news/story/0,6903,726271,00.html> Accessed 25 September 2004.

Comaroff, Jean, and John L. Comaroff. 2000. Millennial capitalism: First thoughts on a second coming. (Special Issue: Millennial capitalism and the culture of neoliberalism). *Public Culture* 12(2): 291–343.

Davenport, Justin. 2002. New evidence on Thames torso boy. *ThisisLondon*, 21 September. <http://www.thisislondon.co.uk/news/articles/1266665> Accessed 25 September 2004.

Flanagan, Jane. 2002. Mandela appeal over torso case. *ThisisLondon*, 19 April. <http://www.thisislondon.co.uk/news/londonlife/articles/445051> Accessed 25 September 2004.

Guardian. 2002. Torso find "consistent" with ritual murder. *The Guardian*, 29 January. <http://www.guardian.co.uk/uk_news/story/0,,641311,00.html> Accessed 25 September 2004.

Gulbrandsen, Ø. 2002. The discourse of "ritual murder": Popular reaction to political leaders in Botswana. *Social Analysis* 46(3): 215–33.

Independent. 2002. Muti. *The Independent*, 15 February. <http://news.independent.co.uk/uk/this_britain/story.jsp?story=120030> Accessed 25 September 2004.

La Fontaine, Jean S. 1998. *Speak of the Devil: Tales of Satanic Abuse in Contemporary England*. Cambridge: Cambridge University Press.

McDougall, Dan. 2002. Is there an evil cult in the UK? *The Scotsman*, 31 January. <http://www.thescotsman.co.uk/print/cfm?id=114872002> Accessed 9 November 2002.

Moore, Henrietta L., and Todd Sanders. 2001. Magical interpretations and material realities: An introduction. In *Magical Interpretations, Material Realities: Modernity, Witchcraft and the Occult in Postcolonial Africa*. Ed. H.L. Moore and T. Sanders. 1–27. London: Routledge.

Nettleton, Philip. 2002. Mandela helps in torso boy case. *ThisisLondon*, 12 April. <http://www.thisislondon.co.uk/news/londonlife/articles/446340> Accessed 25 September 2004.

Oliver, Mark. 2002. Find the lost children. *The Guardian*, 19 April. <http://www.guardian.co.uk/crime/article/0,,687386,00.html> Accessed 25 September 2004.

Peachey, Paul. 2002. Torso in Thames was "ritual sacrifice." *The Independent*, 30 January. <http://news.independent.co.uk/uk/crime/story.jsp?story=117122> Accessed 25 September 2004.

Sanders, Todd. 2001. Save our skins: Structural adjustment, morality and the occult in Tanzania. In *Magical Interpretations, Material Realities: Modernity, Witchcraft and the Occult in Postcolonial Africa*. Ed. H.L. Moore and T. Sanders. 160–83. London: Routledge.

Sawyer, Patrick. 2002. New twist in Thames torso. *ThisisLondon*, 24 May. <http://www.thisislondon.co.uk/news/londonlife/articles/440691> Accessed 25 September 2004.

ThisisLondon. 2001. Witchdoctor lead to torso boy. *ThisisLondon*, 15 October. <http://www.gospelcom.net/apologeticsindex/news1/ano11016-27.html> Accessed 9 November 2002.

———. 2002a. Torso detectives fly to Nigeria. *ThisisLondon*, 24 October. <http://www.thisislondon.co.uk/news/articles/1740881> Accessed 9 November 2002.

———. 2002b. Woman is bailed in torso case. *ThisisLondon*, 11 July. <http://www.thisislondon.co.uk/news/londonlife/articles/434651> Accessed 9 November 2002.

Thompson, Tony. 2002. Thames torso detectives fear repeat killings. *The Observer*, 1 September. <http://observer.guardian.co.uk/uk_news/story/0,6903,784117,00.html> Accessed 25 September 2004.

Vasagar, Jeevan. 2002. New evidence links torso boy to ritual killing theory. *The Guardian*, 26 January. <http://www.guardian.co.uk/uk_news/story/0,,639744,00.html> Accessed 25 September 2004.

Walsh, Nick Paton. 2002. Thames torso link to African rituals. *The Observer*, 27 January. <http://observer.guardian.co.uk/uk_news/story/0,6903,639985,00.html> Accessed 25 September 2004.

9 | WHITE DEVIL AS EXPERT WITNESS[1]

Ted Swedenburg

In October 2002, I found myself testifying in US District Court, Southern District of New York: *Law and Order* country. In the belief system of the plaintiff on whose behalf I was testifying, someone like me might be categorized as a "white devil," one of those who profits off the misery and domination of the majority of the global population. I had to prove that I was not, in fact, a "white devil" but a responsible translator of cultural difference. Although the expert witness role is not entirely unfamiliar to a cultural anthropologist, neither is it an everyday one for most of us. Those anthropologists who do serve as expert witnesses appear not to write much about this part of their professional lives (see Rosen 1977 and Hopper 1990).[2] In our analytical texts, both ethnographic and historical, anthropologists might examine the historical moments and the conditions of power under which "sects" become legitimized as "religions." What is less common is for anthropologists actually to be involved in this process of legitimization. In this case, I was an active player in a legal attempt to contest a hegemonic view that classifies the beliefs of "sects," "cults," or in this instance, "gangs," as unworthy of the recognition owed to citizens who hold recognized religious beliefs.

This chapter concerns my experience during spring and fall 2002, when I served as an expert witness in a suit brought by an inmate named Intelligent Tarref Allah against the New York State Department of Correctional Services (DOCS).[3] Intelligent, a member of the Nation of Gods and Earths (commonly referred to as Five Percenters), had filed suit in order to have his religious rights recognized. The New York State DOCS classified the Nation of Gods and Earths (NGE) not as a religion but as a "security threat" or "unauthorized" group—as a gang, essentially—and, accordingly, denied its members the rights to hold formal meetings, display group symbols, and possess or receive written Nation materials, including central texts and newspapers.[4]

My own work on and interest in the NGE grew out of an abiding concern both for hip-hop and with the subterranean connections between Western and Middle Eastern cultures. The NGE is known in the United

States chiefly as a result of the popularity of rap music produced by its adherents. Rakim Allah of the group Eric B & Rakim was the first major rap artist to bring Five Percent messages to large audiences, through a series of seminal recordings released between 1987 and 1990.[5] Since then a whole host of prominent rap recording artists affiliated in various ways, past or present, with the NGE have emerged. They include, among others, stars like Big Daddy Kane, Erykah Badu, Nas, Poor Righteous Teachers, Brand Nubian, Digable Planets, Gang Starr, Busta Rhymes, Mobb Deep, and all the members of the Wu Tang Clan, including Old Dirty Bastard, Raekwon, Method Man, the RZA, and Ghostface Killah. Over the last 15 years, these artists collectively have moved tens of millions of units and thereby brought the lessons of the Five Percent to the centre of American popular culture. This fact has been little commented upon, however, either in the music press or in the by-now massive body of academic work on hip-hop. Moreover, most of the millions of white American rap music fans remain ignorant of the meanings of Five Percent-inflected rap lyrics, due to their occult and coded nature.

I presented a paper on the NGE, hip-hop, and the NGE's relation to other Islamic groups at the American Anthropological Association in 1996 and then published the revised paper online in 1997 (Swedenburg 1997). I remain one of a handful of American academics to have written on the NGE. My own paper largely relies on textual readings, whereas the best work of other writers trained as academics is based on firsthand experience with the NGE (see Nuruddin 1994, Aidi 2002, and Perkins 1996). After other potential experts declined to testify, I was contacted by three lawyers from the prestigious New York City law firm Sullivan & Cromwell, who had taken on Intelligent Allah's case on a *pro bono* basis.[6]

NATION OF GODS AND EARTHS

The NGE belongs to a much larger trend in the African-American community in the United States, dating back to the early twentieth century, which combines Afro-centrism, pan-Africanism, and Islamic cultural and religious influences. Among the most prominent organizations to emerge out of this current are the Moorish Science Temple (founded by Noble Drew Ali in 1913) and the Nation of Islam (NOI), founded in 1931 by Wallace Fard Muhammad, taken over by Elijah Muhammad in 1934, and now headed by Reverend Louis Farrakhan. The NGE was founded by Clarence 13X, a member of NOI Temple #7 in Harlem (which was headed by Malcolm X during the 1950s). Clarence 13X was expelled from the NOI in 1964 for teaching that the black man collectively is God, in contradistinction to NOI doctrine that God appeared in Detroit in 1930 in the person of Master (Wallace) Fard Muhammed and gave the word to his messenger Elijah Muhammed. After his expulsion from the NOI, Clarence changed his name to Allah and, along with a few followers, began to preach to youth on the streets of Harlem.

Allah, or "The Father" as his followers called him, taught that the Black Men who studied and learned the lessons of Master Fard and came to have knowledge of self—to know their own divinity—constitute 5 per cent of the population (hence the term, Five Percenters). The 85 per cent of the population who lack this knowledge are the mentally deaf, dumb, and blind, whose ignorance makes them ripe for exploitation by the remaining 10 per cent of the population. The 10 per cent, the bloodsuckers of the poor, possess knowledge and understand the truth, but they use this knowledge to mystify and control the 85 per cent. They exercise this control over the masses through their teachings that God is a "spook," a mystery God who exists in heaven, out of sight, not on earth. The 10 per cent include the white devils, the Caucasians, who were created ("grafted"), according to Fard, by the evil scientist Yaqub some 6,000 years ago, as well as the preachers of Christianity and Orthodox Islam, who hoodwink the 85 per cent with their doctrine of the mystery God. (The 85-10-5 formulation is Elijah Muhammad's; the NGE doctrine that Black Man is God is based on statements by Elijah Muhammad as well.) While Black Man is the embodiment of God, Black Woman is "Earth," from whom life emanates. As Earth revolves around the sun, woman is subordinate to man; the black woman NGE member is not a god, but witnesses to the fact that her man is divine.

Allah brought these messages to urban black youth by disseminating, on the street, the secret teachings of Master Fard, known as the 120 Degrees, which the NOI hierarchy had monopolized and kept away from the rank and file. Allah also developed his own system of teachings, known as the Supreme Mathematics and the Supreme Alphabet, which are sets of principles, organized in the form of a catechism, that are attached to numerals and the letters of the alphabet and that serve as keys to understanding how the universe works. Allah was gunned down in 1969 by unknown assassins, but his movement gradually spread to most American urban centres, and it lives on and thrives—although the numbers of adherents are unknown.

EXPERT WITNESS

The plaintiff for whom I testified, Intelligent Tarref Allah, was serving time for homicide. He is one of many African-American prisoners who joined the NGE in prison; he did so in 1994, while awaiting trial at Rikers Island. Lawyers doing *pro bono* work at Sullivan & Cromwell (S & C) often specialize in prisoners' rights cases, and it is in this context that they took on Intelligent's suit against the DOCS. S & C, which has an impressive list of corporate clients (for instance, Microsoft and Goldman Sachs), in fact *uses* its extensive commitment to *pro bono* work to attract socially conscious graduates from top-tier law schools.

The task that Intelligent's lawyers set for me was, first, to produce an "expert report" and then to travel to New York City to be deposed by the US Assistant District Attorney, lawyer for the defendants. Writing a nine-page expert report was a process that involved considerable research on my part as well as intensive collaboration with Intelligent's lawyers. In order to familiarize me with the case, the lawyers sent a box of the pertinent legal documents, which I poured over, frequently bewildered by the legalese. Most useful for my purposes was an almost complete set of *The Five Percenter* published by the Allah School in Mecca (NGE parlance for Harlem), a central NGE institution.

In writing my report, my assigned task was to demonstrate that the NGE constitutes a religion according to conventional anthropological understandings of the term. After consulting with colleague JoAnn D'Alisera, whose expertise is in the field of anthropology of religion, I opted for a definition adapted from John Bowen's (2001) *Religions in Practice: An Approach to the Anthropology of Religion*, a textbook widely used in the United States.[7] The aim was to work with a definition that (1) could be argued to be one that would generally be accepted by anthropologists and (2) could be used to demonstrate, empirically, that the NGE constitutes a set of beliefs and practices that anthropologists would recognize as religious in nature and would therefore constitute a religion. I am aware of, and in full sympathy with, the reasoned critiques of universalist anthropological definitions of religion (Asad 1993). The point of the report, however, was a pragmatic one: to attempt to make effective arguments that might persuade the court to accord NGE members the same religious rights accorded to other recognized faiths. What is to some anthropologists a theoretically outdated universal definition of religion (which is actually much influenced by a historically specific understanding of religion in the context of secular, liberal societies), actually proved quite persuasive, given that we were arguing on the terrain of the secular state.

I argued in my report that, based on a conventional anthropological definition of religion, the NGE can be shown to possess the necessary characteristics. The NGE, as we have seen, preaches a notion of divinity (Black Man = God) and possesses an articulated belief system (contained in the 120 Degrees, the Supreme Mathematics, and the Supreme Alphabet). It observes particular rituals, including regular gatherings known as "parliaments" and "rallies," where lessons are taught, their applications discussed, and community decisions are made. It organizes community celebrations, in particular Show and Prove Science Fairs, where young people present scientific experiments. It also possesses key symbols, in particular the Universal Flag, which consists of an eight-pointed star that contains the number 7, a crescent, and a smaller five-pointed star, and is encircled by the words, "In the Name of Allah." NGE members also observe holy days: the birthday and death day of Allah, as well as the birthdays of Elijah Muhammed and Master Fard Muhammed. NGE members often fast on these holy days; they also observe dietary laws, in particular a proscription against eating pork. They proselytize on the streets, in everyday life, in prisons, and through rap music. The NGE possesses a distinct organizational structure that is decentralized and nonhierarchical—appropriate for a group where all male members are Gods. It is a network of groups found in many major American metropolitan districts, whose local activities are for the most part organized through Allah Schools; the most important of these schools remains the Harlem ("Mecca") Allah School. Although local NGE communities have little by way of formal hierarchy, distinctions exist between elders—older, respected members—and the rest of the membership, which is younger and has less years of experience within the Nation. I also attempted in my report to show the relationship between the NGE and other religions or sects, such as the NOI, Sunni Islam, and heterodox Shi'ite sects like the Druze and the Isma'ilis.

We have already seen some of the important ways in which the NGE both draws on and distinguishes itself from NOI doctrine. Like all Muslims,

NGE members do not eat pork. They draw on the Qur'an as a (secondary source) for lessons. From the perspective of Sunni Muslims, however, the NGE's belief in the divinity of black men constitutes *shirk*, or polytheism. The NGE shares with Ismai'lism and the Druze sect a belief in the mystery of numbers as well as Gnostic tendencies. Such forms of eclectic borrowing are, of course, familiar to anthropologists as *syncretism*. I concluded that, on the basis of the fact that the NGE's beliefs and practices accord with what could be considered a broadly accepted anthropological definition of religion, anthropologists would consider the NGE a religion.

The process of producing the report involved careful reading and editing on the part of the lawyers, numerous drafts, and long telephone conversations. The lawyers I worked with, while not trained in anthropology or religious studies, were incredibly knowledgeable about the NGE as a result of all their diligent work on Intelligent Allah's case. In addition, as a result of other *pro bono* work they have undertaken, they were amazingly knowledgeable about Islam in prisons, in African-American communities, and in New York City. One of the lawyers in particular could have provided graduate students with a number of fascinating research topics on African-American Islam. Due to the input and care taken by the attorneys, my expert report on the NGE (only nine pages in length) was probably written with as much care and heavy editing as anything that I have every produced (Swedenburg 2002a).

My deposition in New York in May 2002 was uneventful, as the defendants' lawyer, the assistant DA, did not probe very deeply. My appearance at trial in October, however, required much more preparation—about six hours each day over the weekend—for my testimony on Monday in District Court. The process of preparation involved: (1) the lawyers turning my report into a carefully scripted set of questions and answers, with me assisting them in refining the script; (2) rehearsing the testimony, over and over, so that it flowed smoothly, I made no mistakes, and forgot nothing; and (3) the production of a large visual aid—a chart mapping the doctrinal relations between the NGE and the NOI, Orthodox Islam, the Isma'ilis, and the Druze. The chart, initiated by one of the lawyers and elaborated with my assistance, was a kind of Venn diagram that showed the NGE and the other Islamic sects as partially overlapping and partially distinct. I put more work and careful preparation into my expert testimony, which ended up lasting about an hour, than for any lecture or job talk I

have ever given. My testimony, I believe, went well. Of particular importance, in addition, was the Venn diagram chart, because it served to powerfully and visually position the NGE within the field of legitimate(d)
religious and theological discourse.[8] The only substantial issues raised by
the counsel for the DOCS was whether or not I had ever attended a
Parliament, Rally, or Show and Prove Science Fair. I had to answer that I
had not. (One of the lawyers and I had planned to attend a Parliament in
Harlem the evening before the trial, but we had to work on rehearsing my
testimony instead.) I don't know whether it was opposing counsel's intent,
but the questioning sounded very much like the empiricist question
frequently posed to anthropologists: were you there?

In addition to testifying, I listened to the testimony of other witnesses
for a day and a half. It was very useful for me, given my continuing
research interests in the NGE, to hear testimony from Five Percenters (the
plaintiff, Intelligent Allah, as well as Cee Aaquil Allah Barnes and Born
Justice Allah, from the Allah Youth Center, which is affiliated with the
Allah School in Mecca) and DOCS corrections officers and officials. I met
some NGE members from New York who were present at the trial. (My
only previous personal contact with NGE members was at a conference on
Islam and hip-hop at the University of Pennsylvania in spring 2001).
Among the things I learned from watching testimony is that Five
Percenters believe that whites are born devilish and are inherently satanic,
but that it is also possible for whites, through their actions, to become "civilized." (But it is not possible for them to become Gods or Earths.) It also
became clearer to me that the focus of NGE teachings is not on white
devilry. As Allah is reported to have said, "We are neither pro-black nor
anti-white. We are pro-righteousness and anti-devilishment." NGE lessons
focus, rather, on the need for African-Americans to exercise self-control,
to strive to educate themselves, to adopt positive behaviours, and to
foreswear negative ones, such as gangbanging, violence, and drug abuse.
By doing so, they will realize the divine capacity within. While NGE
members are very critical of white racist structures in the United States that
produce "negativity," their stress is on the development of self-discipline
and personal responsibility as the means of combating and overcoming the
devilishment inflicted by white hegemony.

It also became clearer from attending trial that the state possesses
tremendous powers to define and constitute groups as it wills. The state

disciplinary mechanisms that treat Five Percent inmates as "security threats" of course also have important valences with dominant American discourses which treat young black males as dangerous, pathological, and violent. Although a number of inmates belonging to the NGE had previously filed suit to have their religious rights recognized, the case of Intelligent was the first in which a Five Percenter plaintiff has received proper representation—due to the fact that the Wall Street firm of S & C was able to commit a great deal of resources in contest with a state that possesses virtually limitless resources when it comes to legal matters.

GODS AND SNIPERS

As chance would have it, I returned from my weekend in New York to find my e-mail and voice messages full of queries from the American mass media—including, among others, CNN, the Today Show, and *USA Today*. The demands of the mass media, and particularly daily news outlets, mean that journalists need to talk to sources immediately and to produce their story *that* day. I therefore missed my chance at 15 minutes of dubious media fame by being away for the weekend. I had been contacted due to the media obsession of the moment—the snipers that had terrorized the greater Washington, DC area and beyond, for the preceding several weeks. Two suspects, John Allen Muhammad and John Lee Malvo, had just been arrested, and reporters were uncovering clues that some thought suggested a connection between the suspects and the NGE. The clues, which included rap cassettes found in the suspects' car, were also said to suggest the influence of Five Percent hiphoppers, like Method Man of the Wu Tang Clan, on Malvo and Muhammad. These connections were asserted in the post-9/11 atmosphere where many observers—inflamed by cases like that of the "American Taliban" John Walker Lindh and José Padilla of "dirty bomb" fame—were raising the specter of a "fifth column" of radical Muslims in American urban minority communities and prison populations with ties to Al-Qaeda and other jihadist Islamic groups (see Aidi 2002).[9] The powerful associations already circulating in the American media and in popular discourses—associations linking hip-hop lyrics, gang violence, and radical African-American Islamic trends—now combined with the discourses of the war on terrorism to create a brief moment of media hysteria about murderous snipers and Five Percenters.

Fortunately, I guess, the story quickly played itself out, and the media herd moved on to its next obsession— probably North Korean nukes or Iraqi weapons of mass destruction—but not before it had wreaked a fair amount of damage. A representative op-ed in *USA Today,* commenting on the reported connection between the sniper suspects and the NGE, characterized the Five Percenters as a "virulently racist black group" that was calling for "race war." The media reports and commentaries on the sniper-Five Percent-hip-hop connections were, predictably, based almost entirely on prevailing prejudices about African-American Islam, on clues sloppily drawn from Internet research, on crudely literalist readings of hip-hop lyrics, and on the almost total absence of any meaningful representation of the points of views of Five Percenters themselves. All of this is depressingly familiar to anyone with any knowledge of mass media portrayals of African-American youth culture. The rush to interpret hip-hop lyrics that deal with violence, whether in the form of revenge fantasy, reportage, or morality, as simply *incitement* seems endemic, particularly at moments of crisis or panic. No doubt there also are parallels here with Talal Asad's observations (2003: 10-11) on current Western discourse about "Islamic terrorism," which presupposes that the Qur'an *constrains* Muslims to act according to it and therefore to kill nonbelievers.

I was contacted by one reporter from the *Richmond Times-Dispatch*, and after about an hour of conversation, I at least partially (I thought) set him straight. He thanked me profusely, saying that if he hadn't spoken to me, he would have produced a much different—and much less accurate—report. I also wrote a piece on the snipers and their purported Five Percent connections that was published on *Middle East Report Online* (Swedenburg 2002b). Again, this was a perfectly ordinary role for an anthropologist to be occupying—attempting to translate and make sense of a "native point of view," to defend an "Other" culture against the charges of irrationality. But this was an attempt at damage control that was mostly too little, too late. The hegemonic depiction—of a deep-rooted link between African-American culture, hip-hop, senseless gang violence, and black-racist Islam—had already been reinforced. (The assertion of the NGE-sniper connection has never come up again, even at Malvo and Muhammad's trials.)

RULING

On 31 July 2003, District Judge Naomi Reice Buchwald finally released her judgement in the case of *Marria v. Broaddus, et al.* Buchwald ruled in favour of the plaintiff, Intelligent Allah, and ordered the DOCS to conform its policies in accord with her ruling. She stated, "We have found that plaintiff is a sincere adherent to a religious belief system that qualifies for First Amendment protection…" (*Marria vs. Broaddus et al.* 2003: 54).[10]

Overall, Judge Buchwald found convincing the evidence brought by Intelligent's lawyers that the NGE constituted a religion and not a gang. This is a rather unique experience for an anthropologist, to be an agent in the broad process of the transformation of a "gang/cult/sect" to a recognized "religion." I was pleased to have been part of the legal team's successful effort, because I support NGE inmates' struggle to have their religious rights recognized and because I am in broad sympathy with the NGE's forceful critique (particularly via rap) of white racism. I am also—it almost goes without saying—critical of a number of NGE tenets, particularly its racialist essentialism. My testimony, however, constituted just a small part of the evidence brought to bear by Intelligent's lawyers. I found the testimony of Intelligent, Cee Aaquil Allah, and Born Justice Allah to be particularly compelling. It was clear that becoming a God radically transformed Intelligent; since joining he has become a vegan, studied for and attained his GED, and was a model prisoner, with no record of disruptive conduct or violence. Cee Aaquil gave a persuasive account of the important activities of the Allah School and its Youth Center, which include field trips outside the ghetto for children, substance abuse programs, and after-school tutoring sessions. My testimony therefore was just one source among many cited by Judge Buchwald throughout her 61-page opinion. For instance, although "syncretism" is a complex term that has been the subject of considerable anthropological debate (see Stewart and Shaw 1994), it seemed to have helped in this instance to persuade the judge that this was a well-established, often identified process of religious transformation, and not something unique to the NGE (*Marria vs. Broaddus et al.* 2003: 6).

CONCLUSION

In her opinion cited above, Buchwald called the plaintiff a *sincere* adherent of a religious belief system. Basing her argument on precedent, and referring to precedent in a case involving the Hare Krishnas, the judge asserted that her task was not to rule on whether the beliefs in question were "appropriate or true" but on the sincerity of belief (*Marria vs. Broaddus et al.* 2003: 20).[11] She made this determination on the basis of observing the plaintiff's "demeanor at trial" as well as his testimony. She noted, in making her judgement, her approval of philosopher William James's definition of religion: "the feelings, acts, and experiences of individual men in their solitude, so far as they apprehend themselves to stand in relation to whatever they may consider the divine" (*Marria vs. Broaddus et al.* 2003: 20; James 1902: 31).

Although Intelligent was asking for a *public* acceptance of the NGE, including the right of assembly and the right to display insignia of membership, the judge resorted to a classically secular definition of religion, one which attempted to confine it to the domain of private solitude and individual belief and to a subjective judgement of "sincerity." The NGE, in fact, is quite deliberately critical of secularist definitions of religion, which restrict it to the domains of the private and the individual. The NGE proclaims that it is *not* a religion but is rather "a way of life." In this way it seeks to distinguish itself from religious traditions that it considers to have accepted their confinement to specified domains. One could read the NGE's assertion that divinity is *present*, within the corporeal reality of black men, as opposed to being a "spook," as an instance of such a critique. In my report and testimony, I argued that the NGE's assertion that it was not a religion but a way of life paradoxically confirmed its religious status. The claim, I stated, could only be interpreted as a "religious" argument, articulated within a discourse of religious argumentation.

To reiterate, although I am in agreement with recent anthropological critiques of universalist definitions of religion, I felt compelled to work with such a definition in my expert testimony. When working within the boundaries imposed by the state and the law, in this case at least, it seemed imperative to deploy rather than to critique (from outside) modernist categories. Members of the NGE are, in a sense, caught in the same bind. While asserting that the NGE is *not* a religion, at the same time they cannot *not* want the NGE to be recognized *as a religion* by the state, particularly inside the prison system.

Based on my experience, I subsequently received two more queries about possibly appearing as a witness in cases involving Five Percenters, but in neither instance did I ultimately appear in court. I have received the occasional communication from various Gods (members of the NGE) ever since I posted my piece on the web, much—but not all—of it positive. Since my testimony and the publication of my "sniper" commentary, I have received more correspondence, and it is possible that I may in future be involved in some way in efforts to get the NGE recognized as a legitimate religion in other state prison systems. (Unfortunately, because I live quite far from any urban centre with NGE communities, I have not been able to conduct further field research.) Given the continued likelihood of future panics over African-Americans, violence, and Islam, further fieldwork and testimony by other would-be "civilized white devils" on behalf of the NGE and related groups will no doubt be necessary and, in fact, urgent. Such research and witnessing may, at times, require anthropologists to work within and critically engage state and legal systems, and therefore, to operate *within* the modernist paradigms which we at the same time so persistently critique.

NOTES

1 Thanks to the editors of this volume, Donna J. Young and especially Anne Meneley, for their invaluable assistance in developing and clarifying my arguments.

2 Anthropologists testifying at land claims cases for First Nations peoples are often, in fact, restricted from publishing about their testimony, at least until the land claim is settled.

3 The case is known as *Marria v. Broaddus, et al*. The plaintiff Intelligent Allah was formerly known as Rashaad Marria; he legally changed his name in 2001.

4 At least three other states with significant Five Percenter inmate populations, Virginia, New Jersey, and South Carolina, also treat them as "security threats."

5 To wit, *Paid in Full* (1987), *Follow the Leader* (1988), and *Let the Rhythm Hit 'Em* (1990).

6 Sullivan & Cromwell (S & C), founded in 1879, played a crucial role in the formation of the Panama Canal and presidential approval for its construction; John Foster Dulles was managing partner of the firm before becoming President Eisenhower's Secretary of State. It currently employs 475 attorneys. S & C does not pay expert witnesses, so for anyone living on the East Coast, the amount of work involved was probably not worth it. For a resident of Northwest Arkansas, however, two expenses-paid trips to New York City seemed to me to represent ample compensation. (Naively, I had no idea how much work was actually involved, as discussed below.)

7 Bowen 2001. Here are key excerpts from my citations of Bowen: he "defines religion as 'ideas and practices that postulate reality beyond that which is immediately available to the senses.' In addition, Bowen views religious traditions as 'ever-changing complexes of beliefs (including those authoritative beliefs called "doctrine"), practices (including formalized rituals), and social institutions.' Bowen […] is also very concerned with religious practices […] Bowen takes care to explain: What we call religion may look quite different from one society to another…" (Swedenburg 2002a: 3–4, 5).

8   One also wonders whether the scientific origins of Venn diagrams—they were invented and developed by the famous mathematician John Venn, most notably in his famous book *Symbolic Logic* (1881)—did not also lend weight to the empirical truth of the testimony. I doubt that most cultural anthropologists would think of representing the NGE in such a manner. Since NGE members see their belief system as distinct, I wasn't sure that they would find the chart appropriate. One Earth—a public school teacher—who I met after my testimony, however, loved it and wanted a copy for educational purposes.

9   Lindh, prior to his departure for Afghanistan, was a hip-hop fan and something of an extreme Wigger (in Norman Mailer's parlance, a White Negro), who posed as an African-American on-line. Padilla, a former gang member, first encountered Islam while in prison (Aidi 2002).

10 Buchwald went on to state, "[we] are also prepared to accept for the purposes of this decision DOCS' claims that prison inmates identified as 'Five Percenters' have been associated with instances of violence and disruption. This raises the possibility that 'the Five Percenters' may somewhat uniquely connote both a religion and a gang in the New York State prison system (though the sincere religious adherents and gang members may not be the same inmates)." This concession to the DOCS claims did not, however, detract substantially from Buchwald's broad ruling in favour of Intelligent.

11 *Marria v. Broaddus et al.*, 97 Civ. 8291 (NRB), p. 20 (S.D.N.Y. 2003). In fact, Buchwald states (p. 3) in her opinion that "several of [the Nation's tenets] we find repugnant to the principles of tolerance and equality that are fundamental to our Constitution and the ethos of our country" (*Marria v. Broaddus et al.* 2003: 3).

WORKS CITED

Aidi, Hisham. 2002. Jihadis in the hood: Race, urban Islam and the War on Terror. *Middle East Report* 224 (Fall): <http://www.merip.org/mer/mer224/224_aidi.html>.

Asad, Talal. 1993 [1983]. The construction of religion as an anthropological category. In *Genealogies of Religion*. 27–54. Baltimore, MD: Johns Hopkins University Press.

———. 2003. *Formations of the Secular: Christianity, Islam, Modernity*. Stanford, CA: Stanford University Press.

Bowen, John. 2001. *Religions in Practice: An Approach to the Anthropology of Religion*. 2nd ed. Boston, MA: Allyn and Bacon.

Hopper, Kim. 1990. Research Findings as testimony: The ethnographer as expert witness. *Human Organization* 49(2):110-13.

James, William. 1902. *The Varieties of Religious Experience*. New York, NY: Longmans, Green. Marria v. Broaddus et al. 2003. 97 Civ. 8291 NRB. SDNY.

Nuruddin, Yusuf. 1994. The Five Percenters: A teenage Nation of Gods and Earths. In *Muslim Communities in North America*. Ed. Yvonne Yazbeck Haddad and Jane Idleman Smith. 109–33. Albany, NY: State University of New York Press.

Perkins, William Eric (ed.). *Droppin' Science: Critical Essays on Rap Music and Hip Hop Culture*. Philadelphia, PN: Temple University Press, 1996.

Rosen, Lawrence. 1977. The anthropologist as expert witness. *American Anthropologist* 79: 555–78.

Stewart, Charles, and Rosalind Shaw (eds.). 1994. *Syncretism/Anti-Syncretism*. New York, NY: Routledge.

Swedenburg, Ted. 1977. Islam in the mix: Lessons of the Five Percent. <http://comp.uark.edu/%7Etsweden/5per.html>.

———. 2002a. Expert report of Ted Swedenburg, May 22. *Marria v. Broaddus et al.* 2003. 97 Civ. 8291 NRB. SDNY.

———. 2002b. Snipers and the panic over Five Percent Islamic hip-hop. *Middle East Report Online* 10 November 10. <http://www.merip.org/mero/mero111002.html>.

Venn, John. 1881. Symbolic Logic. London: Macmillan.

PART IV | DISCIPLINING THE ACADEMY

HERE WE EXAMINE THE WAYS various funding and political institutions attempt to influence universities and to reshape the particular practices of academics. As Joan Vincent (1991) noted, the powerful critique of representation in the 1980s ignored the actual circumstances in which we write and the conditions under which we work. As institutions increasingly think of themselves as corporations in a competitive market, they package themselves in ways that will sell to clients and patrons. Often, academics are asked to embrace values in their professional activities they find objectionable as intellectuals.

Urciuoli examines the ways in which the policies of neo-liberalism play out in the context of a liberal arts university. She discusses the infiltration of neo-liberal discourse about citizenship and corporate workers into the everyday, seemingly benign life of students. The language of ethnicity and individualism comes to saturate their participation in voluntary associations and to reshape the ways they think about their own identities. In the process, complex historical relations are flattened and erased. As we negotiate our place in a university that seems increasingly willing to cater to the political whims of governments and private interests in exchange for hard cash, we need to ask ourselves about the ways we come to endorse political programs that run contrary to the values we espouse in the classroom.

Sometimes, in a heated political environment, universities and the academics working there are confronted more directly. David McMurray discusses the assault on academic freedoms that followed the terrorist attacks on New York and Washington of September 11, 2001 (9/11). Caught in the wider power plays of global politics, scholars of the Middle East were simultaneously accused of failing to recognize threats to the United States and of indulging in anti-American sentiment. In retrospect, our debates about representation probably imputed far more power to our anthropological texts than they deserved. Post 9/11, the idea of our texts having any impact on the world seems quite illusory, as McMurray's chapter indicates. In any event, whatever the flaws of anthropological discourse, it now looks considerably better than other forms of knowledge produced, at least about the Middle East. It is other discourses that appeal to those who plan and implement invasions. This is not to say that we should abandon a concern with representation, but merely to remind ourselves that the power of our texts is considerably more modest than we once might have thought.

McMurray shows that when academic freedoms and intellectual work are so profoundly disturbed and threatened, the university typically rallies. However, as an institution, it seems better positioned to combat blatant threats from without than to stop the gradual erosion of academic autonomy brought about by dependence on corporate and government funding initiatives, as discussed by Urciuoli. So much for the impermeable Ivory Tower!

WORKS CITED

Vincent, Joan. 1991. Engaging historicism. *Recapturing Anthropology: Working in the Present*. Ed. Richard G. Fox. 45–58. Santa Fe, NM: School of American Research Press.

10 | TEAM DIVERSITY: AN ETHNOGRAPHY OF INSTITUTIONAL VALUES[1]

Bonnie Urciuoli

ETHNOGRAPHY AND SEMIOTICS

This is a brief sketch of how the liberal arts college where I work views itself as a "diverse institution" and what that tells us about the college's place in American corporatized culture. What I describe here came about as a by-product of a larger project. Since 1995, I have been engaged in a study of how notions of *diversity* and *multiculturalism* are produced in college life. This was triggered by earlier work I had done on Puerto Rican bilingualism in Manhattan and the Bronx, which I wrote while teaching where I am now. As I wrote that work, I noticed many students who could easily have been younger relatives of the people I worked with in New York. I grew interested in the identity transition they seemed to experience, from a specific ethnic/national identity to a generalized sense of being *Latino/a*. After a number of curious and casual conversations about this, I began a series of interviews with students about their experience of that transition with questions like, "When you were in high school, did you think of yourself as *Latino/a*? As *multicultural* or *diverse*? If not, how did you think of yourself? When and how did you start applying the term *Latino/a* to yourself?" Typically, students came to college thinking of themselves as Puerto Rican, Dominican, Ecuadoran, and so on, and while they may have checked off *Latino/a* on a form they filled out, they generally saw it as an "official" or "school" category. It became personal when they became active in the school's Latino organization. *Multicultural* and *diverse* were similarly on the horizon but not personal until students became involved in college activities.

The questions I had begun to ask should be considered in the context of the school itself, a rural northeastern American liberal arts college with about 1,750 students. Six per cent of the student body self-identifies as black or African-American, 1 per cent as Native American, 6 per cent as Asian/Pacific Islander, and 3 per cent as Latino or Hispanic. Sixty-one per cent went to public schools. The college was founded almost 200 years ago and is heavily networked into the corporate and government world. This information forms an important backdrop to the structures of student life. As I began paying more attention to those structures, and to the structures of the rest of the school, I was struck by several points, none of which are unique to this college. First, college recruiting and publicity foregrounds the resonance between college and corporate life. Both assert that college provides opportunities for leadership, emphasizes the acquisition of trans-ferable skills, and reinforces the value of teamwork. Moreover, the partici-pant structures of student life are presented as a kind of training ground for participation in corporate life, e.g., experience in student organizations and activities translates into student activity résumés. Second, raising the school's student *diversity* profile has become a mandate. The director of admissions explained to me how the college's peer schools compete for high "diversity numbers" although those numbers are not explicitly part of the *U.S. News and World Report* ranking system. (*U.S. News* does post a "diversity index" on its website along with its ranking of "best" colleges.) Third, *multicultural* and *diverse* are not complete synonyms, particularly not in the school's recruiting, marketing, and fundraising activities. In the references to *lead-ership*, *skill*, and *excellence* that saturate the language of student recruitment, *multiculturalism* is used less frequently and more specifically (i.e., denoting *Asian*, *Latino*, or *Black/African-American*) than *diversity*. For example, in speeches about the college, its president has often referred to the college's commitment to increasing diversity because of the enrichment brought to the community by a diverse population. The school's website describes its diversity as "A diversity of cultures, ideas and activities [which] permeates every aspect of the [College's] community. The College encourages respect for intellectual and cultural diversity because such respect promotes free and open inquiry, independent thought and mutual understanding."

The semiotically minded reader might, at this point, note a certain inde-terminacy of meaning in these uses of the word *diversity*: sometimes it's about race and synonymous with *multiculturalism*; sometimes it's not. This is not an accident. We routinely find indeterminacy built into the nature of meaning and the social function of reference. In a recent article (Urciuoli 2003), I argued for the existence of what I call *strategically deployable shifters* or SDSs, by which I mean words and expressions used across different fields of discourse in ways that seem the same (i.e., the words are formally the same) but have different social implications and, to an extent, different meanings. *Shifters*, in grammatical theory, are morphemes or words that create an alignment between the speaker and another aspect of context. They don't have dictionary meaning in a strict sense because their primary function is this alignment: examples include past tense markers or such pronouns as *I*, *we*, *you*, and (aside from their substitution function) *he*, *she*, *it*, *they*—all of which are only fully meaningful when taken in context. Think about the alignments that can be implied by *us* versus *them*. I am extending this idea of alignment into what most people think of as vocabulary with fixed meaning (especially nouns and adjectives), and I am arguing that our ordinary language is full of vocabulary that is *strategically deployable*, that people use as much to align their own position as to provide information in any objective sense. (One important consequence of this, although not a major point in this paper, is that everyday semanticity is much looser and more flexible than most people think. Were that not the case, words would not easily change meaning, and they do change meaning continually.)

This happens in discourses where people share key viewpoints and values. Political, religious, and other value-oriented discourses are filled with words that take on specialized, often oppositional functions, depending on who's using it with whom and why: *family*, *evolution*, *welfare*, to name a few obvious ones. But language is full of less obvious examples. In corporate circles, *communication* means information transmission in organizational interactions that promote the best interests of the company or of those running it. *Communication*, when used with other corporate-oriented SDSs such as *skill*, *flexible*, and *team*, indicates alignment with a management perspective. (By contrast, when linguistic anthropologists like me say *communication*, we refer to open-ended and complexly meaningful interchange among people generally, whatever the outcome and whether it is task-oriented or not, and it indicates alignment with a certain theoretical perspective.) This phenomenon includes what linguists call *register*, that is, a set of terms and ways of using those terms specific to that social group and its activities (different occupations routinely have their own registers), but SDS usage goes well beyond that into a sense of aligned values. Terms such as *leadership*, *diversity*, *excellence*, *flexible*, *team*, *skills*, and *communication* belong to a corporate register. Moreover, they are routinely used as a cluster in ways that foreground the values and viewpoints underpinning a corporate worldview. Indeed, they do not simply foreground them, they are manifestations of the hegemony underlying that worldview, representing the interests of a powerful social sector in ways that routinely saturate people's consciousness with a sense that things are just naturally "that way." Whether or not people like how things are, they accept things "as is" (Williams 1977). Over the past 10 to 15 years, higher education has become increasingly saturated with this corporate register in ways that manifest a general corporate hegemony. Thus, people's use of *leadership*, *diversity*, and so on in higher education administrative and promotional discourse are not simply borrowings from the corporate register. Rather, they indicate a hegemonic entrenchment of corporate notions of what learning should be, and what good students as proto-employees should be, in ways that saturate practices, attitudes, and forms of organization throughout the academy.

This saturation is most evident in the parts of the academy that students and faculty loosely term "the administration," i.e., that which oversees and represents: the offices of the president (overseeing and representing the whole school) and the dean of faculty (overseeing faculty business), student and residential life (overseeing the structure and regulation of student life), and Admissions, and Communications and Development (representing the school to the outside, recruiting students, tracking alumni, raising money, and making the school visible to the world at large). The recasting of what was once *race* or *minority* as *multicultural* and then *diverse* takes on meaning in this institutional context. And in this way, what began as a study of students' shifting sense of ethnic identity became a study of the institutional structures and attitudes encompassing those students' lives.

STUDENT AND RESIDENTIAL LIFE: PLAYING WELL WITH OTHERS

Judging from interviews with students, officership in student organizations at this (and similar) schools involves a sort of management-training program in budgeting, space allotment, program planning, and time management. In fact, in student life "participation" seems increasingly oriented toward the inculcation of team skills, the capacity for several people to pool expertise in carrying out tasks without explicit direction. This is even more apparent in residential life activities and goals, which stress the design and implementation of student living arrangements that facilitate and enhance the emergence of specific forms of sociality. This has been a particular concern at this college, which, like most of its kind, has had fraternity houses and other forms of off-campus living. In 1995, the College's Board of

Trustees and president decided to close fraternity houses without disbanding fraternities and to integrate all students into participation in a common residential community. Fraternities would no longer hold and distribute their unique form of symbolic capital (status and prestige) through control over residential and dining space and, above all, party space. Instead, the college would designate spaces for living, eating, and partying on an all-inclusive basis, through housing lotteries, full meal plans, and applications for use of social spaces. Fraternities and sororities would continue to exist as (ideally) one of many kinds of clubs students might join, but they would no longer dominate student sociality. The college would establish the rules for use of social space, and the student government would administer them. The new regime was based on the hope (buoyed by survey results) that "higher ability students" would be attracted to a school less dominated by frat party life. It was concomitantly assumed and widely asserted that these better students would also be attracted by "higher diversity numbers."

This plan for regulated, diverse, and team-oriented student sociality is mapped out and overseen by the offices of student and residential life and held together "on the ground" by a system of Resident Advisors—RAs for short. In the RA training manual, the RA's *community building* job is conceptualized and mapped out as a task structure. The introduction, "Getting ready for the RA position: Preparing the foundation for community building," begins as follows:

> So you are going to be a resident assistant. Welcome to a *community* of *learners* who are as *diverse* as the *global community*, who possess a myriad of *individual skills* and *talents* and who use their *differences* to *come together* in a *commitment* to make residence living a *positive learning experience*. [Emphasis added]

The italicized elements are terms typical of the Residential Life register. They are also SDSs in that they have specialized meanings that emerge from this institutional perspective and operate as a system of connected concepts. Take for example the idea of RAs as "a *community of learners* ... as *diverse* as the *global community*." The word *community* has a range of possible referents: people who live together, or work together, or have the same interests, or the same occupations; people who live in a small interactive society; or people who never meet. Here it refers to a collective of people enacting the same role, as RA, but it does not actually refer to everyone living together on a dorm floor. *Learners* could refer to any student, but here it has a specialized sense of someone willing to learn a task in coordination with others (all assumed to be *learners* like oneself). *Diverse* may (though it is unclear) refer to racial or ethnic difference. However, what *diversity* does have is a sense of being skill-like insofar as it plays an instrumental role in community building. As we will see shortly, this is quite compatible with the way in which *diversity* is currently conceptualized in corporate practice. But *diversity* in the RA training manual, unlike its corporate use, also retains some sense of race-like historical specificity and some sense that it should be respected in and of itself. The manual states that the RA should "role model an appreciation for multiculturalism and diversity" and should actively pursue policies and activities to create an inclusive environment through meeting attendance, movie showings, discussion groups, conversation, and so on, aimed at fostering mutual understanding and appreciation. This is consistent with the manual's definition of the RA role as that of facilitator, as agent of change and growth:

> Being a part of the administration means that you can have a very *significant* and *positive impact* on the lives of those in your hall *community* ... *Programming* should provide students with *opportunities* for *learning* and *growth* during their residential living and academic experiences at The College. [Emphasis added]

In short, the RA role is that of apprentice social engineer. Since the late 1800s, the manager's job has been to use techniques and procedures that sustain organizational operation and meet its goals. Although the compartmentalized management structures of classic modernism have shifted in recent decades toward a flexible team leader model, what has become firmly established is the definition of the management role as occupied by a person who uses a skill set to bring about results: a cause-and-effect model. It is no accident that residential life administrative discourse has become utterly saturated with such references and assumptions. Thus, the RA manual explains the RA role in terms of, e.g., *time management*, *programming*, *handling confrontation*, and *conflict resolution*, all conceptualized as *skills*, as techniques that can be learned and which, if done correctly, should provide consistent outcomes. The training manual conceptualizes each of the aspects of the RA role as techniques that build on other techniques: there are lists of tips and exercises for time management that should in turn facilitate program planning, and techniques for structuring how one talks and interacts so as to facilitate conflict management and resolution. Underlying these conceptions of action is a fundamental belief that people can plan outcomes and make them happen and that students acting in concert can create a peaceful well-behaved residence hall full of students actively learning outside and inside the classroom.

DIVERSITY AND FLEXIBILITY: THE EMERGENT MODEL

In the social psychological model analyzed here, people are imagined in terms of defining traits or qualities and as rational and responsive to beneficial choices and clear communication. This blueprint-like conception makes social engineering feasible. Much the same social psychology is presupposed in the human relations literature on building workplace diversity and the related literature on team building. For example, Loden (1996) lays out strategies for shifting company culture toward *valuing diversity*. She approaches diversity as "those important human characteristics that impact individuals' values, opportunities and perceptions of self and others at work" (1996: 14). These include core traits—age, ethnicity, gender, mental/physical abilities and characteristics, race, sexual orientation—and secondary traits— "communication style, education, family status, military experience, organizational role and level, religion, first language, geographic location, income, work experience, work style" (1996: 15). The core traits, of which everyone has some version, form the basis for aggregation into larger groups. Traits are thus dry-cleaned of residue from history, structural inequality, and discrimination. Such residue is seen as "EEO/AA" (Equal Employment Opportunity/Affirmative Action) business for which federal regulations exist. Valuing diversity means that employees learn to stop seeing diversity as barriers and start seeing them as contributions, the proper approach for "today's more flexible, empowering, team-focused organization" (1996: 32). Training manuals are even clearer about the need to downplay social history. Rasmussen (1995) decries EEO/AA "quota filling" as a "detrimental and divisive" approach which "only adds to conflict and reinforces stereotypes" (1995: 4) and defines *diversity* as "the mosaic of people who bring a variety of backgrounds, styles, perspectives, values and beliefs as assets to the groups and organizations with which they interact," a definition which "applies to and includes everyone" (1995: 8). All this is a preface to a book of exercises including "games, questionnaires, group activities" (1995: 3) designed to foster a climate that values diversity in the ways outlined above.

To some extent, the key assumptions underlying this approach to diversity implementation turn up in residential life community planning and, in more dilute form, in student organizational life generally: diversity as a set of traits that contributes to the whole; the importance of teamwork; an investment in analyses that have instrumental applications; an understanding of human social situations as problems that can be solved rationally through strategies and clear communication; and, organizing everything else, a firm belief that people can and will want to acquire social techniques that can bring about desired outcomes and that can be orchestrated into coherent plans with predictable outcomes. But corporate diversity planning and student life do differ. Students are not employees with jobs to lose if they don't cooperate. They are, as college administrators often put it, "paying customers" who live together in a 17- to 22-year-old world.

Students do not have the same investment in outcomes that employees do. And up to now, not much has kept them from forming their own little groups, especially since fraternities and sororities remain alive and well. In student life, the diversity-as-contribution-to-the-whole model has featured significantly in the print and web literature of cultural organizations. For example, the Afro-Latino student organization lists as its goal "to help preserve the cultural identities of Black and Latin students at the College"; the international student organization "introduces and stimulates interest in the various cultures represented within the College community"; the Middle East organization "seeks to educate the College community about Middle Eastern culture"; the West African and African organization lists as one of its aims "educating the College Community on issues affecting those regions"; the Latino organization "educates the College community about the political situations and diverse cultures of Central America, South America and the Caribbean." By contrast, the fraternity-sorority council states as its purpose "to serve as the student governing body for all recognized private societies ... promote the academic goals and mission of The College ... work toward internal organization and self-regulation of all activities and strive for enhanced community and communication amongst all recognized private societies ... (and to) work toward a complimentary [sic] educational experience for the development of skills in leadership, scholarship, friendship, and community service." (All statements cited from the college's student activities website). There is no reference to *skills* or *leadership* in any of the multicultural organization statements and, not surprisingly, no reference to culture or educating the community in the fraternity-sorority council statement.

There is, however, a new model in town, one which pulls all these SDSs together much more tightly into a corporate alignment. About four years before this writing, the school joined the Boston chapter of the Posse Program (there are also chapters in Chicago, New York, and Los Angeles). Posse was established in 1989 on the premise that students of colour would best succeed in predominantly white colleges if they went through in a close cohort or "posse" (the term was consciously appropriated from urban slang). Posse recruits students from the chapter area, and Posse's subscriber schools take cohorts of ten students per year. Students receive scholarships covering 75 per cent of their total fees. Posse's 2001 Annual Report (p.2) states its mission as follows:

> The Posse Foundation identifies public high school students with *extraordinary academic and leadership potential* who may be overlooked by the traditional college-selection process. *Working with its partner universities*, the Foundation extends to these students the opportunity to pursue personal achievement and academic *excellence* by awarding them four-year scholarships and placing them in supportive, multi-cultural *teams* ("posses") of ten students.... The concept of a posse works for both students and college campuses, and is rooted in the belief that a small, diverse group of talented students—a posse—*carefully selected and trained, can serve as a catalyst for increased individual and community development.* As the United States becomes an increasingly multi-cultural society, Posse believes that *leaders* in this new century should reflect the country's rich demographic mix, and that the key to a promising future for our nation rests on the *ability of strong leaders from diverse backgrounds to develop consensus solutions to complex social problems.* One of the primary aims of the Posse Program is to train these leaders of tomorrow.

I have italicized phrases and clauses that especially resonate with a corporate register and underlined elements that foreground cause-and-effect, the social engineering elements. I particularly draw the reader's attention to the SDS *leader/leadership*. The specialized meaning that emerges here is the notion of *leader* as change facilitator through team action, rather than, as is the case in student life more generally, service as club officer or athletic captain. Compare Posse's language to this selection from the website <http://www.innovativebrains.com/leadershipteamwork.htm]: "Our team-building and leadership programs incorporate individual and group development training initiatives, individual development exercises and discussion as tools to catalyze personal and group growth." The website continues, "These benefits result from learning team skills that include heightened abilities in the areas of … " followed by this list: Communication, Trust, Respect, Honesty, Problem-solving, Decision-making, Capitalizing on diversity, Effective leadership, and Effective followership. The site continues, "People empowered with these skills can meet challenges with better and more creative solutions.… "

These basic premises of team and leadership training saturate the Posse Program design. Posse recruits for articulateness, confidence, the drive to succeed, leadership potential, and the capacity to work in teams and with different kinds of people (Sutton 2002). Team-building is a key theme in their program, as one of the annual Posse Plus retreat facilitators explained to me recently. The chapter to which each participating school belongs sends a facilitator team to that school once a year to administer an off-campus weekend retreat for that school's Posse students plus two or three non-Posse invitees. This retreat opened with a message about the importance of community building as a means of addressing campus diversity issues. The ensuing group sessions used role-play and highly structured discussion to explore and reinforce themes of overcoming stereotypes, working together toward a common goal, and developing a college identity. Especially striking (to me and to a number of students) was the thematic repetition across the different sessions (why was a college identity important, how was it formed, how was its formation inhibited by stereotypes) and the rigourousness with which the trainers monitored and reinforced the discussion rules (such as taking turns at precisely one-minute intervals). While students questioned these rules to each other, I did not see them question the trainers. After the retreat, a colleague versed in team training techniques confirmed to me that the exercises and the monitoring of process were common practice with some trainers.

What strikes me most about this program is how coherently it is engineered. Previous multicultural recruitments have focussed on leadership in campus activities, often played out by "educating the public" as the multicultural organization websites indicate. Posse is strongly oriented toward the production of specific outcomes: the inculcation of a sense of diversity as an element of team formation and leadership and the inculcation of a sense of organizational identity that might be expected to transfer readily from the college to the workplace, built as it is around a team identity. Finally, in the Posse Annual Report, *diverse/diversity* appeared both more frequently than *multicultural* (by seven to two) and more semantically flexible: the Posse team and American society are referred to as *multicultural*, while *diverse/diversity* is used in conjunction with backgrounds, with students generally, or on its own. This pattern matches that which I described for the college's administrative discourse. Thus, we see *diversity* emerge as the more general term, the one more compatible with qualities desired by the corporate world.

WHO AND WHAT IS EDUCATION FOR?

I have traced the spread of corporate-oriented discourse organization (especially SDSs) into different aspects of college life. The social management register has come to saturate the "officialdom" of student life much as it saturates the "officialdom" of corporate life. The use of words like *skills* and *team* function as SDSs indicating their alignment. But there are differences in how *diversity* is used. In the corporate world, *diversity* is heavily integrated with *skill* and *team* in notions of flexible management: individuals, especially when organized in teams, have diverse traits that (skill-like) optimize their productivity. The RA manual language tends toward this usage. But students writing for student organization websites tend to separate *diversity* from *skills* discourses. Cultural organization websites equate *diversity* and *multiculturalism* with group identity—*African-American/black*, *Latino*, *Asian*. The sorority-fraternity council website connects *skills*, *leadership*, and *communication* with its assertion of self-regulation. *Team* rarely surfaces in student-authored web language whereas the non-student authors of residential life manuals do tend to integrate usage of *diversity* with *skill*, *leadership*, and *teamwork*. The Posse program language provides the tightest discursive fit with corporate usage. Residential life and Posse language use *diversity* in ways that sound more like individual-embodied traits than an historically shaped group identity. *Diversity*, like *skills*, becomes something possessed by an individual.

Why has corporate discourse spread into college life? Spring (1998: 150ff) raises this question in the context of growing globalization. As an increasing proportion of the college-age population pursues a four-year degree, college increasingly fulfills the function of socializing the potential workforce toward the needs of the workplace. Reports underwritten by major corporations call for colleges to train students in skills useful for the global economy and increase pressure to orient course content toward that end. Unlike training-oriented college programs like business administration, the dilemma for students in liberal arts schools is: what on earth does one learn in English or anthropology or music courses that one can "use" in a career? Not really the course content. By and large, liberal arts education initiates students into ways of thinking about what knowledge is, how it fits together, how the world works, and who they are in that world. Such knowledge may include specific skills but cannot, en masse, be reduced to a skill set. Yet such reduction dominates much writing about liberal arts, even by liberal arts institutions. College publications routinely list, as the goals of education, skills transferable from schoolroom to workplace, such as *critical thinking*, *communication*, *time-management*, *writing skills*, *math skills*, *analytical skills*, *research skills*, and *problem-solving*. Lost here is the older division in educational philosophy between (skills-based) training and (knowledge-based) learning. How did this easy typological equation come about? How does *critical thinking*, once a sign of intellectual independence and mastery, come to be parallelled with *time-management*, a discipline steeped in the industrial tradition of Scientific Management? Such equation marks a shift toward a new form of workerhood—the middle-class flexible self-manager.

In *Flexible Bodies* (1994), Emily Martin tracks the emergence of the notion of flexibility in discourses of immunity and discourses of work. She posits *flexibility* as an important new element in the American construction of self. She extends this idea in a recent article, describing the worker's internalization of corporate culture as "an 'other' inside managing many parts of the self" (Martin 1997: 249). Ideally this would result in fluid, self-regulating groups "guided by flexible corporate policies" toward "achieving a flexible corporate culture" (1997: 251). This internalization is central to the "new" corporate culture of flexibility that has, over the past 30 or so years, arisen as the cost-effective organizational model. It has ideologically displaced the old ideal of businesses organized like a flow chart into compartments, each with a specialized manager and employees doing fixed tasks. I say "ideologically" because in real-world terms, much of the top-down control remains firmly in place. What is expected of workers is the capacity to fit their own abilities, or *skills*, to the task structure as needed, instead of limiting their work to task structures that fit their specific capabilities. The creation of this flexible self begins years before people hit the job market. It is well underway in college life, with the stress on residential programming, the refrain that students learn as much (or more) outside as (or than) inside the classroom, the valuing of transferable skills over subject-specific content, and the résumé-like quality of involvement in extracurricular college activities. Posse's business venture into diversity recruitment follows the favoured corporate pattern: the diverse self as the flexible self as the team self. The concomitant reconstruction of *diversity* is based on the idea that there is no value to those elements of identity forged in the historical inequities of appropriated or exploited labour, but that value can be inserted into identity in proportion to the worker's worth to the company.

NOTES

[1] My thanks to Henry Rutz and Susan Mason for suggestions and background information.

WORKS CITED

Loden, Marilyn. 1996. *Implementing Diversity*. Chicago, IL: Irwin Professional Publishers.

Martin, Emily. 1994. *Flexible Bodies*. Boston, MA: Beacon Press.

———. 1997. Managing Americans: Policy and changes in the meaning of work and self. In *Anthropology of Policy: Critical Perspectives on Governance and Power*. Ed. Chris Shore and Susan Wright. 239-57. London: Routledge.

The Posse Foundation, Inc. Annual Report 2001.

Rasmussen, Tina. 1995. *Diversity: The ASTD Trainer's Sourcebook*. Hightstown, NJ: McGraw Hill.

Spring, Joel. 1998. *Education and the Rise of the Global Economy*. Mahwah, NJ: Lawrence Erlbaum.

Sutton, Jennifer. 2002. Posse Power. In *Vermont Magazine* January-February.

Urciuoli, Bonnie. 2003. Excellence, leadership, skills, diversity: Marketing liberal arts education." In *Language and Communication* 23: 385-408.

Williams, Raymond. 1977. *Marxism and Literature*. New York and Oxford: Oxford University Press.

Websites cited

http://www.usnews.com/usnews/edu/college/rankings/brief/libartco/libartco_campdiv_brief.php

http://www.hamilton.edu/admission/diversity/

http://www.hamilton.edu/college/Student_Activities/

11 | CENSORSHIP, SURVEILLANCE, AND MIDDLE EAST STUDIES IN THE CONTEMPORARY UNITED STATES

David A. McMurray

THE GUYS IN THE BACK

Every evening since 9/11 a rag-tag bunch of middle-aged pacifists gather at 5 o'clock in front of our small town courthouse to wave peace flags and hold up posters with hand-painted messages telling passing motorists to "Bring the Troops Home," or "Peace Is Patriotic," or some other such antiwar message. I was there one day in the fall of 2003 holding up a sign when a pickup truck stopped in the middle of traffic. An angry college student in the military reserve got out and yelled over at us, "You all make me sick! I served for ten years in the army so that you pukes could enjoy the freedom to stand there and tear down our country." He said something more, but I was too confused to catch it. Wasn't he making our point? Wasn't he deriding us for exercising the freedoms he claimed we all enjoyed thanks to him? Someone on our side, no doubt more hardened to this kind of confrontation, shouted back, "Get a haircut." The irony of that remark cracked us up. Yet I left the courthouse that night unable to figure out what made the student so angry—even as he seemed to recognize our right to be there protesting.

The next day in my college introductory anthropology class on the Middle East I asked the students to help me think through what the reservist meant. There were maybe 30 students in the room. Most were there because the course fulfilled a distribution requirement in the undergraduate curriculum. Nonetheless, I assumed that they shared my general sympathy and curiosity—if not enthusiasm—for the peoples and cultures of the Middle East. I assumed that at least the attempt to understand how other people lived presented an interesting challenge to the students or they wouldn't take the course.

Now I think I was being naïve. The row of males sitting along the back wall began the confrontation. "The guy was probably sick at the sight of people questioning what our troops are doing, right now, while soldiers are being killed," one of them said. Another chimed in to back him up, "Yeah, they put their lives on the line. At least people back home can shut up and support them." I sputtered on about having rights that are never exercised or about the way questioning war policies might actually save lives. Another student summed it up with an interesting, very American, simile. He said, "It's like a sports team. When you get on the field, you want all of your fans behind you. You want to know that they're rooting for you. You need to know that they approve of what you're doing; that they want you to win. Otherwise you might as well be cheering for the other side, you know, the Arabs."

I never really recovered the class's good will after that. I felt a yawning chasm had opened up between how I thought about rights and education and the Middle East and how my students thought of these subjects. My left/progressive gut reaction was to sympathize with the downtrodden and suspect authority. The guys along the back wall had grown to respond in almost the exact opposite fashion. I decided to start looking into these differences more closely and came to discover that there had been a serious intrusion of reactionary, jingoistic political forces into the university. This was particularly true when it came to teaching and researching about the Middle East or the Arab and Islamic worlds. My research into the sources as well as repercussions of right-wing attacks against Middle East Studies on American campuses forms the subject of this chapter. Though I do not want to suggest that they are a part of any organized movement, I guess I do have the boys in the back to thank for opening my eyes to the presence of such forces.

THE NATURE OF THE ATTACKS

Conservative assaults on Middle East Studies shifted into high gear after 9/11, with the emergence of a two-pronged attack strategy, which combined a demonization of the whole field with the targeting of individual specialists. A well-organized publicity campaign was launched, which outlined the "failings" of Middle Eastern studies within the academy. A year later a highly contentious list, naming the most egregious offenders, began circulating.

I want to discuss the nature of these attacks, that is, the "naming of names" campaign associated with the right-wing pundit Daniel Pipes and his "Campus Watch" website, as well as the general charges of programmatic failure aimed at the field of Middle East studies as a whole and which are associated with Martin Kramer's book, *Ivory Towers on Sand: The Future of Middle East Studies in America* (2001). Second, I want briefly to lay out the sources and tactics used in these attacks. Finally, I want to sketch out their short- and long-term effects, paying special attention to whether or not the pressures exerted by higher levels of intimidation, censorship, and surveillance have brought about changes in the production of knowledge in the field in the form of altered teaching, writing, and research interests.

Kramer published *Ivory Towers* in the month after 9/11. He levels several related charges against Middle East Studies, one of which is that the field ignores American national interests. This is particularly the case, he states, when it comes to the threat posed by political Islam, which Middle East experts spend more time excusing than analyzing. Kramer also criticizes the field for snubbing hard-nosed, empiricist, policy-oriented analysis and instead flirting with arcane theory, particularly post-colonial theory associated with Edward Said's work, *Orientalism*. He also levels the charge that mountains of money and time have been wasted on researching civil society in the Middle East and looking for democratizing forces while ignoring or making apologies for the continued power of the authoritarian states that dominate the region.

As a solution to these symptoms of corruption within Middle East Studies, Kramer proposed that the government "attach strings" to its Title VI funding of Middle East Centers. This proposal represented an alarming development for many professors associated with area studies centres because, no matter whether they were affiliated with Latin American, African, East Asian, or Middle Eastern centres, they have traditionally received a share of their operating budgets and a good number of student scholarships from Title VI and thus did not want to see these important funds jeopardized. As an aside, let me briefly explain that area studies centres developed early in the twentieth century in American Ivy League universities as an outgrowth of American evangelism. The Cold War was the next historical moment when more secular and imperialistic motives led to a desire to develop local experts via the expansion of area centres (Prashad 2003). "Title VI" refers to the "Language Development" section of the National Defense Education Act (NDEA) which was passed by Congress in 1958 and which "recognized that the defense and security of the nation were inseparably bound with education" (Scarfo 1997). This act continues to be a major source of funding for the study of non-Western languages in the United States.

In September 2002, partly inspired by Kramer's book, Daniel Pipes launched the website "Campus Watch," which, according to one of his admirers, was to act as "a corrective to what [Pipes] called, 'the intellectual failure of Middle East studies, the tendency toward political extremism, the intolerance of alternative viewpoints, the apologetics, and the abuse of power toward students.' The site included a compilation of dossiers on eight offending professors, and a page inviting students to fink on teachers who cross the line" (Cavanaugh 2002).

The launching of the Campus Watch site was met with protest in Middle East Studies circles and with approval and delight in the right-wing media. Pipes's attempts at character assassination were compared to McCarthyite tactics by some commentators, which seemed to have had an effect. By the end of the month the "dossiers" of the original eight offenders had been quietly removed. The call for students to report on offences committed by their professors remained up. It was joined by a new section devoted to listing the names of the first hundred or so academics who petitioned the Campus Watch website to be listed as supporters in solidarity with the original eight.

SOURCES OF THE ATTACKS

The loss of Republican seats in the 1982 elections, the defeat of Judge Bork's nomination to the Supreme Court in 1987, and the election of Clinton to the presidency in 1992 put the conservative movement into ideological overdrive. These events helped elevate into positions of leadership the most activist right-wing elements of the Republican Party. They were the ones, led by Representative Newt Gingrich of Georgia, who understood that this was war. They were the ones who perfected the strategy of defining the political struggles of the day as battles over moral values. They excelled at demonizing their adversaries and canonizing their leaders.

The spread of a paranoiac, pessimistic, anti-statist Manicheism within the American conservative movement no doubt provided much of the fertile soil for the growth of the political thinking of pundits like Pipes and Kramer. The millions of dollars flowing out of various conservative foundations and corporations into the coffers of right-wing think tanks, organizations, institutions, and journals has helped Pipes and Kramer earn accolades and their livings as intellectual agitators for conservative causes.

Now that right-wing hawks control much of the Bush administration, the government has got into the act of doling out honours to those who would toe the conservative line. Witness the fact that Daniel Pipes was given a recess appointment by President George W. Bush in August 2003 to the government board known as the United States Institute of Peace. Presumably he got the appointment in part because his work as a campus watchdog had not gone unappreciated by those above him in conservative ranks. His reputation for Islam-bashing did cause a few Democratic senators to hold up his nomination during the regular session, but that was not seen as an impediment within the Bush administration, and so he was given a recess appointment.

But most importantly, Pipes, and to a lesser extent Kramer, were touted in right-wing circles because they helped in the larger move to provide a viable, post-Soviet external threat in the form of Arabs and Islam. Their alarm cries over the dangers posed to America by Islamic forces on the outside and academic sympathizers on the inside struck just the right chord, particularly after the terrorist attacks of 9/11 and the increased demonization of Muslims which followed (Barry and Lobe 2002).

TACTICS

In terms of tactics, the post-9/11 attacks on the political biases of Middle East Studies practitioners, combined with the use of student monitors to carry out classroom surveillance, are a continuation of the "Culture Wars" initiated during the Reagan decade. Authors on the right, such as Dinesh D'Souza (*Illiberal Education*, 1991) and Lynne Cheney (*Telling the Truth*, 1996), challenged the new concerns with race, gender, and non-Western societies, which were working their way into curricula and politicizing the social sciences and humanities (Kors and Silverglate 1988: 5). The solution, according to such conservative intellectuals, was for parents, civic leaders, alumni, administrators, and college trustees to confront the tyranny of "tenured radicals" and to reassert control over what constitutes a liberal education (Menand 1996: 19 fn.1). To that end, Reed Irvine, founder of the right-wing media monitoring group, Accuracy in Media, set up a sister organization, Accuracy in Academia (AIA), in 1985. He sought, in his words, to "document and oppose political bias in the classroom" via the use of volunteer student monitors (Hunter 1991: 214–15).

The call to defund Middle East Studies and its centres, or at least to establish an oversight board, plausibly gets its inspiration from the 1995 right-wing movement to "defund the left" that grew out of Newt Gingrich's "Contract with America." One of Gingrich's henchman at the time, Grover Norquist, was quoting as saying, "We will hunt [these liberal groups] down one by one and extinguish their funding sources" (People for the American Way 1996).

The specific tactic of developing a blacklist of Middle East scholars, such as the one used on Pipes's original Campus Watch website, may owe some of its inspiration and impetus to the immediate post-9/11 appearance of a report by Senator Joe Lieberman's and Lynne Cheney's organization called the American Council of Trustees and Alumni (ACTA, founded in 1995). The report, entitled "Defending Civilization: How Our Universities Are Failing America and What Can Be Done about It," accuses scholars who do not defend American foreign policy of "giving comfort to its adversaries" (Gonzalez 2001). The original report goes on to cite 100 cases of professors who made statements, or carried out actions in reference to 9/11, which the report finds to be anti-American.

Perhaps the most important inspiration for Pipes's Campus Watch initiative was the success in general in recent years of conservative "watch" groups dedicated to ferreting out liberal bias in all aspects of government, the media, and private life. The most influential and effective has proven to be the "ABA Watch" initiated by the arch-conservative Federalist Society. The group is dedicated to attacking so-called liberal judicial bias, as well as "documenting the American Bar Association's allegedly liberal stands on abortion, the death penalty and gun control" (Alterman 2003: 250). So successful has this group been that President George W. Bush even pushed the American Bar Association out of the judicial nomination vetting process in favour of the Federalist Society.

The "ABA Watch" was joined after 9/11 by two less influential but no less partisan watch programs launched by journals, namely, the "Kumbaya Watch" initiated by the *National Review* and the "Idiocy Watch" begun by the *New Republic*. Both were intended to heap satirical scorn on liberals and progressives in the aftermath of the terrorist attacks.

EFFECTS OF THE ATTACKS

Let us turn to an analysis of the effects of Kramer's and Pipes's attacks, starting first with Kramer's assaults on Middle East Studies. Remember, Kramer claimed that the field ignores American national interests, downplays the threat posed by political Islam (which Middle East experts spend more time excusing than analyzing), slavishly subscribes to post-colonial theory associated with Edward Said, and focusses on civil society and democratic potential while ignoring or making apologies for the continued power of authoritarian states. I would say that some of his charges have had an influence within the field; some have not. For example, Lisa Anderson, past president of the Middle East Studies Association, seemed to agree with Kramer's charge that the field peddled a certain rosy image of the Middle East and concentrated on civil society at the expense of authoritarianism. She stated that she thought the practitioners of Middle East Studies were purposefully under-reporting the extent of the social, political, cultural, and economic degradation suffered by the peoples of the region over the last two decades. Professors remained silent, she said, in order to preserve their ties to the region or to protect colleagues there. But regardless of the rationale behind their collective silence, Anderson said, it still constituted a professional abdication of responsibility (Anderson 2003). Plausibly, the attacks of outsiders like Kramer and Pipes were behind the decision to publish her negative assessment of this aspect of Middle East Studies.

Or take the example of Prof. Henry Munson, a respected scholar of Islam and North Africa, who wrote an evaluation of Pipes's charge that the field of Middle East Studies coddled Islam by celebrating its virtues while ignoring the threat of radicalism. Munson confined his evaluation to a comparison of Pipes's work with that of John Esposito, a prolific compiler of a dozen books on contemporary Islamic subjects and thus one of the most widely read authorities in the field. Munson determined that, yes, there existed a romanticized, apologetic portrayal of Islamic militancy and that Esposito embodied it. He declared, "Reading Esposito, one would never know that anti-Semitism is indeed a serious problem in the Islamic world. Pipes demonizes Islamic militancy without analyzing the various social, nationalistic, and religious grievances that fuel it. Esposito idealizes Islamic militancy while downplaying the bigotry, fanaticism, and violence associated with it. Students of Islamic militancy need to avoid both Pipes's demonization and Esposito's idealization" (Munson 2002: 8). Obviously, again, Munson's assessment has been influenced directly by the charges of our pundit duo.

On the other hand, most commentators have rejected Kramer's charge that arcane theory dominates the field of Middle East Studies. This is the position of Middle Eastern history professor Juan Cole of the University of Michigan, one of the original Campus Watch targets. He argued (in a rebuttal to similar charges made by Kramer's fellow traveller Stanley Kurtz), that the majority of Middle East Studies scholars are quite mainstream (Cole 2003).

Turning to the charges that the field promotes policy irrelevant research, coddles Islam, and is insufficiently concerned with national interests such as the threats posed by Islamic fundamentalists—all of these charges are considered by several of my informants to be disingenuous.

A professor of political science who specializes in the Middle East reported to me that pre-9/11 coverage of Islamist groups did in fact tend to focus on militant activists such as al-Qaida, the Taliban, Hamas, Hezbollah, the GIA, etc.. The more politically oriented movements such as the Jordanian Islamists are the ones who received short shrift. Another professor of Middle East political science told me that, contrary to what Kramer, Pipes, and others might imagine, there is very little policy relevance pressure in political science circles anywhere in the American academy. As for Kramer's charge that Middle East Studies missed the threat posed by Islamic militancy, one interviewee pointed out that "The Israelis with all of their highly touted military intelligence capabilities missed forecasting the 1973 October War. Are professors of Middle East Studies in the United States to be held to a higher standard?"

Let me turn now to a brief evaluation of the effects of Pipes's Campus Watch and his follow-up "Apologists" list.

Most of the original eight targeted by Pipes lamented the fact that their e-mail systems had been rendered useless by the inundation of hate mail in the months following their appearance on the Campus Watch list. A few had also received death threats in the wake of the publicity. A couple of them also noted with chagrin that these highly contentious charges against them had spread worldwide and were thus impossible to retract or rebut.

Columbia's Hamid Dabashi, Chair of the Department of Middle East and Asian Languages and Cultures, worried not about himself in the aftermath of Campus Watch, but about the campus climate. "It preempts the possibilities of civilized dissent, civil discourse, and public debate…" he said. Debashi also pointed to the concerted efforts spearheaded by some alumni and Columbia's Hillel Center to harass him and get him into trouble with the university administration. He continues his pro-Palestinian activities, he claims, but with fairly constant outside interference and with only tepid backing from Columbia's administrators (Dabashi 2003). Shahid

Alam and Rashid Khalidi, both of the original eight, decry the way the Campus Watch site urges students to take classes so as to monitor them for political content. Khalidi equates this tactic with the kinds of security arrangements found under police state dictatorships.

The last group to be publicly cited by the Campus Watch are the so-called "Apologists." These are the hundred odd faculty members from around the country who e-mailed in their support for the original eight. I surveyed a dozen of the named fellow travellers and discovered a wide variety of experiences. While some had suffered no effects one way or the other, a couple had been tarred and feathered in their local campus papers and via e-mail during the year following the publication of their names. One of them, an untenured faculty member, was more seriously alarmed by an alumni-led assault directly tied to Campus Watch. His department chair and then the dean eventually stepped in to protect him and get the campaign against him derailed.

CONCLUSION

It would appear that Kramer and Pipes on their own have not had a profound effect on the field or on the practitioners of Middle East Studies. In spite of their advocacy, altering the research being done so that it becomes more policy relevant does not seem to be happening. Focussing studies of Islamist groups so that militant factions receive greater coverage is already par for the course. Limiting the popularity of so-called arcane theory is probably another non-starter for the simple reason that arcane theory has a rather small purchase on the field of Middle East Studies to begin with.

The second thrust associated with Pipes, that is, the naming of names so as to draw attention to academics who are supposedly anti-American, Pro-Muslim, or anti-Israel, has had slightly better success. Some practitioners in the field have had to suffer the inconveniences and insults that followed upon their names being made public. However, none of them claim that the unwanted publicity caused them to change their worldview, teaching methods, or politics.

I do not want to leave the impression that nothing influential has happened. No doubt the level of self-censorship goes up during traumatic periods, such as in the aftermath of 9/11. When well-publicized assaults on professors get added into the mix, the effects are surely important and traumatic for many who are involved. It is just that anxiety and self-censorship are difficult things to measure. Signs and symptoms remain vague and impressionistic.

One professor of Middle East Studies in the United States did relate to me that the personal blacklist attacks coupled with the urging of students to monitor classroom activities had given her pause. She now felt less secure and more concerned about her course contents. "What am I teaching? How is it presented? Is it fair? What are the risks?" she said were all questions that crossed her mind with greater frequency than in the pre Pipes/Kramer era.

On the other hand, passivity and quiescence are openly encouraged within the ranks of the professorate in the United States. Internalizing censorship, remaining above the political fray, and learning how to "go along to get along" form important aspects of one's professional training (Schmidt 2000). My just-mentioned colleague, when questioned along these lines, could not say that she normally sought to speak her mind in class or that she thought of herself as routinely exercising her right to free speech, so I am not sure her case provides much in the way of evidence of any change due specifically to Kramer and Pipes.

The assessments above apply to the attacks of Kramer and Pipes alone. When they are placed back into the larger context of a hawkish conservative assault on Middle East Studies, they should perhaps be judged differently. It is impossible to identify which of the numerous attacks on the field has done the most to slowly sway perceptions of what Middle East Studies is all about, but it does seem to be the case that perceptions are shifting, at least within the Washington Beltway. One of my informants mentioned that even though funding for Middle East Centers jumped 20 per cent in the aftermath of 9/11, the way the funding would be carried out in future appeared to be under scrutiny. Some of it, he speculated, would now be run through the National Security Agency, an intelligence branch of the government, with government service requirements tacked on, similar to those that apply to Congressman Boren's NSEP program (a controversial scholarship program set up in 1992 which offered funds in exchange for recipients going into government service after graduation). More unsettling is the gossip within Center circles that future funds will be run through the Department of Homeland Security.

At the least, and thanks especially to Kramer, Pipes, and their fellow Middle Eastern Studies basher, Stanley Kurtz, centres receiving Title VI funds may soon have their budgets scrutinized by a national supervisory board. In Kurtz's congressional testimony on 19 June 2003, he suggested that, since "Title VI-funded programs in Middle Eastern Studies (and other area studies) tend to purvey extreme and one-sided criticisms of American foreign policy…1) Congress needs to create a supervisory board to manage Title VI…. 2) Congress needs to pass an amendment that would take funding out of the hands of any Title VI center that engages in or abets a boycott of national security related scholarships. 3) …Congress needs to reduce the funding for Title VI. Specifically, the twenty million dollars of funding added to Title VI in the wake of September 11…" (Kurtz 2003).

Congressional subcommittee hearings during the summer culminated on 21 October 2003 with the House of Representatives passing The International Studies in Higher Education Act (H.R. 3077), which is a re-authorization of Title VI funding for international studies and which incorporated some of Kurtz's suggestions. Specifically, the bill has a provision to set up an advisory board to manage Title VI. Amy Newhall, Executive Director of the Middle East Studies Association, claims that, in fact, the bill is meant to target Middle East programs. She claims that it creates an oversight committee, which will be "an investigative body rather than an advisory group" (Craig 2003).

So, in sum, it would appear that pundits who specialize in attacking Middle East Studies have had mixed results when it comes to affecting professors, research, or the larger field. However, something more serious may be shaping up at the institutional level. Wealthier, more powerful, and autonomous universities may be able to stave off the worst effects of politically directed funding. Professors at more vulnerable public universities may have a harder time halting the spread by the radical right of the ideological culture wars into their Middle East Studies careers and classrooms.

That this trend is spreading beyond the confines of Middle East Studies is testified to by the fact that in early 2004, Republicans in the House of Representatives introduced legislation calling for a version of an "Academic Bill of Rights." This follows a model of legislation developed by a fellow right-wing agitator of Kramer and Pipes named David Horowitz, president of his own Center for the Study of Popular Culture. Under the guise of advocating *balance*, Horowitz and others on the right want to see additional conservative scholars hired at publicly funded universities. They also advocate for the creation of student watchdog committees to be set up to expose leftist bias in the classroom. Some of them even want rules put in place to forbid professors from introducing controversial topics unrelated to their courses. Students at Occidental College, Utah State, and Wichita State have successfully introduced such measures (Hebel 2004: A19). How far it will spread beyond these campuses remains to be seen.

WORKS CITED

Alterman, Eric. 2003. *What Liberal Media?: The Truth about Bias and the News*. New York, NY: Basic Books.

Anderson, Lisa. 2003. MESA Newsletter, February. <http://fp.arizona.edu/mesas-soc/Onlinenews/03presletter.htm>.

Barry, Tom, and Jim Lobe. 2002. US foreign policy—attention, right face, forward march.. *Policy Report*. Foreign Policy in Focus. April. <http://www.fpif.org/papers/02right/index.html>.

Cavanaugh, Tim. 2002. A bogus controversy over McCarthyism continues." Reasononline 28 October. <http://www.reason.com/hod/tc102802.shtml>.

Cheney, Lynne V. 1996. *Telling the Truth: Why Our Culture and Our Country Have Stopped Making Sense, and What We Can Do About It*. New York: Simon and Schuster.

Cole, Juan. 2003. Why are arch conservatives ganging up on the Middle East Studies Association?" History News Network. 20 January 20. <http://hnn.us/articles/1218.html>.

Craig, Bruce (ed.). 2003. NCH Washington update 9(41) 24 October. National Coalition for History [NCH] <http://www2.h-net.msu.edu/~nch>.

D'Souza, Dinesh. 1991. *Illiberal Education: The Politics of Race and Sex on Campus*. New York, NY: Free Press.

Dabashi, Hamid. 2003. Forget reds under the bed, there's Arabs in the attic. *The Times Higher Education Supplement*, 17 October. <http://www.thesis.co.uk/current_edition/story.aspx?story_id=2005019&window_type=print>.

Gonzalez, Robert J. 2001. Lynne Cheney-Joe Lieberman group puts out a black-list. *San Jose Mercury News* 31 December. Reprinted in Common Dreams News Center. <http://www.campus-watch-watch.com/>.

Hebel, Sara. 2004. Patrolling Professors' politics. *The Chronicle of Higher Education* 50(3) 13 February: A18–A19.

Hunter, James D. 1991. *Culture Wars: The Struggle to Define America*. New York, NY: Basic Books.

Kors, Alan Charles, and Harvey A. Silverglate. 1998. *The Shadow University: The Betrayal of Liberty on America's Campuses*. New York, NY: The Free Press.

Kramer, Martin. 2001. *Ivory Towers on Sand: The Future of Middle East Studies in America*. Washington, DC: The Washington Institute for Near East Policy.

Kurtz, Stanley. 2003. Statement of Stanley Kurtz before the Subcommittee on Select Education, Committee on Education and the Workforce. U.S. House of Representatives. June 19. <http://edworkforce.house.gov/hearings/108th/sed/titlevi61903/kurtz.htm>.

Menand, Louis (ed.). 1996. The limits of academic freedom. In *The Future of Academic Freedom*. Chicago, IL: University of Chicago Press.

Munson, Henry. 2002. Between Pipes and Esposito. *ISIM Newsletter* 10. July.

People for the American Way. 1996. Buying a movement: Right-wing foundations and American politics. <http://www.pfaw.org/pfaw/general/default.aspx?oid=2052>.

Pipes, Daniel. 2003. On being Borked. *New York Post* 26 August. <http://www.meforum.org/article/pipes/1220>.

Prashad, Vijay. 2002. Confronting the evangelical imperialists. *Counter Punch* 13 November. <http://www.counterpunch.org/prashad11132003.html>.

Said, Edward. 1979. *Orientalism*. New York, NY: Vintage Press.

Scarfo, Richard D. 1997. *The History of Title VI and Fulbright-Hays*. International Education in the New Global Era: Proceedings of a National Policy Conference on the Higher Education Act, Title VI, and Fulbright Hays Programs. <http://www.isop.ucla.edu/pacrim/title6>.

Schmidt, Jeff. 2000. *Disciplined Minds: A Critical Look at Salaried Professionals and the Soul-Battering System that Shapes Their Lives*. Lanham, MD: Rowman and Littlefield.

PART V | DEPARTURES

WHILE ANTHROPOLOGISTS SPEND MUCH TIME preparing their students for the culture shock of their fieldwork initiation, little ink has been spilled exploring the extreme dissonance that often attends our departures from the field. Fieldwork is often described as a rite of passage, yet that rite of passage needs, eventually, to be legitimized via the production of a dissertation, otherwise it just does not count. Whatever our romanticism regarding fieldwork, it is the ability to write in a conventional fashion that makes us professional anthropologists. Indeed, and contrary to what many think, one can become an anthropologist without doing fieldwork at all, but if you hope to land a job, you need a PhD and publications.

As Graeber notes, while reflexive anthropology and the debates around "writing culture" drew attention to the politics surrounding fieldwork, little attention was paid to the phase of writing the research up, and the politics that attend that process, back in our universities. Yet this is perhaps the most liminal of phases for academics. In fact, few actually complete the cycle. Dissertation writing is a time when most graduate students are likely to be penniless (scholarships typically dry up before the dissertation is completed) and vulnerable (they are often wracked by self doubt in this phase and feel utterly reliant on the good will, advice, letters of reference, and connections of supervisors and committee members). Their dearest friends become sibling rivals, as they all try to land scarce academic jobs. Those who fail in their quest to become *bona fide* anthropologists remain permanently liminal or vanish from the collective memory of the initiated, the employed. It is this fear that haunts the anxious graduate student that Graeber describes. Graeber also considers why a form of activism based on anarchist principles is not as easily routinized in the university system as are other political philosophies, even those concerned with possibilities of social transformation like Marxism. He explores the question of whether academics who are also anarchists can find a space within the academy or whether their political activism will make it more likely that they will be forced out.

Young reflects on the difficulties of ever leaving the field when one does fieldwork at home. She notes that when one works at home, it is often difficult to disentangle oneself enough from relationships made in the field in order to be able to write. The longer she remained "in the field," the more complex her relations with people became. Although her knowledge deepened, in one sense, the less certain she became, in another sense. And the professional risks became greater and greater as this liminal stage continued.

As Pratt (1986) notes, the need of anthropologists to establish themselves as professionals and to distinguish themselves from amateurs, the "other" foreigners found in the places where they work (such as missionaries, travellers, colonial administrators, and volunteers), is very strong. Too often, the result is recourse to a style of writing that is, in many ways, deeply boring. Gibb probes this long-recognized tender spot about what kind of writing is authoritative in anthropology and the pain of feeling compelled to write about her experiences in ways constrained by anthropological conventions. In between the lines is the fear of being excluded—by virtue of a writing style—from a profession that inculcates a sense of personhood and that is really more of a sensibility than a science.

Gibb's reflections on her intense relationships with people she meets while doing fieldwork and the unfathomable sadness that accompanies her departure from the field will surely resonate for anyone who has ever done fieldwork or suffered the loss that follows the end of an intense experience elsewhere. But such reflections had no place in her dissertation in Social Anthropology at Oxford. Yet we believe her chapter offers a truly redemptive moment for anthropology, as it explores the less contrived and honest relationship that she builds with her friend, Doctor Hassan, long after she leaves the field and the profession to become a creative writer. Doctor Hassan comes to know Gibb differently by reading her novels, and their relationship deepens.

In giving Doctor Hassan this opportunity to learn about her world, she honours their friendship by reciprocating in kind. All cross-cultural communication involves risk, but the world is full of curious and accepting people willing to learn about other people and ways of living. Anthropological curiosity flowing in all directions can only strengthen our relations with others.

WORKS CITED

Pratt, Mary Louise. 1986. Fieldwork in Common Places. In *Writing Culture: The Poetics and Politics of Ethnography*. Ed. James Clifford and George E. Marcus. 234–61. Berkeley, CA: University of California Press.

12 | THE AUTO-ETHNOGRAPHY THAT CAN NEVER BE AND THE ACTIVIST'S ETHNOGRAPHY THAT MIGHT BE

DAVID GRAEBER

MY FIRST REACTION WHEN ASKED to contribute to this volume is that an auto-ethnography of the academy was simply impossible.

My logic was this. During the 1980s, we all became used to the idea of reflexive anthropology, the effort to probe behind the apparent authority of ethnographic texts to reveal the complex relations of power and domination that went into making them. The result was an outpouring of ethnographic meditations on the politics of fieldwork. But even as a graduate student, it always seemed to me there was something oddly missing here. Ethnographic texts, after all, are not actually written in the field. They are written at universities. Reflexive anthropology, however, almost never had anything to say about the power relations under which these texts were actually composed. In retrospect the reason seems simple enough: when one is in the field, all the power is on one side—or at least, could easily be imagined as being so. To meditate on one's own power is not going to offend anyone (in fact, it's something of a classic upper-middle-class preoccupation), and, even if it does, there's little those who are offended by your representations of them can to do about it. The moment one returns from the field and begins writing, however, the power relations are reversed. While one is writing one's dissertation, one is, typically, a penniless graduate student, whose entire career could very possibly be destroyed by an impolitic interaction with a committee member. While one is transforming the dissertation into a book, one is typically an adjunct or untenured assistant professor, desperately trying not to step on any powerful toes before landing a permanent job. Any anthropologist in such a situation will likely spend many hours developing complex and agonizingly detailed ethnographic analyses of the power relations this entails, but that critique can never be published without fear of committing academic suicide. One can only imagine the fate of, say, a female graduate student who wrote an essay documenting the sexual politics of her department, let alone the sexual overtures of her committee members. Or, say, one of working-class background who published a description of the practices of Marxist professors, who regularly cite Pierre Bourdieu's analyses of the reproduction of class privilege in academic settings and then in their everyday lives act as if Bourdieu had been writing a how-to book instead of a critique. By the time one is a senior faculty member, absolutely secure in one's position, one might be able to get away with publishing such an analysis. But by then—unless one is reminiscing—one's very situation of power guarantees the object can no longer be perceived.

My conclusion was that it would be safer to admit to being an anarchist than to write an honest auto-ethnography of the academy.

On the other hand, I am an anarchist. And it strikes me the dilemmas that have come out of that provide an interesting commentary on the academy in themselves.

CONSENSUS AND DIRECT DEMOCRACY

I conducted my doctoral research in a rural community in Madagascar, during a period in the late 1980s and early 1990s in which most of the countryside there had been largely abandoned by the state. Rural communities, and even towns, were to a large degree self-governing: no one was really paying taxes; if a crime was committed, the police would not come. Public decisions tended to be made by a kind of informal consensus process. I wrote a little bit about the latter in my dissertation, but I couldn't think of all that much interesting to say about it.

In fact, I only really came to understand what was interesting about consensus retrospectively, when ten years later, I became an activist in New York. By that time almost all North American anarchist groups operated by some form of consensus process, and the process works so well—it really seems about the only form of decision-making fully consistent with non-top-down styles of organization—that it has been widely adopted by anyone interested in direct democracy. There's enormous variation among different styles and forms of consensus, but one thing almost all the North American variants have in common is that they are organized in conscious opposition to the style of organization and, especially, of debate typical of the classical sectarian Marxist group. Where the latter are invariably organized around some Master Theoretician, who offers a comprehensive analysis of the world situation and, usually, of human history as a whole, but very little theoretical reflection on more immediate questions of organization and practice, anarchist-inspired groups tend to operate on the assumption that no one could, or probably should, ever convert another person completely to one's own point of view; that decision-making structures are ways of managing diversity; and, therefore, that one should concentrate instead on maintaining egalitarian process and considering immediate questions of action in the present. One of the fundamental principles of political debate is that one is obliged to give other participants the benefit of the doubt for honesty and good intentions, whatever else one might think of their arguments. In part, too, this emerges from the style of debate consensus decision-making encourages: where voting encourages one to reduce one's opponent's position to a hostile caricature, a consensus process is built on principles of compromise and creativity where one is constantly changing proposals around until one can come up with something everyone can at least live with. Therefore, the incentive is always to put the best possible construction on other's arguments.

All this reminded me of what I had witnessed in Madagascar. The main difference was that since American activists were learning all this from scratch, it all had to be spelled out explicitly. So, although the activist experience did throw some new light on my original ethnography, it mainly brought home to me just how much ordinary intellectual practice—the kind of thing I was trained to do at the University of Chicago, for example—resembles just the sort of sectarian modes of debate anarchists are trying to avoid. One of the things that had most disturbed me about my training was precisely the way we were encouraged to read other theorists' arguments: in the least charitable way possible. I had sometimes wondered how this could be reconciled with an idea that intellectual practice was, ultimately, a common enterprise in pursuit of truth. In fact, academic discourse often seems an almost exact reproduction of style of intellectual debate typical of the most ridiculous vanguardist sects. I ended up compiling a kind of checklist:

1. the tendency, if there are two ways to read a sentence written by someone with a point of view differing from one's own, one of which assumes the author had at least an iota of common sense, to always to choose the other one.

2. the tendency to carry around in one's head a list of "32 different ways to be wrong" and to listen to points of view differing from one's own only as long as it takes to figure out which variety of wrongness to plug them into. We have probably all had the experience of having

someone explain to us, in detail, what *we* think: "You like coops? You are a cooperativist. You believe that X and Y and Z. But you are wrong because cooperativism is utopian and reformist." "You use the word 'clarity' approvingly? You are a Habermassian…"

3. the tendency to treat often minor intellectual differences not only as tokens of belonging to some imagined "ism" but as profound moral flaws; one is thus revealed to be racist, or sexist, or bourgeois, or something similarly execrable.

ANARCHISM AND THE ACADEMY

All this helps to explain something else: why there are so few anarchists in the academy. As a political philosophy, anarchism is going through a veritable renaissance. Anarchist principles—autonomy, voluntary association, self-organization, direct democracy, mutual aid—have become the basis for organizing new social movements from Karnataka to Buenos Aires, even if their exponents are as likely to actually call themselves Autonomists, Associationalists, Horizontalists, or Zapatistas. Yet most academics seem to have only the vaguest idea about this and tend still to dismiss the very idea of anarchism with stupid jokes ("Anarchist organization! But isn't that a contradiction in terms?"). There are thousands of academic Marxists, but no more than three or four well-known academic anarchists.

I don't think this is because academics are slow on the ball. It seems to me that Marxism has always had an affinity with the academy that anarchism never could. It is, after all, probably the only social movement to be invented by a man who had submitted a doctoral dissertation, and there's always been something about its spirit that fits that of the academy. Anarchism on the other hand was never really invented by anyone. True, historians usually treat it as if it were, constructing the history of anarchism as if it's basically a creature identical in its nature to Marxism: it was created by specific nineteenth-century thinkers (Proudhon, Bakunin, Kropotkin), it inspired working-class organizations, and it became enmeshed in political struggles. In fact the analogy is strained. The nineteenth-century thinkers generally credited with inventing anarchism didn't consider themselves to have invented anything particularly new. They saw anarchism more as a kind of moral faith, a rejection of all forms of structural violence, inequality, or domination (anarchism literally means "without rulers"), and a belief that humans would be perfectly capable of getting on without them. In this sense, there have always been anarchists and, presumably, always will be.

One need only compare the historical schools of Marxism and anarchism, then, to see we are dealing with a fundamentally different sort of thing. Marxist schools have authors. Just as Marxism sprang from the mind of Marx, so we have Leninists, Maoists, Trotksyites, Gramscians, and Althusserians. Note how the list starts with heads of state and grades almost seamlessly into French professors. Pierre Bourdieu once noted that if the academic field is a game in which scholars strive for dominance, then you know you have won when other scholars start wondering how to make an adjective out of your name (1988). It is, presumably, to preserve the possibility of "winning the game"—of being recognized as an intellectual titan or, at least, being able to sit at the feet of one—that intellectuals insist on continuing to employ just the sort of Great Man theories of history they would scoff at in discussing just about anything else. Foucault's ideas, like Trotsky's, are never treated as primarily the products of a certain intellectual milieu, as something emerging from endless conversations and arguments in cafes and classrooms, but always as if they emerged from a single man's genius. Here, too, Marxism seems entirely within the spirit of the academy.

Schools of anarchism, in contrast, always emerge from some kind of organizational principle or form of practice: Anarcho-Syndicalists and Anarcho-Communists, Insurrectionists and Platformists, Cooperativists, Individualists, and so on.[1] Anarchists are distinguished by what they do and how they organize themselves to do it. They have never been much interested in the kinds of broad strategic or philosophical questions that preoccupy Marxists such as: "Are the peasants a potentially revolutionary class?" (anarchists tend to think this something for peasants to decide) or "What is the nature of the commodity form?" Rather, they argue about what is the truly democratic way to go about a meeting, or at what point organization stops empowering people and starts squelching individual freedom. Is "leadership" necessarily a bad thing? Or, alternately, they argue about the ethics of opposing power: What is direct action? Should one condemn someone who assassinates a head of state? Is it ever okay to break a window?

Marxism, then, has tended to be a theoretical or analytical discourse about revolutionary strategy. Anarchism has tended to be an ethical discourse about revolutionary practice.

Now, this does imply that there is a lot of potential complementarity between the two. There is no reason one couldn't write Marxist theory and simultaneously engage in anarchist practice; in fact, many people have, including me.[2] But if anarchism is an ethics of practice, it means nothing to say you are an anarchist unless you are doing something. It is a form of ethics that insists, before anything else, that one's means must be consonant with one's ends. That one cannot create freedom through authoritarian means. That as much as possible, one must embody the society one wishes to create. Therefore, it's very difficult to imagine how one could do this in a university without getting into serious trouble.

I once asked Immanuel Wallerstein why he thought academics engaged in such sectarian styles of debate. The answer was, to him, obvious: "Well, the academy. It's a perfect feudalism." In fact, the modern university system is about the only institution—other than the British monarchy and Catholic Church—to have survived more or less intact from the High Middle Ages.[3] What would it mean to act like an anarchist in an environment full of deans and provosts and people wearing funny robes, conference-hopping in luxurious hotels, and doing intellectual battle in language so arcane that no one who hasn't spent at least two or three years in graduate school would ever understand it? At the very least it would mean challenging the university structure in some way. So we are back to the problem with which I began. To act like an anarchist would be academic suicide. Thus, it is not at all clear what an anarchist academic could actually *do*.

REVOLUTIONARIES AND THE UNIVERSITY

If one were to follow Wallerstein's lead, it would be possible to write a history of academic sectarianism, starting perhaps with the theological quarrels between Dominicans and Franciscans in the thirteenth century— that is, when the quarrels were literally between rival sects—and tracing it down to the origins of the modern university system in Prussia in the early nineteenth century. As Randall Collins has pointed out (1998), the reformers who created the modern university system, mainly by putting philosophy in the place formerly held by theology as master discipline and tying the institution to a newly centralizing state, were almost all exponents of one or another form of philosophical Idealism. His argument seems a trifle cynical, but the pattern was repeated in so many places—with

Idealism becoming the dominant philosophical mode at exactly the moment the universities were reformed, first in Germany, then England, the United States, Italy, Scandinavia, Japan; it's difficult to deny something is going on here:

> When Kant proposed to make the philosophy faculty arbiter of the other disciplines, he was carrying out a line which made academic careers in themselves superior to careers within the church... When Fichte envisioned university professors as a new species of philosopher-king, he was putting in the most flamboyant form the tendency for academic degree holders to monopolize entry into government administration. The basis for these arguments had to be worked out in the concepts of philosophical discourse; but the motivation for creating these concepts came from the realistic assessment that the structure was moving in a direction favorable to a self-governing intellectual elite. (Collins 1998: 650)

If so, this explains why followers of Marx, that great rebel against German Idealism, can form such a perfect complement to the spirit of the academy— even its mirror image and even while serving as a bridge over which habits of argument once typical of theologians are carried over into domains of politics.

Some would argue (I think Collins would) that these sectarian divisions are simply inevitable features of intellectual life. New ideas can only emerge from a welter of contending schools. This may be true, but I think it rather misses the point. First of all, the sort of consensus-based groups I described earlier put a premium on diversity of perspectives too. They just don't see discussion as a contest in which one theory or perspective should, ultimately, win. That's why discussion always focusses on what people are going to do. Second, sectarian modes of debate are hardly conducive to fostering intellectual creativity. It's hard to see how a strategy of systematically misrepresenting other scholars' arguments could actually contribute to the furtherance of human knowledge. It is useful only if one sees oneself as fighting a battle and the only object is to win. One uses such techniques to impress an audience. Of course, in academic battles, there is often no audience—other than one's graduate students or other feudal retainers— which might seem rather pointless, but that doesn't seem to bother anyone.

Academic warriors will play to non-existent audiences in the same way that minuscule Trotskyite sects of seven or eight members will invariably pretend to be governments-in-waiting and thus feel it is their responsibility to lay out their positions on everything from gay marriage to how best to resolve ethnic tensions in Kashmir. It might seem ridiculous. Actually, it is ridiculous. But, apparently, it is the best way to guarantee victory in those odd knightly tournaments that have become the hallmark of Collins's "self-governing intellectual elite."

ON THE IDEA OF THE AVANT GARDE

I seem to have argued myself into something of a box here. Anarchists overcome sectarian habits by always keeping the focus on what they have in common, which is what they want to *do* (smash the state, create new forms of community …). What academics want to do, for the most part, is to establish their relative position.

Perhaps it might be best to take it, then, from the other side. Anarchists have a word for this sort of sectarian behaviour. They call it "vanguardism," and it is typical of those who believe that the role of intellectuals is to come up with the correct theoretical analysis of the world situation, so as to be able to lead the masses on a truly revolutionary path. One salutary effect of the popularity of anarchism within revolutionary circles is that this position is considered nowadays definitively passé. The problem is, then, what is the role of revolutionary intellectual in fact to be? Or how can we get past our vanguardist habits?

Untwining social theory from vanguardist habits might seem a difficult task because, historically, modern social theory and the idea of the vanguard were born more or less together. Actually, so was the idea of an artistic avant garde, and the relation between the three suggests some unexpected possibilities.

The term avant garde was actually coined by Henri de Saint-Simon. Like his one-time secretary and later rival Auguste Comte, Saint-Simon was writing in the wake of the French Revolution; both were asking what had gone wrong. Both reached the same conclusion: modern, industrial society lacked any institution that could provide the ideological cohesion and social integration afforded feudal society by the medieval Catholic Church. Each ended up proposing a new religion: Saint-Simon's called his the "New Christianity," Comte, the "New Catholicism." In the first, artists were to play the role of the priesthood. St. Simon produced an imaginary dialogue in which a representative of the artists explains to the scientists how, in their role of imagining possible futures and inspiring the public, they will play the role of an "avant garde," a "truly priestly function" in the coming society; artists will hatch the visions that scientists and industrialists will put into effect. Eventually, the state itself, as a coercive mechanism, would simply fade away.[4]

Comte, of course, is most famous as the founder of sociology. He invented the term to describe what he saw as the master-discipline that could both understand and direct society. He took a far more authoritarian approach by proposing the regulation and control of almost all aspects of human life according to scientific principles, with the priestly role in his New Catholicism being played by the sociologists themselves.

This is a particularly fascinating opposition because, in the early twentieth century, the positions were effectively reversed. Instead of the left-wing Saint-Simonians looking to artists for leadership, while the right-wing Comtians fancied themselves scientists, we had fascist leaders like Hitler and Mussolini who imagined themselves as great artists inspiring the masses and sculpting society according to their grandiose imaginings, and the Marxist vanguard claiming the role of scientists.

The Saint Simonians at any rate actively sought to recruit artists for their various ventures, salons, and utopian communities, although many within "avant garde" artistic circles preferred the more anarchistic Fourierists and, later, one or another branch of outright anarchists. Actually, the number of nineteenth-century artists with anarchist sympathies is quite staggering, ranging from Pissaro to Tolstoy to Oscar Wilde, not to mention almost all early twentieth-century artists who later became Communists, from Malevich to Picasso. Rather than a political vanguard leading the way to a future society, radical artists almost invariably saw themselves as exploring new and less alienated modes of life. The really significant development in the nineteenth century was less the idea of a vanguard than that of Bohemia (a term first coined by Balzac in 1838): marginal communities living in more or less voluntary poverty seeing themselves as dedicated to the pursuit of creative, unalienated forms of experience and united by a profound hatred of bourgeois life and everything it stood for. Ideologically, they were about equally likely to be proponents of "art for art's sake" or social revolutionaries. And in fact they seem to have been drawn from almost precisely the same social conjuncture as most nineteenth-century revolutionaries or current ones for that matter: a kind of meeting between certain elements of (intentionally) downwardly mobile professional classes, in broad rejection of bourgeois values, and upwardly mobile children of the working class—the sort who managed to get themselves a bourgeois level of education only to discover this didn't mean actual entry into the bourgeoisie.

In the nineteenth century the term "vanguard" could be used for anyone seen as exploring the path to a future, free society. Radical newspapers— even anarchist ones—often called themselves "The Avant Garde." Marx began to change the idea by introducing the notion that the proletariat were the true revolutionary class—he didn't actually use the term "vanguard" in his own writing—because they were the one that was the most oppressed or, as he put it, "negated" by capitalism and therefore had the least to lose by its abolition. In doing so, he ruled out the possibility that less alienated enclaves, whether of artists or the sort of artisans and independent producers who tended to form the backbone of anarchism, had anything significant to offer. The results we all know. The idea of a vanguard party dedicated to both organizing and providing an intellectual project for that most-oppressed class chosen as the agent of history, but also, actually sparking the revolution through their willingness to employ violence, was first outlined by Lenin in 1902 in *What Is to Be Done?* It has echoed endlessly, to the point where in the late 1960s groups like Students for a Democratic Society ended up in furious debates over whether the Black Panther Party should be considered the vanguard of The Movement as the leaders of its most oppressed element. All this in turn had a curious effect on the artistic avant garde who increasingly started to organize themselves like vanguard parties, beginning with the Dadaists and Futurists, publishing their own manifestos, communiqués, purging one another, and otherwise making themselves (sometimes quite intentional) parodies of revolutionary sects.[5] The ultimate fusion came with the Surrealists and then finally the Situationist International, which on the one hand was the most systematic in trying to develop a theory of revolutionary action according to the spirit of Bohemia, thinking about what it might actually mean to destroy the boundaries between art and life, but on the other hand, in its own internal organization, displayed a kind of insane sectarianism full of so many splits, purges, and bitter denunciations that Guy Debord finally remarked that the only logical conclusion was for the International to be finally reduced to two members, one of whom would purge the other and then commit suicide. (Which is actually not too far from what actually ended up happening.)

NON-ALIENATED PRODUCTION

For me the really intriguing question here is: why have artists so often been drawn to revolutionary politics to begin with? It does seem to be the case that, even in times and places when there is next to no other constituency for revolutionary change, the one place one is most likely to find it is among artists, authors, and musicians, even more than among professional intellectuals. It seems to me the answer must have something to do with alienation. There would appear to be a direct link between the experience of first imagining things and then bringing them into being (individually or collectively)—that is, the experience of certain forms of unalienated production—and the ability to imagine social alternatives, particularly if that alternative is the possibility of a society which is itself premised on less alienated forms of creativity. This would allow us to see the historical shift between seeing the vanguard as the relatively unalienated artists (or perhaps intellectuals) to seeing them as the representatives of the "most oppressed" in a new light. In fact, I would suggest, revolutionary coalitions always tend to consist of an alliance between a society's least alienated and its most oppressed. And this is less elitist a formulation than it might sound, because it also seems to be the case that actual revolutions tend to occur when these two categories overlap. That would at any rate explain why it almost always is peasants and craftspeople—or alternately, newly proletarianized former peasants and craftspeople—who actually rise up and overthrow capitalist regimes and not those inured to generations of wage labour. Finally, I suspect this would also help explain the extraordinary importance of indigenous people's struggles in that planetary uprising usually referred to as the "anti-globalization" movement: such people tend to be simultaneously the very least alienated and most oppressed people on earth. Once it is technologically possible to include them in revolutionary coalitions, it is almost inevitable that they should take a leading role.

The role of indigenous peoples, curiously, leads us back to the role of ethnography. Now, it seems to me that in political terms, ethnography has received a somewhat raw deal. It is often assumed to be intrinsically a tool of domination, the kind of technique traditionally employed by foreign conquerors or colonial governments. In fact, as I've argued elsewhere (Graeber 2001: 325), the use of ethnography by European colonial governments is something of an anomaly: in the ancient world, for example, one sees a burst of ethnographic curiosity at the time of Herodotus which vanishes the moment gigantic multi-cultural empires come on the scene. Periods of great ethnographic curiosity have tended to be periods of rapid social change and at least potential revolution. What's more, one could argue that under normal conditions, ethnography is less likely to be employed by the powerful than as a weapon of the weak. All those graduate students constructing elaborate ethnographies of their departments that they can never publish are really doing, perhaps in a more theoretically informed way, something that everyone in such a position tends to do. Servants, hirelings, slaves, secretaries, concubines, kitchen workers— anyone dependent on the whims of someone living in a different moral or cultural universe is, for obvious reasons, constantly trying to figure out what that person is thinking and how people like that tend to think in order to decipher their weird rituals or understand how they get on with their relatives. It's not like it happens much the other way around.[6]

Of course, ethnography is a little more than that. Ideally, ethnography is about teasing out the hidden symbolic, moral, or pragmatic logics that underlie certain types of social action—the way people's habits and actions make sense in ways of which they are not themselves completely aware. But it seems to me this provides a potential role for the radical, non-vanguardist intellectual. The first thing we need to do is to look at those who are creating viable alternatives on the ground and try to figure out what might be the larger implications of what they are (already) doing.

Obviously what I am proposing would only work if it were, ultimately, a form of auto-ethnography—in the sense of examining movements to which one has, in fact, made some kind of commitment, in which one feels oneself a part. It would also have to be combined with a certain degree of utopian extrapolation: a matter of teasing out the tacit logic or principles underlying certain forms of radical practice and then not only offering the analysis back to those communities, but using them to formulate new visions ("If one applied the same principles you are applying to political organization to economics, might it not look something like this?"). These visions would have to be offered as potential gifts, not definitive analyses or impositions. Here, too, there are suggestive parallels in the history of radical artistic movements, which became movements precisely as they became their own critics;[7] there are also intellectuals already trying to do precisely this sort of auto-ethnographic work. However, I say all this not so much to provide models as to open up a field for discussion, first of all, by emphasizing that even the notion of vanguardism is itself far richer in its history, and full of alternative possibilities, than most of us would ever be given to expect. And it provides at least one possible answer to the question of what an anarchist anthropologist is to do.

No doubt there are many others.

NOTES

[1] Significantly, those Marxist tendencies that are *not* named after individuals, like Autonomism or Council Communism, are themselves the closest to anarchism.

[2] Even Mikhail Bakunin, for all his endless battles with Marx over practical questions, also personally translated Marx's *Capital* into Russian. I also should point out that I am aware I am being a bit hypocritical here by indulging in some of the same sort of sectarian reasoning I'm otherwise critiquing: there are schools of Marxism which are far more open-minded and tolerant, and democratically organized, and there are anarchist groups which are insanely sectarian. Bakunin himself was hardly a model for democracy by any standards. My only excuse for the simplification is that, since I am arguably a Marxist theorist myself, I am basically making fun of myself as much as anyone else here.

[3] In fact, a medieval historian tells me that at least in many parts of Europe, medieval universities were actually more democratic than they are now, since students often elected the professors.

[4] Saint-Simon was also perhaps the first to conceive the notion of the withering away of the state: once it had become clear that the authorities were operating for the good of the public, one would no more need force to compel the public to heed their advice than one needed it to compel patients to take the advice of their doctors. Government would pass away into, at most, some minor police functions.

[5] Note, however, that these groups always defined themselves, like anarchists, by a certain form of practice rather than after some heroic founder, presumably in part because any artist who admitted to being simply the follower of another artist would abandon any hope of being seen as a significant historical figure by doing so.

[6] Take, for example, Todorov's famous essay on Cortes, who, he argues, was an amateur ethnographer who sought to understand the Aztecs in order to conquer them. It is rarely noted that Cortes tried to understand the Aztecs precisely as long as their army outnumbered his something like 100 to 1. The moment he defeated them, his ethnographic curiosity appears to have vanished

[7] Of course the idea of self-criticism took on a very different, and more ominous, tone within Marxist politics.

WORKS CITED

Bourdieu, Pierre. 1988. *Homo Academicus*. Trans. Peter Collier. Cambridge, UK : Polity Press.

Collins, Randall. 1998. *Sociology of Philosophies : A Global Theory of Intellectual Change*. Cambridge, MA.: Harvard University Press, 1998.

Graeber, David. 2001. *Toward an Anthropological Theory of Value: the False Coin of our Own Dreams*. New York, NY: Palgrave.

Todorov, Tzvetan. 1984. *Conquest of America : The Question of the Other*. Trans. Richard Howard. New York, NY: Harper and Row.

13 | WRITING AGAINST THE NATIVE POINT OF VIEW[1]

Donna J. Young

> Time that is intolerant…
> Worships language and forgives
> Everyone by whom it lives;
> Pardons cowardice, conceit…

—W.H. Auden, "In Memory of W.B. Yeats"

Abigail, her mother, and her stepfather came to my house for tea. We ate fresh strawberries on tea biscuits with lots of whipped cream. It was the long weekend in June in a new millennium. Abigail's parents had travelled from their home in New Brunswick to visit her in Halifax. They had no idea she had recently been diagnosed with multiple sclerosis (MS), and she had organized this outing to tell them so. Her mother seemed to sense something unpleasant in the offing and appeared wary. Her stepfather clearly resented being dragged to my house on this holiday weekend. I was feeling impatient. Why did Abigail have to make such a production out of everything? And why was my presence required? It all seemed unnecessary and cruel. I urged her to cut to the chase, to say what she had to say.

Abigail's voice faltered as she told them about her disease. As always, she had done her research on the Internet and could trace the exact origins of her present predicament. She has a modernist turn of mind. According to her, the sources of her disease were exposure to mercury and vitamin D deficiency as a child. "Mom, remember when Daddy used to bring mercury home from the fertilizer plant so we could play with it? You would put the bucket of mercury in the middle of the floor, and it would entertain us for hours." Scarlet, Abigail's mother, looked uncertain, but was determined to be agreeable. After all, she was a guest in my home. "Yes, I think so," she ventured. Abigail carried on, "And you never made us drink milk, because you didn't like it when you were little. Do you remember that?" Scarlet nodded, tentatively. Joe, her husband, could suppress his hostility no longer. "Oh for god's sake Abigail, how do you know you have MS? Is this a lifestyle disease? Look at you: if you just lost some weight and got a job, you'd be fine."

If Abigail believed holding this meeting at my house would curb Joe's tongue, she was mistaken. Did she seek an anthropologist as witness? Or had she simply sought the moral support of a friend? Certainly, she had placed her mother in an awkward situation. Scarlet tried to run interference between her husband and her daughter, while appearing the good guest, the good wife, the good mother—all at that moment, in this family, mutually exclusive categories. And in the end, to diffuse the situation, she would have to admit neglect as a parent who had allowed her children to play with mercury and refused them vitamin-rich milk. I am pretty confident such ironies were lost on those present.

In a huff, Joe went outside to smoke. From my window, I caught him scowling at my drooping peonies and sunny English buttercups. Unlike us, he was not born in the Maritimes or, for that matter, Canada. We, the women, ended the visit by gossiping about people and things "up home," by which we refer to the small settlement in the northeastern corner of New Brunswick from which Abigail and her mother come and in which I conducted ethnographic fieldwork for the better part of two-and-a-half years in the early 1990s. We exchanged recipes and laughed until our sides hurt. They chose the pseudonyms Scarlet and Abigail for my work. But the repartee constantly threatened to dissolve into accusations of blame, complaining and lamenting, stubborn refusals and tight-jawed resignation. That night, Scarlet went back to her daughter's apartment and scrubbed floors until one in the morning, but still she could not sleep. The next day she took her daughter shopping, a typical response from this woman who prides herself on never shedding a tear. Eventually, the gloves would come off, and acrimonious phone calls and recriminations between mother and daughter would continue throughout the summer and fall, ruining yet another family Christmas.

For me, one particularly disturbing idea attended the fallout of my tea party. At the core of the arguments waged between Abigail and her mother over the following months was Scarlet's wish to talk to Abigail's doctor and Abigail's refusal to grant it. Scarlet phoned me to complain that Abigail had been a hypochondriac from the time she was a small child. She found Abigail's story fishy, but she knew I had a tender heart and did not want me to worry needlessly. According to Abigail, Scarlet was meddling in her life. I countered that I thought her mother was deeply concerned and thought her request, to talk to Abigail's doctor, reasonable. Further, I argued, the doctor would put an end to her mother's suspicion that she was making the whole thing up. Abigail said I didn't understand how spiteful her mother could be and that Scarlet would convince the doctor his diagnosis was wrong. I asked how that was possible, as I understood the tests were conclusive? Abigail told me that when it came to her mother, anything was possible; I should not underestimate her. I dropped the subject and have not broached it since, but seeds of doubt had been planted in my mind.

And I am still trying to figure out why I should have found such doubts about the *real* state of my friend's health troubling in the least, for I thought myself beyond this obsession with literal truth. I grasp the significance of the distinction between illness and disease, and as an anthropologist attend to the former rather than the latter (Kleinman, *et al.* 1997; Lambek and Antze 1996, 2003). My chief concern is with the interpretation of culturally mediated narratives of self-understanding. Indeed, I credit Abigail and her relations with having taught me much on the subject of narrative truth and have learned—admittedly, with a good deal of effort—to adopt an ironic sensibility as I listen to and analyze their stories and talk. By this I mean that I have made a deliberate attempt to achieve a degree of respectful detachment, to be sensitive to contradictory and contentious takes on the subject of truth so as not to succumb to absolute certainties that would diminish the experiences of some while elevating those of others. I try not to take sides and to withhold judgement, for I firmly believe we all make our realities out of language and are subject to its whims and fancy.

But the tea party and the conversations that followed threatened to undermine this hard-won sensibility. When I began fieldwork in the early 1990s, Abigail was undergoing therapy, and we spent a considerable amount of time discussing her recovered memories of sexual and satanic abuse. I even helped her search the shoreline for a cave where she believed we would find the skeletal remains of sacrificed babies. I was open to the idea that such recovered memories might help to explain her nightmares and depression. The ethnographic encounter is predicated on such openness, and such ideas were prevalent at the time. While in the field, Abigail gave me her journal to read, which she said I could treat as a life history. Several years later she would come to my office and record another life history, radically altering her interpretation of her life so as to erase the ritual abuse stories. We had both come to think about such things differently. At the tea party, she began again to rearrange the events of her life history in light of fresh ideas. But this time I began to suspect Abigail of a degree of calculation and out-right dishonesty that went beyond the niceties of shifting narrative truths and a native point of view.

NATIVE POINTS OF VIEW

The idea of a seamless "native point of view" has been with anthropology since Malinowski. According to Stocking, Malinowski was well aware of "the problem of informant variation" and the "hopelessly inadequate and contradictory answers" with which the natives responded to his questions. Stocking writes: "Temperamentally disinclined to allow them to contradict him rather than each other, Malinowski's solution—arrived at *ex post facto* in the analysis of his field data—was to distinguish between 'social ideas and dogmas'" embodied in cultural institutions and "opinions or interpretations that might be offered by individuals, groups of specialists, or even the majority of the members of a community" (Stocking 1983: 99). As Stocking notes, "Though it apparently privileged a customary or institutional realm where native belief was homogenous, it gave tremendous weight to the conflict of cultural rule and individual impulse which made savage society 'not a consistent logical scheme, but rather a seething mixture of conflicting principles'" (1983:100). My own society, by this definition, is wildly savage, as my memories and fieldnotes are nothing if not a "seething mixture of conflicting principles." The natives (and I include myself in this category) could agree on very little. Thankfully, post-structuralism refocussed anthropology's attention on the contradictory and, so, in a sense, rescued me from the tyranny of finding an all-encompassing native point of view, which I could find nowhere.

Instead, I have tried to make sense of the arguments and dissenting opinions expressed by the people I knew. Trying to figure out the context and wider significance of their arguments became the key focus of my work. Puzzling through my own falling out with Abigail has been one of the most telling aspects of this work, as it so neatly highlights some of the difficulties and contradictions at the heart of ethnographic fieldwork. My reflections on our eventual estrangement are the subject of this essay. Not only did our quarrel bring an abrupt halt to a long friendship, it brought closure to fieldwork, which I had been unable to accomplish on my own.

My involvement with the people of whom I write continued long after I left the settlement. Critiques of the idea of bounded communities aside, subjects jumping our fences can pose practical difficulties for the anthropologist who works at home. When I think about my fieldwork experiences, I do so with the knowledge of how it all ended. It colours my memories and shapes my interpretation. Our falling out marked my departure from the field, although I never left home.

ANTHROPOLOGY CLOSE TO HOME

I began graduate school when the post-colonial critique of anthropology was at a fever pitch. Anthropologists everywhere were struggling with the ethical implications of fieldwork practices and forms of representation (Clifford and Marcus 1986). We were schooled to recognize the ways in which anthropology had come to represent the lives of others as belonging to places distant and distinct. Such distance was conceived of in spatial, temporal, and cultural terms. Like Conrad's Marlowe, whose journey up the Congo River "was like travelling back to the beginnings of the world" (Conrad 1995: 59), the anthropologist's journey to other places was cast in metaphors and tropes that implied a radical otherness somehow lost in time. Johannes Fabian (1983) argued that in this way anthropology ignored the coeval nature of the historical times in which both the anthropologist and the "other" lived, the very history that brought them together.

My response to such criticism was to argue for an anthropology at home, one in which the legacies of colonialist and racist ideologies that haunt our relationships with people in other parts of the world, or with those colonized at home, might be avoided. By some peculiar logic, I reasoned that, if one took the radical otherness, or the exotic, out of anthropology, it would cease to make objects of its subjects. I agreed with Augé, who wrote that "if anthropology was not possible everywhere, it was not possible anywhere" (1994: xiii). I still do. But if I thought studying one's own would ease the ethical and representational dilemmas of ethnographic fieldwork and writing, or overcome the epistemological hurdles that attend our most prominent, if troubling, method of participant observation, I was soon to learn otherwise.

Do not misunderstand me: I greatly value the insights to be gained from participant observation research and worry that the current strictures placed upon our discipline by ethics review boards and unsympathetic positivists threaten to undermine the subtleties of our knowledge of others and of ourselves. Perhaps the thing I value most about participant observation is its unerring ability to undermine the elegant simplicities of our theories. Participant observation forces us to confront the limits of our knowledge and understanding. The knowledge we produce tends to be tentative, and occasionally, at least to friends, we admit to self-doubt about the deceptions, collusion, and complicity that become an aspect of our ethnographic endeavours, despite our efforts to be forthright and ethical. This is inevitable because our very presence contaminates the field, muddies the waters. We go where we don't belong.

Even as natives, we go where we don't belong, we transgress borders. And that is the funny thing about "native anthropology." Even when we work at home, we tend to respond and to write *as if* we were outsiders. That is, we continue to translate the ways of one group of people for another group of people. We don't assume a native audience, we assume an academic audience. As both Kirin Narayan and Marilyn Strathern note, in becoming academics, we become outsiders (Narayan 1995; Strathern 1987). Indeed, as Eduardo Viveiros de Castro so brilliantly observes: "Nobody is born an anthropologist, and, curious though this may seem, still less is anyone born a native" (2003: 9). Framing it thus does more than draw attention to the negotiation of reality that attends the ethnographic encounter (Crapanzano 1980), it underscores the particular type of social relationship involved in that negotiation, a negotiation that positions the anthropologist *vis-à-vis* her subject.

But those who become the subject of our discourse may be less inclined to mark this tricky relationship if they are able to place us within their world. I grew up in New Brunswick, and whether in the settlements, or interviewing retired nuns who once worked there, conversations would inevitably begin with an attempt to locate me geographically and according to kin. "Now, to which branch of the Young family do you belong?" "And who did you say your mother was?" Surprisingly, we were often able to find a connection. "Of course I remember the Young's turkey farm." "So you were in grade two with my brother's boy." No matter how distant, it mattered. It both made me less suspect and bound me more closely to acceptable codes of behaviour.

I often wondered if someone truly "other" would have been given more leeway in terms of ethnographically "poking and prying with purpose"

(Hurston 1942: 174). When my husband, African-born in a strictly exogamous society, came to spend the summer with me, I noticed that his queries were tolerated with a lot more humour and good will than were mine. They met his impertinent curiosity about "life in the bush and incestuous marriage patterns" with their own about "life in the jungle and polygamy." Neither side revealed a thing about the complexities of their personal lives and seemed quite happy to play the exotic for each other. Both were convinced that the other did not work and wondered how they mysteriously supported themselves. Although I know each found the other quite peculiar, they seemed satisfied with their stereotypical understandings of each other and did not, in any serious manner, pry into the other's business. Ironically, in this manner, both respected the privacies and autonomy of the other. But our discipline disrespects the personal limits of others in the name of science. It is an impolite discipline.

I have, some would say too often, dealt with my discomfort in this regard by allowing those who have been the focus of my own curiosity to reciprocate in kind. It makes for a great deal of confusion, even if it facilitates ethnographic fieldwork. I can't imagine a more contaminated *scientific* endeavour. In the process of building the personal relationships required to carry out ethnographic fieldwork, both the researcher and the subjects of research let their guard down, revealing more than they had intended once they begin to relate more as friends and neighbours. This process is anathema to those who conceive of ethical responsibilities in narrow terms. But for me it is where the real work of making sense of another's life begins, and it reshapes the ways I think about our world.

A FAMILY QUARREL

The summer before my tea party, Abigail lay disconsolate for months in my spare bedroom, her few possessions lying in boxes around her bed. She was deeply depressed and had nowhere to go. I made frantic phone calls to social workers, but no one seemed willing to take her on. Years before she had done the circuit as a satanic abuse victim, and therapists told me they found her "too needy." Finally, a group of her lesbian friends intervened and found her an apartment in a non-profit, public housing building for women only. They put her in touch with social services, and she was given meagre social assistance on which to live. She was in a terrible situation.

She knew she could not work; she felt abandoned by her family, not to mention her anthropologist; and she could not pay for even the most basic necessities of life.

Abigail went to her doctor, who suspected she might be suffering from MS. That winter we spent hours on the phone discussing symptoms and rewriting her history in light of her possible new medical condition. Suddenly her old sleep disorders, her inability to hold a job for more than a few months, her inability to cope with life, were given a sound medical explanation. And this medical explanation erased the need to examine all the less savoury aspects of her life, such as a childhood in poverty; childhood sexual abuse; a history of school failure; living with the fear that someone would discover that the credentials she listed on her resume were falsified; her complete disdain for authority; and her quick temper, which led to troubled relations with employers, friends, and family. MS was a godsend. Abigail told me it was such a relief to know she was really, really sick and not insane. And I agreed. I found myself in the ridiculous position of wishing my friend ill health. We both crossed our fingers, and she applied for a disability pension. In the meantime, she decided it was time to break the news to her mother when she came to visit over the long weekend in June.

But, as I have noted, the news of Abigail's illness was not so readily embraced by Scarlet. Initially, I chalked this up to Scarlet's inability to bear such dreadful news about her daughter's health, but I soon came to understand that her suspicions stemmed from their troubled relationship. At the tea party, the spin that Abigail placed on the story of her illness was brand new to me. It placed the blame entirely at Scarlet's feet. Indeed, the structure of Abigail's discovery and disclosure of MS was the same as her earlier discovery and disclosure of satanic and childhood sexual abuse (Young 1996). I began to detect a disturbing repetition in Abigail's stories, in which she accused her mother of neglect and abuse and demanded attention and retribution. No wonder Scarlet's reaction was hostile. No wonder I felt ambivalent, uneasy.

I confess that, had Abigail's last story been her first, had I heard the story about the buckets of mercury brought home from the fertilizer plant *before* I heard the story of satanic cults, my interpretation of its significance would have been completely different. For starters, I would have taken it at face value. It alludes to the changes in the regional economy I had been primed to investigate. Taken literally, it could have so perfectly illustrated the plight of an undereducated and exploited working poor not properly trained to handle toxic chemicals. Such things are common enough. But I no longer think it is the significant point. Abigail's life stories rarely allude to the workplace at all, but illness as a consequence of childhood neglect, in one form or another, is always central to her narrative.

I will never know if Abigail *really* has MS. But even if she is the author of her illness, it is only to the extent that she is able to creatively carve out new spaces from which to speak as a subject in need. I can easily celebrate her ability to recast her story in an acceptable therapeutic language (especially at a time when the language of repressed memory had been roundly discredited) so as to receive housing and medical attention. However, in drawing attention to the ways in which discursive regimes create subjects as victims, I do not mean to imply that victims are merely opportunists. We all live our lives through language and are culturally implicated. She is hardly exceptional in this regard. Socializing in the field frequently involved commiserating over illness and misfortune. As related to me, illness was often a pivotal experience in one's life, marking the end of a relationship, the end of the ability to work, and the beginning of one form of trouble or another. Often illness initiated intense scrutiny on the part of the state, as the welfare worker began a series of home visits to process claims for disability welfare insurance. This was an extremely stressful, but oddly hopeful, time for those being "processed" by what Habermas calls the "therapeutocracies" of the welfare state (Habermas 1984: 530-40). If you could prove you were really ill, you would be given enough on which to survive. Otherwise, you were out of luck. Such are the meagre needs of the truly desperate.

Still, it was the twist Abigail placed on her story that morning at the tea party that made me uneasy. Had I not heard several different versions of Abigail's life history, I would have missed its underlying structure to focus on details I now find suspect. The longer I knew Abigail and her family, the less certain I became of anything as factual. I am left with stories, which constantly shift as people struggle to make-do and to make sense of their lives and relationships. While I can do little more than trace the historicity of their understanding, its continuities and breaks, I remain uneasy about the discrepancies in their interpretations of their lives as they dredge the landscapes of memory for the telling bits that explore the unbearable weight of their family's history, a history as much shaped by an excess of signification as it is by terrible privation.

A FALLING OUT

Following the tea party, I began to note an accusatory tone in Abigail's voice when she phoned to chat, and I felt guilty for not having called her first. She seemed increasingly suspicious and querulous when I turned the discussion away from her present concerns to ask for news of family and friends up home. She grew impatient with me. I believe Abigail could sense my disbelief, and we began to grow apart. Initially, I welcomed this distance as I had found it nearly impossible to write about my ethnographic experiences under her increasingly disapproving gaze. When I returned to the Maritimes in the late 1990s, Abigail twice relocated to the cities in which I lived and worked. She would come find me in my office on campus, and I would scurry to hide confidential documents and fieldnotes. I never knew the appropriate way to introduce her to the others in my midst. When she moved, lock-stock-and-barrel, into my home for a summer, I was forced to put my work away and unable to write at all. I was greatly relieved when she eventually moved out and achieved a measure of independence, which a disability pension from social services eventually secured for her.

I was very surprised when, almost two years later, she began to date a student in the university department in which I taught. Still, I was happy she had met somebody for whom she cared. It was when she began calling me to reveal things about other students, or to report things they said about *me*, that I became concerned. I told her I could not have such conversations and refused any involvement that would include her new partner and friends. Abigail made it clear that she resented this, and to an extent I understood her anger. As an anthropologist, I had exploited our friendship to gain a foothold in the community where I conducted fieldwork. Was she not simply reversing the order of things?

Soon after that conversation an essay I had written about Abigail's family was read in a class given by a colleague. A day before I was to visit that class to discuss the essay with students, I received a letter from Abigail accusing me of unethical practice. She was embarrassed by things she had once said, which were now recorded for posterity and out there in the public domain for her friends to read. I am not unsympathetic. Writing in the ethnographic present is intended to capture a moment in time, but I concede that in doing so we risk leaving the impression that those we write about are forever caught in that time. Meanwhile, we allow ourselves the privilege of after-thought. When our subjects read what we write they must be startled by the fact that our voices are newly altered so as to be measured and thoughtful, while their voices remain raw. It is a betrayal of sorts that has absolutely nothing to do with obtaining consent.

Abigail also took umbrage with my publishing the essay without her permission and accused me of concealing its publication. It is true that I did not seek her permission to publish, but I did take her, all expenses paid, to a conference where I had presented the same essay long before it was published. At that time, I even asked if she would like to write a rebuttal to be included with the essay. Back then, she claimed to understand my point of view and declined my offer. Still, she was unprepared for what was to come. As was I. I too felt betrayed, for I had not intended to conceal my work and over the years had often spoken to Abigail about my changing perspectives.

I meet my ethical obligations to those I write about by never, ever revealing their identities. For the most part, I even avoid place names. Sometimes I invent composite characters by merging the details of several people's lives into a single identity. I have even toyed with the idea of splitting Abigail into several people, as she has not only changed her story several times, but suggested different pseudonyms with each retelling. Because Abigail's revisionist history became my most perplexing theoretical problem, she remains one person. Despite this writing process, the *factions*,[2] if you will, are culled from actual events and the stuff of real people's lives. I stray from the strictly factual to protect identities and to clarify the points I hope to make. After all, it is the underlying social and cultural processes that most concern me. However, only the anthropologist, not those of whom she writes, is bound by the conventions of the profession. Unfortunately, Abigail had revealed her identity, as a subject of my research, to her new friends. In the past, this had not been a problem, as my ethnographic domain had simply broadened to include all those I met through her. Then our worlds collided. Not only did the distance between home and field dissolve into thin air, so did the distinctions between research, teaching, and friendship. The various domains of my profession, typically kept apart, collapsed into each other, raising a series of ethical and practical difficulties seldom acknowledged, let alone discussed, in anthropology.

In confronting this collapse, I came to appreciate anew the ways in which the antinomies that structure the discipline of anthropology grew out of a very specific set of historical conditions in which the relationship between the anthropologist (the self) and her subject (the other) belonged to very different worlds, worlds separated by cultural, class, ethnic, and/or national borders. Paradoxically, I wish neither to maintain the antinomy between *us and them* (which was, and is still, formed by deeply unequal political structures), nor believe it can be intellectually transcended (either by assuming an ability to overcome my own social positioning and subjectivity, or by adopting a theoretical position that would neatly bury contradictions and messiness under a veneer of total understanding and/or revolutionary politics). The possibility of resolving the very real social and cultural disparities that create the gap between self and other—the key antinomy at the heart of our discipline—through a transcendent philosophical manoeuvre seems dishonest to me. I might claim solidarity with Abigail, and I sincerely regret the social inequities that shaped our encounter and desire their demise, but in the end we both felt caught and caught out.[3] I can think of no comforting theoretical or philosophical resolution to our deeply interpersonal conundrum, which came to fruition when I stopped participating (an intersubjective process) and withdrew to write (an objectifying process). So, instead, I try to be as frank as possible and acknowledge the jarring contradictions and historical and social processes that shaped my encounter with Abigail and her family and friends. Abigail told me to stop writing about her world and then disappeared from my life. But beneath the cacophony and discord I do detect patterns, and I am unwilling to be silenced. As it turns out, I'm more like Malinowski than I once thought. As for Abigail, she is a storyteller. We share that compulsion. I hope she understands this, even though she has cause to resent it.

NOTES

[1] Thanks to Michael Lambek, Anne Meneley, and Sandra Widmer for thoughtfully commenting on earlier drafts of this essay. Jean Young and Uzoma Esonwanne offered support of various kinds, for which I am truly grateful.

[2] "Faction" is Uzoma Esonwanne's term for what he thinks I do. He uses the term to signify the slipperiness between fact and fiction that attends my ethnographic writing. What intrigues him is my compulsion to bury my evidence and theoretical concerns in an ethnographic narrative that tells a story, which is a form of invention. I have to concede the point. Nevertheless, ethnographies are not novels, regardless of what our students write. James Clifford drew attention to the elements of fiction in ethnographic writing in his essay "Introduction: Partial Truths" (Clifford and Marcus 1986).

[3] As Lindsay Dubois often tells me, structure outs every time.

WORKS CITED

Antze, Paul, and Michael Lambek (eds.). 1996. *Tense Past: Cultural Essays in Trauma and Memory*. New York and London: Routledge. 1996.

Clifford, James, and George E. Marcus (eds.). 1986. *Writing Culture: The Poetics and Politics of Ethnography*. Berkeley, CA: University of California Press.

Conrad, Joseph. 1995. *Heart of Darkness*. London: Penguin Books.

Crapanzano, Vincent. 1980. *Tuhami*. Chicago and London: The University of Chicago Press.

De Castro, Eduardo Viveiros. 2003. And. *Manchester Papers in Social Anthropology* 7: 1–17.

Fabian, Johannes. 1983. *Time and the Other: How Anthropology Makes its Other*. New York, NY: Columbia University Press.

Habermas, Jürgen. 1984. *The Theory of Communicative Action*. Vol. 1. Trans. Thomas McCarthy. Boston, MA: Beacon Press.

Hurston, Zora Neale. 1984 (1942). *Dust Tracks on the Road: An Autobiography*. Urbana and Chicago, IL: University of Illinois Press.

Kleinman, Arthur, Veena Das and Margaret Lock (eds.). 1977. Social Suffering. Berkeley, CA: University of California Press.

Lambek, Michael and Paul Antze (eds.). 2003. *Illness and Irony: On the Ambiguity of Suffering in Culture*. New York and Oxford: Berghahn Books.

Narayan, Kirin. 1977. How native is the native anthropologist? In *Situated Lives*. Eds. Louise Lamphere, Helena Ragoné and Patricia Zavella. 23–41. New York, NY: Routledge.

Stocking, George W. 1983. The ethnographer's magic: Fieldwork in British anthropology from Tylor to Malinowski. In *Observers Observed: Essays on Ethnographic Fieldwork*. Ed. George W. Stocking. Madison, WI: University of Wisconsin Press.

Strathern, Marilyn. 1987. The limits of auto-ethnography. In *Anthropology at Home*. Ed. Anthony Jackson. 16–37. London: Tavistock Publications.

Young, Donna J. 1996. Remembering trouble: Three lives, three stories." In *Cultural Essays in Trauma and Memory*. Ed. Paul Antze and Michael Lambek. New York and London: Routledge, 1996.

14 | AN ANTHROPOLOGIST UNDONE

Camilla Gibb

FIELD[1]

I'm squatting in a white hallway, waiting in line for my medication—
"Smartie time" the Glaswegian woman with the greasy hair ahead of me
calls this nightly ritual. I'm turning my hands over and over, staring at the
black of my palms, when the woman behind me interrupts my private
agonizing to ask me how I burned my hands. I'm about to object, I'm
working up to words:

*They're not burnt. It's henna. Henna that my friend Nuria and I darkened
with gasoline and then slathered on our palms and the soles of our feet so that
we would look beautiful at her sister Nimute's wedding. We were bridesmaids
last week, veiled and ululating in a city in the eastern highlands of Ethiopia.*

I don't speak it   the story just sounds too implausible, like the stories of
all the other people here. *Last week I was a bridesmaid. This week I am crazy.*

* * *

In the brief journey between the walls of an Ethiopian city and those of an
English psychiatric hospital, I am alone. I take airplanes, drink much wine,
compensating for a year of abstinence; blurring the passage between the
blues and oranges of East Africa and the crushing, familiar grey that is
Oxford, that is home.

Home is a swamp waiting to swallow. I've been neck deep in its mud
before—depressed enough to have been hospitalized; wild enough to be
diagnosed manic; depressed and wild enough that when I left for Ethiopia
to conduct fieldwork, I took two duffle bags: one full of clothes, the other
full of pills, because they didn't have lithium where I was going.

I've been back for a day now, and I walk around Sainsbury's with the
boyfriend who has waited for me all this time. I cry at the sight of chick-
ens—pasty poultry suffocating under plastic—frozen vegetables, foul-
mouthed toddlers, and fluorescent lights. I think of ritualized slaughter,
halal meat stewed with fenugreek, and peppers and pumpkins taken from

the fertile earth beyond the city walls. Women huddled over a fire, food shared between hands. The fights that would break out over whose turn it was to suck the marrow from the bone.

Ted is beside me, and there is Marmite, and Earl Grey tea, and pasteurized milk for miles, but life's former essentials seem unnecessary now, unwanted.

We carry our bags full of pathetic vegetables down our street, passing door after closed door. Life here is the weak light behind shutters, the faint smell of cooking oil, graffiti and broken car windows, and the footsteps of men making their way to the damp pub at the bottom of the hill.

England rains its way into the next day, when I have an outpatient appointment at the psychiatric hospital. I am resuming a weekly ritual from which I had been spared during my time in Ethiopia. I am trying to explain to the row of doctors in front of me that I am not crying because I am crazy, but because I'm suffering from something called reverse culture shock. But there's no entry for this in their DSM.

"Does it look bleak? Does it look hopeless?" they ask.

"Honestly? Yes it does. It looks terribly sad, devoid of any colour, all meaning."

The switch in worlds is unequivocally abrupt, so devastating that I am breaking up into pixels, stretched across oceans, unable to reconcile being here and being there. I tell the truth: I say things that an anthropologist, a traveller, a dreamer, a refugee or immigrant might understand. But these are doctors, not travellers. This is psychiatry, not poetry. I am mentally ill, not heartbroken and disoriented. *Last week I was a bridesmaid. This week I am crazy.*

* * *

Three hundred people are crammed into a domed shrine to celebrate the miracles of the patron saint of the city of Harar. We are awake and buzzing; drumming, clapping and chanting our way through a monotonous series of religious verses into the wee hours of the morning. We are fuelled by qat—green leaves with the effect of a mild narcotic—cut earlier in the day from squat bushes on the farms surrounding the city. We have masticated leaves stuck between our teeth, green film accumulating at the corners of our mouths; we have reached the state of *mirqana*; we are high.

As high as I am, I'm taking notes. I am an anthropologist: this is my job. I'm studying the religious practices of members of a community known for feeding hyenas and worshipping saints. I am veiled, abstinent, conversant in Arabic and increasingly in Harari, the local language. I'm an aberration, the only foreigner for miles with the exception of a scattering of Somali refugees.

I've been adopted into Fatima's cluster of 12 children. She and her visiting sisters and all their female children eat, sleep, and pray together in one room; her husband, Mohammed, and their sons in another. There is little interaction between these two rooms; the world is cleaved in two. I am a girl by definition because I am unmarried. I must observe a curfew, I must wear a veil outside the household compound, I must not be alone with a man.

Somewhere though, somewhere under this veil, there is a woman who used to be me. The one who lives with her boyfriend in England, struggles with sanity, drinks too many pints at the pub, and wears short skirts and steel-toed boots. They don't want her here, and I certainly don't want her here. Several months into this, and I've all but forgotten her and the place she comes from. The one reminder that she is still here somewhere is the 1,200 milligrams of lithium I have to remember to feed her every day. The essence of *her* is captured in these white pills.

I am not at all depressed here, but I am, like most people who live in the city, chronically ill. There is the brown, intermittent supply of water that the neighbourhood shares. We drink it, we cook with it, we wash dishes in it, we bathe in it, and then we throw it out into the street where it trickles downhill and seeps into the ground. We throw waste into the street as well, including animal remains, trusting that the hyenas roaming the city streets at night will have licked the pavement clean by morning.

We eat stew that has been made with the brown water. Four or eight or ten of us break pieces with our right hands from a large, unleavened bitter pancake over which the stew has been poured. We scoop up the stew with pieces of injera, pop these morsels into our mouths. Breakfast, lunch, and dinner—three times a day, every day except Friday when we honour the Prophet and, thanks to a brief Italian occupation of Ethiopia in the 1940s, eat spaghetti (with our hands) for lunch.

There is the square patch of dirt behind the storage shed in our compound where we go to the bathroom, tiptoeing in flip-flops around the fly-covered excrement of our kin. There are flying cockroaches. There is leprosy, TB, hepatitis, HIV. We all have bloated, gaseous bellies and severe diarrhea, courtesy of intestinal parasites. We routinely kill the parasites by taking pink pills that are sold singly alongside pieces of chewing gum and individual cigarettes in the makeshift stalls that line the main street.

I get better at interpreting the early signs of parasitic invasion, but I don't always catch it in time. When I fail to, I get dizzy, and my vision begins to blur. I assume this happens to everyone, except that on the worst of these occasions, I'm suffering differently. My hands have begun to tremble just like they did in the early days of taking lithium. The drug is toxic, and I'm pretty sure the dehydration that results from chronic diarrhoea has increased the lithium concentration in my blood. I'm showing all the signs of blood poisoning, and now I'm scared.

I go to the local hospital in the hope that some form of testing might be possible. I pay the mandatory hospital fee and wait for hours before meeting the doctor—Dr. Hassan Abdulnasser, a gentle 24-year-old with an incredible command of English. He has had only one training session in psychiatric illness and no clinical practice in the subject, but he compensates for this with his bedside manner.

He can offer no means of testing my lithium levels, but he listens and empathizes as I reveal a deeply incriminating secret: a mental illness in a country where the crazy are those who sit alongside the lepers and beg on the streets. I am telling him something about the woman I left behind, the woman who has no place here, the woman under this veil.

His kindness is enough to make me feel calmer, and feeling calmer, I realize the only option is to simply stop taking lithium for a while. Bring on the depression: I'd rather take that risk than die here from blood poisoning.

* * *

Hassan Abdulnasser. Exceedingly handsome—six feet two, as black as black can be, with a soft voice that contradicts his size. He wears a grey suit under his white coat and proper laced-up shoes as opposed to the flip-flops I wear and think of as national dress. *Hassan Abdulnasser.* Back in his hometown after four years of medical training at Addis Ababa university. A local boy done good. He dreams of doing specialized training in pediatrics in the United States. He's preparing for exams he's going to take in Cairo in a year's time, the final stage in a special scholarship competition for African doctors. He's made it this far; he thinks he stands a chance.

* * *

I am sick for a week and a half as the lithium leaves my system. I want to lie in the dark with a sheet over my head, sleep in silence, daydream about Hassan, but this is not the Harari way. No, to be alone is to invite evil spirits, so the women in the neighbourhood keep me company, sit around my prostrate body, sing songs together, weave baskets, burn incense, sort through grains. A tiny girl, a girl from the neighbourhood whom they call Biscutti, crawls over me, tickles me, hides under the sheet.

Fatima tells me the reason I am sick is because when I first arrived I did not wear trousers under my skirts. Someone must have resented my bare skin and cursed me with the Evil Eye. Aini, her sister, tells me the reason I am sick is because I am not Muslim enough. She throws a prayer rug down and points in the direction of Mecca. "But I'm not Muslim at all," I protest weakly. "When then?" they shout. "What more proof do you need?"

Finally, I feel better, and much to my relief, my mood hasn't plummeted. I am eager to get back to work. I'm interviewing local midwives now, trying to gain some understanding of whether they consider the female circumcision they perform to be part of Muslim practice.

I start by interviewing the one midwife I know: Biscutti's grandmother. Biscutti and her mother are supported by the grandmother's paltry income, and the three of them are desperately poor. They love Biscutti, but she is clearly suffering from malnutrition. I often find her during the day sitting alone in the road and eating dirt. She must be about two-and-a-half years old but she hasn't started speaking yet, she doesn't play with other children, she still breastfeeds, and she has open wounds on her face that refuse to heal.

She's taken to spending a couple of hours with me nearly every day. I give her crayons, fill buckets with hot water that I've warmed over the fire so she can bathe. She's aggressive: a wordless holy terror, eating crayons, splashing water, and tearing up my notebooks when I'm not looking. She leaves for home when she realizes that no amount of tugging on my breast is going to yield the milk she needs.

The sores on her face get worse, not better. It's been two months since I've seen Dr. Hassan, but I decide to take Biscutti to him. He gives me some antibiotic ointment to apply twice a day, and while I hold her, he paints her face with purple anaesthetic. We are as close as two people can be with a baby between them.

He invites me to a *bercha'a* on the weekend—a qat party, where people recline on pillows, drink tea, tell stories, and chew their way into *mirqana*.

I think about him for the rest of the week. *What if we married? Would I become Harari? What if we adopted Biscutti and went back to my country, Canada, and you could be a doctor there?*

The *bercha'a* at his house is a sultry affair. It is conducted in a hidden room because the company is mixed sex, young men and women, highly charged. It is conducted in the dark because Hassan has something very rare: a television and a VCR. We watch an American thriller, the name of which I forget because all I am conscious of is Hassan, cross-legged and breathing beside me in the dark.

When the lights come on, we talk about my work with midwives. Hassan does not believe in female circumcision. He believes it only causes harm and that it has no basis in Islam. He believes, as I believe, that the answer lies not in preaching or prohibiting it, but in educating women so that they have ways to achieve status other than through being wives and mothers. He offers to accompany me on visits to the midwives I have not been able to interview because they speak Oromiffa, a neighbouring language he, like most Hararis, speaks.

We do interviews together every Saturday after that, and at the house of the last Oromo midwife I interview I marvel as Hassan strokes the foreheads of two girls who have just undergone the operation. Their legs are tied together to prevent them from moving and to promote the formation of scar tissue. Their requests for water are denied because it's best if they urinate as little as possible. Each has had her clitoris and labia minora removed with a razor blade, her labia majora scraped out and sewn together with a row of thorns. There is a matchstick held in place between her labia, so there will at least be a small hole out of which her urine and eventually her menstrual blood can flow. On her wedding night, her husband will force himself through this barrier that has kept his bride a virgin. Hassan tells the two girls they are brave, and I feed them honey by the spoonful.

At his *bercha'a* the next day he finds my hand in the dark. His hand is large and warm. He writes a note: *I love you.* I write back: *I love you too.* We cannot speak. In fact, we will not ever speak, because we are not simply in love, we are in love with things far more complicated than each other.

And I am leaving soon. I'm taking lithium again, preparing for re-entry.

I'm snapping photos of people, wanting to take them with me. Many of them actually ask me to, saying, "Take me with you. Sponsor me. Get me a visa." I try not to make promises I cannot keep. Some people treat me as if I have already left; Biscutti, for instance, has stopped coming to visit. Her mother, Nunu, says it's because she knows I'm leaving.

"But how can she know?"

"Because you're taking her photograph," Nunu says. "Don't leave her. Take her to England with you."

When I tell Nunu that I can't take her daughter from her, she responds with an accusation. "You don't really love her," she says.

"She's being realistic," Hassan says later. "She wants a better life for her child. And you could give her that."

Realistic? The only way I can imagine this reality is if we married and adopted Biscutti together. We could be black and white, Harari, African, Muslim, English, Canadian. Hybrids, hyphenated, our disparate worlds joined. I can think of no other way of holding all this together, containing Biscutti and you and me—both the veiled and unveiled—in one place.

In reality, the Canadian Embassy says, "Not a chance. She has parents, both alive." I lamely defer to government in order to sanction my relief, though my guilt will never quite be assuaged. I will carry the fantasy of an Ethiopian baby with me well into my thirties. And Hassan and I will write for years, signing our letters "your friend," because there is no word within the discourse of anthropology, no word in English at all for being *rrata*— like a piece of meat stuck between one's teeth.

ACADEMY

None of this makes its way into my thesis. It doesn't make its way into conversations with my supervisor or fellow graduate students either. We, "the returned," maintain the posture of ethnographic success, project the picture of anthropological health, even if, in truth, our return home is far more traumatic than our arrival in the field ever was.

I wring the notes of the previous year between my hands like wet laundry. My thesis swims in the puddle at my feet. The right brain figures out the logistical problem of how to get that puddle into a bucket. The left brain dresses in those damp clothes and writes short stories about people and their goats and men in African prisons and women seduced by Arab men on

North African shores, stories full of fantasy and torment and ambiguity and sex, things a thesis cannot bear.

The dry dispassionate tome, meanwhile, lands with a thud on a desk. It requires no changes, but all of us, my examiners included, look upon it with slight disdain. I have "acquitted myself" in their words and am thus released into the world. I am certifiably sane, officially qualified, utterly utterly hollow. I am capable, quite capable, but what have I just done? And for whose purpose? And what now?

What now is returning to Canada and looking for job. What now is that strange purgatory of being a Doctor Without Borders. A Canadian doctor of the 1990s: a travelling salesperson willing to offer service to any university within commuting distance of Toronto; four years of newly minted doctors on either side of you, making exactly the same rounds until they land a job or take up a post-doc in Australia, or otherwise quietly disappear.

I don't think of disappearing as an option. No one does. But I do fantasize about writing fiction. I fantasize about it all the time and feast in secret like a bulimic, although I dismiss pursuing it in any serious way. Totally unrealistic. Possibly even fatal. Definitely dangerous. I feel rebellious and liberated and empowered when engaging in this illicit activity, and like any addict, I do not always have a choice.

There are two languages talking at once: a sophisticated, acquired language and a raw, untrained native tongue. I have been taught to value the former—I am a believer in education, while I dismiss my creative writing because I have not "learned to write." I don't have a PhD in this subject. Furthermore, I've just had offers of a post doc and a job—my career as an anthropologist is evolving as it should.

A man I know takes one look at me and states the obvious. "You're not happy."

I can't deny it.

"What would make you happy?" he asks.

"I wish I could be a writer," I tell him, as if admitting a dirty secret.

"And why can't you be a writer?"

Because I'm supposed to be an anthropologist, I think. I don't say this aloud: I know it would sound pathetic, like saying "because my parents would be disappointed." But the truth is, they would. And so would my supervisor. And so would my Ethiopian colleagues who value the existence of an ethnography of religious practice in Harar. And so, I fear, would

Hassan. And I would feel I'd failed at something which I was capable of doing. You don't choose to leave academia, not when you have worked this long and hard to get there.

I decide upon a compromise: I'll quit my current job and give myself over to writing for six months and *then* take up the post doc. The latter will allow me more time to make a decision about the job, it will give me the support to start research among Hararis in the diaspora, it will give me an opportunity to publish and build my academic c.v.

And so I leave the university and take up residence in my brother's trailer in eastern Ontario. I start hammering out a short story called *Mouthing the Words* on a laptop plugged into the trailer's little stove. The story refuses to end, carries me, writes itself, writes me. By the end of the summer, it looks suspiciously like a novel, and I am relieved and purged: ready to take up a "proper" place, a place within the academy—albeit loose, albeit temporary—again.

I love doing research again, but doing research at home is a very different matter. It is not as easy to separate your fieldwork persona from the rest of your life when the rest of your life is all around you. There are moments of profound dissonance, like the stinking hot day when my friend Anne Meneley and I are sitting on a Bloor Street patio sipping martinis in the middle of the afternoon, both of us in black miniskirts, both of us smoking, and I hear, in a Harari voice, my name.

Dear God. It's my friend Mohammed who is secretary of the Toronto-based Harari Community Organization. *Busted.*

Anne, who knows exactly what's going on, thanks Allah that the Muslim community with whom she worked in Yemen is virtually non-existent in Toronto. Doing fieldwork at home forces you to confront the invention of your fieldwork persona. It breaks down the borders you have constructed in order to do your work. It messes things up.

In my case, it is not just the fieldwork persona which is being challenged, but the construct of the professional anthropologist. At a departmental party I casually mention to one professor that I like to write short stories. He suggests I might want to keep that quiet. "No one will take you seriously as an academic," he warns.

No one will take you seriously. Because you dare to put an ounce of energy elsewhere? Because you dare find pleasure or power in any other language? Because you dare to seek, to find, an audience beyond the academy? Because you dare to find another way of telling the truth?

For fiction is truth telling. It takes us into people's lives, offers us privileged insight into their innermost thoughts, their internal wars, their private worlds. It explores the madness and messiness and joys of being human and offers us far more intimate, far more emotionally resonant portraits of ourselves—representations that are often far more "real," ironically, than those we find in non-fiction.

In method and purpose, fiction is not unlike anthropology. Both demand standing at a certain remove in order to observe and make creative connections between actions and words; both struggle to find ways of representing human experience. Both situate their agents on the periphery: anthropology and literature are two disciplines which attract and cultivate outsiders because alienation, as Ato Quayson has argued, is critical to their business. Alienation is a central theme of both literature and the fieldwork experience (Quayson 2003: 5). It is where fieldwork begins, the point from which we move toward familiarity, knowledge, and understanding. However, as Quayson points out, alienation all but disappears from the ethnographic text; it is expunged as "fieldwork is turned into an object of scientific knowledge" (Quayson citing Rosaldo 1993: 168-72). To do otherwise—to be post modern about it—is to risk being engaged in forms that are dismissed as "dead-end self-indulgence and narcissism" (Quayson 2003: 7).

Hence my dry, dispassionate thesis. Hence the fact that I indulge myself and my narcissism elsewhere. Fiction might be the language of the anthropologist unbound from the narrative conventions of the discipline, the conventions of critique, the contextual and theoretical positioning which more often appear to obfuscate and alienate than they do illuminate and include.

I want, quite simply, to include. I want to include Hassan and Biscutti in my work, as both potential characters and potential readers. I want the room to speak plainly and speak of hearts. When I read fiction I demand an experience, not an intellectual exercise. Empathy is not an intellectual decision, it's an emotional response, and literature, like music, like visual art, invites us to know this capacity in ourselves.

WORLD

I did not quietly disappear. I stepped quietly sideways as fiction blanketed my academic work. And nobody really cared; the world takes no notice of the loss of one neophyte anthropologist, in fact, nor do most anthropologists.

I'm sure the disappearance of one comes as something of a relief to other recent PhDs fighting for footing in the same very limited space.

I chose to leave because that novel born in the trailer park was published two years later. Published in 15 countries. Not in Amharic or Harari or Oromiffa or Arabic but in languages I know not a word of: Hebrew, Polish, Czech, Japanese, Thai. I cannot read the translations, I simply have to trust that the story is being told in a way that makes sense to the particular audience.

I no longer ask the questions: whose stories are we telling and for whose benefit? What impact does this have in the wider world? Who will possibly read them? The questions no longer seem to matter. I've found my native tongue and discovered, much to my surprise, that I'm a talker. I chose to leave academia because nothing will shut the fiction up.

I wrote another novel and, only then, started to call myself a writer. In becoming a writer you have to rewrite your history accordingly. You have to create your origin myth, locate your roots. Mine begins: When I was six I started writing poetry and short stories. When I was 18 I told my English teacher I wanted to be a writer, and he told me that was all fine and good but that I'd better go and have a life first. Then I would have something to say.

And so I went and had a life. And Hassan and Biscutti were part of it. Are part of it. And so is anthropology. In fact, I feel now that I became an anthropologist in order to become a writer. Because I became an anthropologist, I now have things to say as a writer.

* * *

I was reluctant at first to tell Hassan that I had left academia—I worried he would see it as me leaving Harar somehow, abandoning him, his people. I worried that, for all the ambiguity of our relationship, it had ostensibly been framed as one of anthropologist and informant—I did not know who we would be to each other outside the safety of that frame.

Hassan hasn't left Ethiopia. He didn't get that scholarship to study medicine in the United States. What he got instead was very religious after returning from the Haj and, shortly thereafter, very married. His wife is now pregnant with their second child.

The Internet, meanwhile, comes to Ethiopia. Hassan has e-mail and orders my first novel. He e-mails me to say he has learned something about female experience, about England and English childhoods. He says both that he is disturbed by the book and that he is very proud. There appears to be no contradiction. It's a strange moment. I was one person in the field and am quite another at home. Hassan was the only one who knew anything of the latter, but he did not know me as a writer, he did not know me as someone whose work is often rich in profanities and sarcasm and sex. There are characters in my books who are strippers. There are lesbians, tattoo artists, feminist lawyers, and child abusers. And Hararis can order my books over the internet. I can't hide, and I find it an extraordinary relief. Moving beyond anthropology has allowed the relationship with Hassan to develop into something much simpler and more honest.

I send Hassan the second novel. He e-mails:

> My genius friend, I read your book. It is marvilous work and I am really happy for you. Congra!!! You deserve all the praises and even more. I don't have enough vocabulary and combination of words to fully express my appreciation. I had to get a new dictionary to get the meaning of some the words. Besides, there were couple of paragraphes in which I had to consult my dictionary five times for the new vocabulary … The other thing that has impressed me most is the combination of words (hypenated words). For me this is something which is unseen before and unparalelled. In summary you are taking literature to a higher level. Somebody has said that you use words like knife that is true but the usage is not like an ordinary person, rather like a well-experienced Chinese karatist (karate-man).
>
> Camilla, regarding the theme of the story, I have a lot of queries but not as many as your first novel. We may discuss about it in the future.

The future. My next novel is the story of a relationship between a young British Muslim woman and an Ethiopian doctor, set against the backdrop of the 1974 revolution, when Emperor Haile Selassie was deposed. I want to dedicate the book to Hassan, but I feel I should ask him first if he minds, if his wife will mind.

"I am very much honoured," he writes. "You are killing me with joy!"

NOTES

[1] The section "Field" was originally published as "Her Eyes Follow" in Barclay and Logan 2003.

WORKS CITED

Barclay, Jennifer, and Amy Logan (eds.). 2003. *AWOL: Tales for Travel-Inspired Minds*. New York, NY: Vintage.

Quayson, Ato. 2003. *Calibrations: Reading for the Social*. Minneapolis, MN: University of Minnesota Press.

| # OUR SUBJECTS/OURSELVES: A VIEW FROM THE BACK SEAT

Michael Lambek

SHIFTING GEARS IN AUTO-ETHNOGRAPHY

What would an auto-ethnography have to say about its own production? How does a conference panel transform itself into a book? How is a publisher found, how are refereeing and editing accomplished? What constraints do the publishers impose on the editors, and how do the editors receive and then pass these on to contributors? How do the editors balance the various demands imposed on them in order to line up a series of accomplished papers of just the right length on schedule? How do prospective authors balance the requests of the editors with all the other demands on their time and attention?

An inside line informs me that in this instance the publishers are eager for adoption in undergraduate classes and hence request clarity of writing, ruthless attention to word limits, and purging of long words. I am instructed to avoid some of my favourites. Poiesis, for example, is not very long, but it does have three vowels in a row, and it isn't (so my own undergraduates inform me) found in all dictionaries. (Suddenly I wonder whether they have checked alternate, two-vowel spellings.) The person who advises me to skip poiesis is not one of the editors but the contributor with whom I am on most intimate terms. The editors, I know, are relieved. Intimates can get away with confronting you with truths that other colleagues might prefer to avoid mentioning. Anthropology as practiced in many households has something of a family quality. We take kinship literally. But even outside the literal household, the practice of anthropology has an incestuous feel to it, worthy of a novel by, say, Camilla Gibb. We are a discipline crammed into the family auto. It's probably of Japanese or European make, definitely road-worthy, but not all that roomy inside.

There is more. The rules of the game are that the editors should release control when it comes to the Afterword. They are taking a risk; insurance coverage does not extend to this zone.[1] As for me, upon reading these essays I am surprised to find myself for the first time in the position of the native, the ethnographic subject. Of course, I am not merely a subject, I'm also an interested party, a collaborator in the endeavour, and one privileged to immediately talk back to the anthropologists who have just diagnosed my condition. Moreover, the ethics of the afterword writer, if such exist, compel me to add that I have prior and ongoing relationships (of varying kinds) with a number of the contributors. So let's think of my place in this vehicle, this collective auto-ethnography, as the back seat. Think of my voice not as the observant mechanic wryly summing up his diagnosis from the outside but as the complicit back seat driver.

SO WHAT DRIVES AUTO-ETHNOGRAPHY?

As the editors indicate, the genre is not really new, and it has come in a number of models. The essays in this collection do not conform to a single model—they are neither standard nor automatic, neither vintage nor obviously this year's make. For the most part they provide opportunities for the authors to cast a critical eye on aspects of their own practice. In some cases the direction is towards the self-critical, in others to the institutional context "context" here ranging from explicit neo-conservative American politics (David McMurray), through tacit—even hegemonic—neo-liberal formations of students as workers (Bonnie Urciuoli), to the expectations for interdisciplinary teaching and research (Julia Harrison and Anne Meneley) increasingly advocated by research councils and university administrations on the basis of rather mysterious reasoning. The situation thoughtfully laid out by McMurray is particularly troubling; one can only hope it will dissipate once a more enlightened federal administration takes office south of my border[2] and that Kurtz will be sent back up the river. However, the long-standing support of foreign language training through the American National Defence Education Act (Title VI funding) suggests that there are deeper issues to be worked out.

Jacqueline Solway, interestingly, locates herself not with respect to the academy at home, but in relation to the changing political and intellectual climate of her country of research, Botswana, noting the difference that the growth of a local professional and intellectual class has made on the sense of entitlement of foreign scholars there. Maggie Cummings points to the changing consciousness of research subjects in Vanuatu who have learned not only to separate and objectify a part of their culture but to associate that realm—and only that realm—with anthropologists. The irony here is that while she protests that she does not wish to study *kastom*, she ends up studying "kastom," that is, the thing reconfigured as discourse, a discourse in which "anthropology," too, plays a central role.

David Graeber takes us to the "sectarian" production and contestation of ideas in the academy and to the feudal retainer status and perhaps paranoid structure of feeling (the latter depiction is mine) characteristic of graduate students. Graeber queries (ironically) the "self-governing intellectual elite" (citing Randall Collins) who appear to be the very enemy targeted for other reasons by the neo-conservatives as described by McMurray. Graeber is out to change the world through consensus building whereas Pauline Gardiner Barber appears to eschew such consensus-building practices (at least when imposed on others in the form of "participatory appraisals") for more abstract theorizing. Barber implicitly values the lone researcher, located at arm's length from the sins and seductions of collaboration (in her case with ecologically-minded development studies) whereas Solway and Cummings both collaborate (albeit each in very different ways) in the projects of their research subjects.

Todd Sanders and Ted Swedenburg each address the collaboration of anthropologists in the public sphere. Sanders bemoans the lack of interest in anthropological expertise, while Swedenburg recounts a surprisingly positive and productive collaboration with hot-shot Manhattan lawyers. For Sanders the anthropologist's voice is often too weak to be heard against powerful forces. Anthropologists who respond to the call of the media risk serious self-parody—or simply being ignored. Swedenburg is heard precisely because his voice is so carefully cultivated by the elite law firm that, for its own reasons, chooses to take on a case *pro bono*. The knowledge and broadmindedness shown by Swedenburg's lawyers—in marked contrast to Sanders' police—give us some room for hope and remind us not to jump to judgement ourselves.

Some of the authors start with objective goals; some are bemused; some ticked off. Instead of engaging with each argument individually, let me suggest that what fuels these auto-ethnographies are at least three forces. One is an anxiety on the part of anthropologists about our identity. Contributors report in varying ways on the problems of being asked and having to answer (as much to themselves as to others) what it is they are doing, and thus, in effect, who they are. If we find these questions extraordinarily difficult to answer (as I often do), we should reflect on how similar they are to the questions we often pose to our subjects—and just how problematic any such fully frontal question is. But I think there is also something specific to anthropology that makes it so difficult to answer. Fieldwork is an existential space whereas the anthropologist is supposedly a known entity. We are caught between the experience of ambiguity and the amorphousness of both self and professional identity in the crucible of the field situation and the experience of being interpellated, fixed, reduced, or overdefined in the audit culture of the academy as well as by professional collaborators in other disciplines, by the public media, and sometimes even by our research subjects, for whom definitions of anthropologists have by now preceded us. Yet how should good anthropology escape the various forms of utilitarian "objectives-and-results" discourse and evaluation described in several of the papers with respect to other kinds of projects and disciplines? Every anthropologist must struggle with the questions of what kinds of difference their work makes, and indeed why they engage in it, as well as with how subtly to pose questions and with what circumspection to establish answers. These issues underlie the whole volume.

A second force driving auto-ethnography is genuine curiosity about small groups and unusual practices—in this case our own—especially when, like other small-scale societies and rarified practices, they appear to be under threat. The owl of Minerva appears at twilight, and anthropology is a discourse of the vanishing.[3] The ethnographer follows on the heels of the colonial agent—in this case, the colonizers of our life world: the new managers of the university, the writers of promotional copy, the imposers of misconstrued ethical reviews, the informers sponsored by right wing "monitoring" groups. And this is the third impetus: an attempt to come to terms with our rapidly changing circumstances. To be an academic of any sort (I don't count the business schools) these days is to be on guard.

It is remarkable that really none of the essays, with the possible exception of Donna J. Young's (ironic in this case because it takes place at home), is driven by the need to respond to immediate post-colonial critique, which, as Young indicates, so affected anthropology during the 1980s. Although tensions remain, from Botswana to Vanuatu, anthropology now appears to be welcome and valued. The situation is a good deal more ambiguous in the Canadian Maritimes, the Toronto gender clinics, and among the Thames Valley police.

Anthropologists want to be appreciated. But we also want to think of our practice as simultaneously more critical and more sophisticated in substance than anything our public can imagine about us. We are also genuinely ambivalent about being labelled "experts," having our own internal critique of the politics of knowledge and truth. What all the authors appear to share is a strong appreciation of ethnography as a complex intellectual and ethical practice.

THE DRIVER'S SEAT

If auto-ethnography puts you (the anthropologist) in the driver's seat, the same cannot be said of ethnography of the other. The pairs of papers that form the bookends of this collection, by Renée Sylvain and by Lesley Gotlib at the front and by Donna J. Young and by Camilla Gibb at the back, beautifully demonstrate the fact that fieldwork is as much passion (in the older sense of that word) as action. The anthropologist is as much acted upon as actor. Her volition and agency are compromised by multiple alternative forces. It is part of the art and craft of fieldwork to know how to welcome such forces and how far to let oneself get carried along before exercising some kind of resistance.[4] Fieldwork styles are as varied as fieldworker personalities, but no anthropologist is going to get anywhere without allowing herself to be taken by surprise.

The balance between passion and action is precisely an ethical one, but it is an ethics far removed from that imagined by the people who think up and monitor ethical regulations and protocols. In this collection, Gotlib shows what is wrong with current ethical review procedures taken in their own terms, even as she juxtaposes the ethical constraints imposed on her own conduct with the licence given to journalists. As she argues, what passes as ethical review is actually about liability. Indeed, I would (and have) gone further than Gotlib to argue that asking (or, more likely, impelling or compelling) subjects to sign informed consent forms is a matter of transferring and evading liability. In the ethics review process the university or granting agency passes on liability to the researchers and the researchers pass it on to their subjects. In my view, this is not merely non-ethical, but unethical.

But the critique of our current ethics regime can go much further than this. The regime is premised on orderly rule-following. What Sylvain shows is that in real life circumstances, especially unexpected ones, following rules doesn't work. Instead, anthropologists are expected to exercise judgement. This is a continuous and contingent process, meeting each new circumstance as it comes up while drawing from the experience of previous ones. In this manner ethnographers cultivate ethical dispositions and in so doing—as Sylvain elegantly demonstrates—cultivate themselves as ethical persons. Although Sylvain does not make the explicit connection, her essay offers an illustration of an Aristotelian virtue-based ethics rather than a rule-based or utilitarian one (the major competing alternatives).

Young's paper is an auto-ethnography focussed precisely on doing the ethnography of the other (or, more precisely, of another). She writes, "The possibility of resolving the very real social and cultural disparities that create the gap between self and other—the key antinomy at the heart of our discipline—through a transcendent philosophical manoeuvre seems dishonest to me." Like Sylvain, Young sees ethnography as an intrinsically practical and ethical endeavour, constituted in her case through direct and often troubling and agonistic encounters with her subjects.

In Solway's case, this ethnographic ethical self-fashioning in the encounter is given an additional interpersonal dimension as she develops her subjectivity also by means of her relationships with anthropological contemporaries and predecessors.

ACADEMIC LIFE

Whose eyes are caught in the rear view mirror? An ethnography of the academy need not refer to anthropology exclusively. By now there is a substantial literature on the practice of science. The editors themselves address questions of the composition of the academy and cite the burgeoning literature on its social reproduction, notably that by Bourdieu.

Anthropologists spend a lot of time exploring the dialectic of structure and agency or power and resistance among our research subjects. What about our own position as academics? What is the balance of subjection and agency, for example, in Pauline Gardiner Barber's uneasy relationship with the development projects that fund her travel?

In this collection Bonnie Urciuoli attends most specifically to the disciplinary practices characteristic of the university, albeit to a specific kind of American liberal arts college. Her paper is less about the direct effects upon academics themselves than upon the context in which they teach. In a critique of the penetration of corporate discourse, she notes the way the administration now makes "critical thinking" commensurable with "time management" and demonstrates the porous boundaries between the way the subjectivities of students and workers are articulated. Ethnography is a "weapon of the weak," suggests Graeber—but it is still a weapon.

The discourses that interest Urciuoli are aimed at students, but professors too are subjected to the equivalent, often precisely with respect to that central and mysterious dimension of academic practice known as teaching. What a complex and sore subject it is. Harrison and Meneley describe the effects of attempts to innovate in this domain in a Ford Foundation-funded international and interdisciplinary teaching project (with elements reminiscent of the participatory appraisals in the "development" field described by Barber) that seems to have left most of its faculty and students conflicted. This chapter (along with Urciuoli's) is the product of perhaps the most deliberate attempt to conduct "auto-ethnography of the academy," and it is doubtless no coincidence that it is also the edgiest. Their subjects being their colleagues and students, the authors are careful to retain an objectivist distance in their account. It is also clear that co-authorship raises its own problems for reflexivity, a factor that needs to be taken into account in all collaborative reports.[5]

Teaching is a subject of pressing interest to all of us. What are we to make of the way it has become reified as technique to which we are expected to submit to training and evaluation by experts, to produce our own formal "statements" and compile our "dossiers"? Should we entice students into our respective disciplines in order to boost enrolments or succumb to the pressure for "statistically better" course evaluations? Or should we appear relatively disinterested in order to ensure the field is left for the truly inspired and dedicated? How are we to respond to students who have become consumers and treat our lectures and personal attention as commodities for which they expect the right to their money's worth? Do we owe them colourful powerpoint presentations in the classroom and lecture notes on the website? What do we know about the informal trade in ritalin that, I am assured, takes place, especially at exam time? (And how can we get in on it?) How do we resist or accommodate to the new technologies and the influx of "soft managers" determined to get us to "improve" our methods? The latter are part of a new class of workers within the university structure painfully needy of our cooperation so that they can show their bosses they have carried out their mandate. A famous memo at my institution invited instructors to a workshop to learn how to construct multiple choice exams. As my son would say, "That is insulting on so many levels." Merely to delete such messages from the inbox seems an imposition on my time.

My practice as an academic includes my location in a university not only as a professor engaging (differently) with graduate and undergraduate students, but—often more saliently—as subject to a complex and often tedious, unrewarding, and ultimately (but generally non-intentionally) duplicitous administrative environment that favours the construction of virtual realities by means of elaborate memos, planning exercises, and reviews. Departmental politics and relationships with colleagues (most with a sense of humour, some capable of far too much mischief, and a few remarkably humourless) inevitably loom large in such a vacuum of either real power or real democracy. The academic year is comprised of a sequence of deadlines: for calendar entries, job searches, course syllabus submission, term papers, marks returned, setting and grading exams, graduate admissions, activity reports, meeting prospective undergraduates, and simply remembering to go to lectures on time. (You laugh.) As I age, these deadlines seem to extend ever further into the summer and to chase each other faster and faster. In return there are the comments of undergraduates who write on their course evaluation forms, "This course changed my life" (or—a first for me this year— "The prof. looks like Sylvester Stallone") and, more compellingly, the students who hand in essays that show it and then who ask for more.

Many of these things are not specific to anthropological practice, but our practice as anthropologists fully or partially employed by universities inevitably includes them. A further issue that all academics face is captured in the "publish or perish" phrase, though clearly its impact varies both with the stage in one's career and with one's generational cohort. (Personally, I find the reach of this admonition into ever earlier phases of the education process quite disturbing.) Publishing practices also seem to vary by discipline. Stephen Bocking is the contributor who addresses this dimension of academic practice through his lucid discussion of editorial peer review. I must admit I thought Bocking was setting up a straw man until it dawned on me that perhaps other disciplines don't see peer review as anthropologists do, that is, as primarily a matter of offering constructive comments (except when we come across a paper we consider unredeemable or are simply too lazy). Conversely, and following here both Sylvain and Solway in reflecting on how my subjectivity has changed over time, I blush to think of my overly earnest and energetic early attempts at peer review. Peer review is inevitably based on judgement, and judgement is inevitably both potentially fallible and ultimately arbitrary. But that doesn't necessarily make the process a bad one. The main criterion for the job of editor is wisdom.

Just as the publish or perish maxim cannot begin to explore the pleasures of writing, so Bocking's topic barely scratches the surface of what is certainly one of the dominant features of academic practice. I refer here not to writing or publishing but to the amount of time we spend simply evaluating one another: grading, ranking students, reading theses and essays, attending doctoral defenses, and responding to colloquia; participating in hiring, pre-tenure, tenure, promotion, merit pay, and chair selection committees; engaging in anonymous refereeing, editing, writing blurbs, and publishing reviews; and writing and reading grant and fellowship evaluations and letters of reference. This is, for better or worse, a central part of our sociality and eventually our subjectivity (thereby informing our sensitivity). As Graeber notes, the socialization process begins early. It is also critical to the social reproduction of the academy

ANTHROPOLOGY

Why is this discipline different from all other disciplines? The wise child answers, because anthropology is a vocation, a life sentence (though Gibb's essay describes an ostensible escape). Anthropology is a vocation, I tell my undergraduate students when I'm playing the enchanter, in which work and life form a unified whole. Anthropological labour is (relatively) unalienated; fieldwork is a chunk of one's life, not a hole in it, and a part of growing up. Phrased another way, more abstractly and by means of one of those obscure words not in the dictionary that I promised I wouldn't use, one could say that anthropology constitutes a distinctive chronotope.[6] It is not only that anthropologists often travel a good distance to conduct their research but that the time of fieldwork is relatively undisrupted by external life factors and the scene of fieldwork is the site of repeated returns. Moreover, fieldwork is ideally a kind of immersion (in life, not the Internet, and preferably without e-mail access) during which the boundaries of work and leisure and the oscillations between public and domestic life characteristic of bourgeois experience are swept away.[7]

This is true so far as it goes. Many of the essays address, albeit at different scales, the temporality of anthropological practice. McMurray, Sanders, and Swedenburg each allude to the increasingly complex calls on our time and attention and their fragmenting quality. Nothing replaces that first year of pure fieldwork whose temporality is evoked by Sylvain. The editors draw attention to the significance of reminiscence on the part of senior scholars. Solway engages both personal reminiscence and the changing reputation of an "ancestral" scholar in the public domain. Barber and Harrison and Meneley reflect on the history of specific projects or programs of research and their implications for the protagonists. Gotlib and Cummings depict moments of entrance to the field, Young and Gibb the exits. Paradoxically, it is only Gibb, in the guise of describing her exit from the profession, who addresses what is actually one of the most salient aspects of the anthropological chronotope, namely, the quality of the long-term, "kin"-based relationships we establish with our subjects or with their communities as well as what it might mean to continue to live our respective lives (both in reality and through fantasy) in mutual context

No other discipline is quite like this, and it deserves to be celebrated. But perhaps it comes—at least for some—at another kind of cost. Gibb shows how what I have just described as the unalienated quality of the anthropologist's life world might equally be depicted perpendicular to this as one of dissociation. Gibb ventures that she is a different person in Ethiopia from who she is in Oxford or Canada, and she is "caught out" by a Harari in Toronto who spots her smoking and drinking martinis one sunny afternoon. The pleasure of living performatively and the privilege of being able to slide in and out of one's field persona needs to be balanced with considerations of sincerity and consistency. This too is an ethical dilemma that can only be worked through in practice. It is easy to romanticize the anthropologist's life, but remember that both Sylvain and Young as well as Gibb point to the betrayal that inevitably accompanies loyalty.

Gibb's essay captures beautifully two dimensions of the anthropological enterprise: knowing how to be open to experience, even how to put oneself in its path, and knowing how to withhold oneself sufficiently in order to record it. As Gibb knows, it is along a third dimension that the writer of fiction and the anthropologist part company, and that is the practice of explicit analysis and abstraction.

David Graeber is the one author in this collection who fixes on this aspect of doing anthropology. Ostensibly about political practice, his essay addresses the agon of theory-making. Graeber remembers graduate school (at Chicago) as learning to read theorists "in the least charitable way possible." But it is in the need for abstraction and, indeed, in the love for theory and argument—which may well equal the need for or love of alternative experience—that the anthropologist is not only an ethnographer. And yet anthropology is not pure theory either. A good anthropologist, true to her ethnographic roots, must be able to analyze and theorize in ways that are simultaneously empirically informed, ontologically attuned, non-reductive, and critically insightful.

ARE WE THERE YET?

It has been a privilege to have the first public word on this extremely well-crafted collection of smart, feisty, and sometimes deeply personal essays. I say "first" rather than "last" word deliberately; an ethnography of academic practice, as well as our own experience, suggests many responses to come—in the form of book reviews, reactions from subjects, discussion by colleagues, and rehearsals and rebuttals from students. It is in this larger conversation, albeit not always face-to-face in the manner of participatory workshops or forged in "collaboration," that anthropology as an intellectual tradition reproduces and renews itself. Indeed, it is both the fact of conversation and the possibility of arm's length and delayed responses (of which peer reviews are but one instance) that establish the conditions for such continuity. Rather like—and even perhaps, precisely another instance of—the logic of the gift, herewith passed on, or back, to you.

NOTES

1 Nevertheless, I'd like to acknowledge that both editors as well as Jackie Solway have made significant improvements to an earlier draft. Responsibility for infelicities remains mine.
2 I write this June 27, 2004, two days after the first appearance of Michael Moore's *Fahrenheit 9/11* on North American screens.
3 I borrow this from Ivy (1995).
4 For my own experience with and reflection on these matters see Lambek (1997).
5 One innovative strategy for co-authorship is the epistolary work. See Clément and Kristeva (2001) for a rare nonfictional example.

6 "Chronotope," literally "time/space," is drawn from Bakhtin (1981) and refers in the
   first instance to the kinds of conjunction of space and time characteristic of the plot
   or action of specific genres of writing. Thus, the English country-house murder
   mystery obeys certain rules of time and space different from those of the spy thriller.
7 That is, or was, the ideal. There is some worry that a whole generation of fieldworkers has now emerged without that liminal experience of not being able to go
   home at night or on weekends.

WORKS CITED

Bakhtin, M.M. 1981. *The Dialogic Imagination: Four Essays*. Ed. M. Holquist. Trans.
   C. Emerson and M. Holquist. Austin, TX: University of Texas Press.

Clément, Catherine, and Julia Kristeva. 2001. *The Feminine and the Sacred*. New
   York: Columbia University Press.

Ivy, Marilyn. 1995. *Discourses of the Vanishing: Modernity, Phantasm, Japan*. Chicago,
   IL: University of Chicago Press.

Lambek, Michael. 1997. Pinching the crocodile's tongue: Affinity and the anxieties
   of influence in fieldwork. In *Fieldwork Revisited: Changing Contexts of
   Ethnographic Practice in the Era of Globalization*. Ed. J. Robbins and S. Bamford.
   Anthropology and Humanism 22: 31–53.

LIST OF CONTRIBUTORS

Stephen Bocking is Associate Professor in the Environmental and Resource Studies Program at Trent University. His books include *Nature's Experts: Science, Politics, and the Environment* (2004); *Ecologists and Environmental Politics: A History of Contemporary Ecology* (1997); and an edited collection, *Biodiversity in Canada: Ecology, Ideas, and Actions* (2000).

Maggie Cummings is a PhD candidate at York University. For her doctoral fieldwork, she explored the meanings and practices of feminine beauty for young women in Vanuatu. She is interested in the intersections of dress, desire, and modernity and the cultural politics of representing women's bodies, both in the Pacific and at home.

Pauline Gardiner Barber is Associate Professor at Dalhousie University. Recent publications explore how migration is transforming Philippine communities as Filipinos develop transnational identities and become global citizens. She co-edits the Ashgate Press Series, *Gender in a Global/Local World*.

Camilla Gibb received a PhD in Social Anthropology from Oxford University. She is the author of three novels: *Mouthing the Words* (winner, 2000 City of Toronto Book Award), *The Petty Details of So- and-so's Life* (2002), and *Sweetness in the Belly* (2005), and is the 2001 winner of the CBC Canadian Literary Award for short story.

Lesley Gotlib recently received her PhD in Anthropology and Gender Studies. Her research was funded by the Wenner-Gren Foundation for Anthropological Research and the Social Sciences and Humanities Research Council of Canada.

David Graeber is an Associate Professor of Anthropology at Yale University. He has written books (some of them published) on Madagascar, value theory, and anarchism, and is currently working on an ethnography of direct action.

Julia Harrison is an Associate Professor of Anthropology and Chair of the Women's Studies Department at Trent University. She is the author of *Being a Tourist: Finding Meaning in Pleasure Travel* (2003). Her recent essays include: "Journeying Home" in *Journeys: International Journal of Travel and Travel Writing* (2002), "Thinking About Tourists" in *International Sociology* (2001), and "Multiple Imaginings of Institutional Identities: A Case Study of a Large Psychiatric Research Hospital" in *Journal of Applied Behavioural Science* (2000).

Michael Lambek is Professor of Anthropology at the University of Toronto at Scarborough. Recent work includes *The Weight of the Past: Living with History in Mahajanga, Madagascar* (2002) and *Irony and Illness* (edited with Paul Antze, 2003).

David A. McMurray is an Associate Professor of Anthropology at Oregon State University. He is the author of *In and Out of Morocco: Smuggling and Migration in a Moroccan Boomtown* (2001). He currently works on comparative popular culture and the politics of music. His most recent work is a textbook entitled *Musics of Resistance and Cultures of Opposition* (2004).

Anne Meneley is an Associate Professor of Anthropology at Trent University. She has published a book *Tournaments of Value: Sociability and Hierarchy in a Yemeni Town* (1996) and is a co-editor (with Don Kulick) of *Fat: The Anthropology of an Obsession* (2005). Her current research explores the production, circulation, and consumption of Tuscan extra-virgin olive oil.

Renée Sylvain is an Assistant Professor in the Department of Sociology and Anthropology at the University of Guelph. Her research on the San in Namibia has been published in *Anthropologica*, the *Journal of South African Studies*, and *American Anthropologist*.

Todd Sanders is an Assistant Professor of Anthropology at the University of Toronto. His research interests include ritual, gender epistemologies, witchcraft, and neoliberalism in Tanzania. He has co-edited: *Transparency and Conspiracy* (2003); *Magical Interpretations, Material Realities: Modernity, Witchcraft and the Occult in Postcolonial Africa* (2001); and *Those Who Play with Fire: Gender, Fertility and Transformation in East and Southern Africa* (1999).

Jacqueline Solway is an Associate Professor in the International Development Studies and Anthropology Departments at Trent University. She has conducted research in North and East Africa but has worked primarily in Botswana, South Africa, studying rural socio-economic change, culture and development, and multiculturalism in the context of liberal democracy. Her articles appear in numerous books and journals including *Current Anthropology, Ethnos, Interventions, Anthropological Quarterly, Journal of Anthropological Research, Development and Change*, and *Journal of Southern African Studies*. She also edited a special issue of *Anthropologica*.

Ted Swedenburg is Professor of Anthropology at the University of Arkansas. He is the author of *Memories of Revolt: The 1936-39 Rebellion and the Palestinian National Past* (1995) and is co-editor (with Smadar Lavie) of *Displacement, Diaspora, and Geographies of Identity* (1996) and (with Rebecca Stein) of *Palestine, Israel, and the Politics of Culture* (2005). He is currently working on a manuscript entitled "Radio Interzone," dealing with popular music flows between the Middle East and the West.

Bonnie Urciuoli is Professor of Anthropology at Hamilton College, Clinton, New York. She wrote *Exposing Prejudice: Puerto Rican Experiences of Language, Race and Class* (1996). She has also published several articles on the experiential complexity of language contact and more recently, on constructions and representations of "multiculturalism" and "diversity" in higher education.

Donna J. Young has published several articles about her research in Northern New Brunswick.

INDEX

Abdulnasser, Hassan (Dr. Hassan), 219,
  220–22, 226–27
"Academic Bill of Rights", 183–84
Academic Instincts, (Garber), 66, 80
academics, 2, 111
  blacklist of Middle East scholars, 178,
    181–82
  Campus Watch, 174, 175–6
  political activism of, 15, 173–74, 187
  power of in anti-intellectual times, 112
  scholarly production of, 9–10, 65–66, 82
academy (the)
  See also post-9/11 atmosphere;
    university (ies)
  American, 3, 10, 81, 380
  anarchism and, 187, 192–94
  assault on academic freedoms, 173–85
  auto-ethnography of, 3–12, 189–202
  Brazilian, 10
  Canadian, 3, 8–9, 16n6, 67, 80, 81, 93n4
  career advancement. *See* career
    advancement
  class structure of, 3, 8, 16n5, 189–90, 194,
    201n3, 231
  diversity and institutional values, 159–72
  funding. *See* funding; government funding
  hiring practices, 2, 8, 67
  ideology of meritocracy, 8–10
  intellectual practice as sectarian modes of
    debate, 191–92, 195
  outside influences on, 111–12, 157–58,
    230, 235
  peer review and, 67, 79
  perceived role of, 12–14
  political economy of, 3, 8–10
  reactionary forces and, 173–85
  sexism in, 1, 6–7, 11, 16n2, 16n11
  social and structural parameters of, 1–2,
    14–15, 234–37
Accuracy in Academia, 177
Accuracy in Media, 177
Achebe, Chinua, on *Heart of Darkness*, 132
African fieldwork
  Botswana, 113–25
  of Isaac Schapera, 117–21

Ju/'hoansi (San [Bushmen] of Omaheke),
  25–38
"African *muti* killing (ritual murder)"
  homogenization of African otherness,
    131–32
  media attention, 127–30
  us versus *them* imagery, 132–34, 136, 137
African otherness, 126–42
Alam, Shahid, 180–81
Ali, Noble Drew, 144
alienation, and unalienated production,
  199–201, 237
  fieldwork experience, 225
Allah, Intelligent Tarref, 143–54, 154n3
American academy, 3, 10, 80, 81, 93n4, 93n5
American conservative movement, 176–78,
  182, 230
American Council of Trustees and Alumni
  (ACTA), 178
anarchism
  the academy and, 187, 190–202
  the avant garde, 196–99
  consensus and direct democracy, 190–92
  history of, 192–94
  intellectual practice as sectarian modes of
    debate, 191–92, 195
  vs. Marxism, 190–91
  revolutionary practice *vs.* revolutionary
    strategy, 193
  role of ethnography and, 199–201
Anderson, Lisa, on Middle East studies, 179
Anderson, Nels, *The Hobo*, 4–5, 6
Annan, Kofi, 117
anonymity
  contradiction between signature and, 24n1
  ethical obligations of, 213
  in peer review, 69
  privacy issues, 47–48, 49n2
anthropological writing
  accessibility in, 6
  autobiographical reflexivity, 3, 7–8
  career advancement and, 6–7, 65
  conventions in, 188, 225
  genres of, 3–12
  native (insider) anthropology, 3, 4–7